NO BACKING DOWN

NO BACKING DOWN

My Story of Suing One of the Largest
Investment Firms in the World and Winning

TAMERON KEYES

A MEMOIR

Ashtad
Publishing

Beverly Hills, California

Note to Readers:
This is a memoir and narrative of events as Tameron Keyes felt the experiences. All names have
been changed except the names of some of the lawyers and law firms involved who are either
well known and/or are public people. Some place names have also been changed.

Library of Congress Cataloging in Publication Data
Keyes, Tameron.
No backing down : my story of suing one of the largest investment firms in the world
and winning : a memoir / Tameron Keyes. p. cm.
LCCN 2010907911
ISBN-13: 978-0-9845831-0-2 • ISBN-10: 0-9845831-0-6

1. Keyes, Tameron. 2. Stockbrokers--United States-- Biography.
3. Investment advisors--United States-- Biography.
4. Actions and defenses--Cases
5. Sex discrimination against women.
I. Title.
HG4928.5.K49 2010   332
QBI10-600128

Ebook ISBN 978-0-9845831-1-9

Printed in the United States
First Edition 2010

Published by Ashtad Publishing, Beverly Hills, California

Contents

ACKNOWLEDGMENTS

A friend reminded me a long time ago that no one ever succeeds alone. In my case, every crumb of support I got was absolutely crucial to moving me to the next place in my journey. My male friends are especially important and I am eternally grateful to them for helping me in so many ways. Without them I probably would not have this story to tell. My deepest gratitude goes to Hassan, for keeping me afloat in my early career and to Michael for his friendship from the very beginning to the present day. I am also grateful to Bob for his strategic input; to RP for his positive attitude and camaraderie, which kept me going during a very dark period; to RL for giving me hope when I really needed it; to M for his knowledge, skill and understanding of my experience; and to Wayne for his friendship and strategic input.

Additionally, this book would not have been realized without many other people who have helped me. I am lucky to have a friend like Andrea. She has been a huge emotional support through-out the writing of this book. I am grateful for that and for her patiently reading my manuscript, and providing invaluable insight and feedback. My thanks also go to Maha and Rita for reading parts of the manuscript and for their suggestions; to Molly for her "good deed for the day"; to Ben for reading part of my manuscript and for his encouragement; and to Amanda for pointing me in the right direction. Of course, my editors were absolutely critical. I am grateful to Becky for wading through that first monster manuscript, to Nasser for introducing me to my second editor Jessie; to Jessie for taking the time to help me even though she was writing her own PhD dissertation; and to Pamela and Abi for their proofreading and willingness to work within my time limitations. Lastly, my thanks go to Patricia who has been much more than a book designer. Thank you all.

To my former clients: I left the business the way I felt I had to leave at the time. I know it upset many of you, especially those of you with whom I had my best and longest relationships. I am truly sorry for that. Thank you all for your business over the years. Without you I wouldn't have had a career.

I

THE BEGINNING
OF THE END

I don't make anything of it, but it was Friday the thirteenth of December 2002. I woke up with a feeling of overwhelming anxiety so intense that I couldn't do anything except try and deal with it. It made me scatter-brained, and I couldn't concentrate on anything for longer than fifteen seconds. I'd start making coffee, forget what I was doing, then start sorting laundry. Literally, after a few seconds, I'd forget I was sorting laundry and go back to the coffee. I walked in circles in my apartment and even caught myself holding my breath a few times. My chest was so tight that it felt like I had a rock perched on my heart. The waiting was nerve-racking, and it was only 9:00 in the morning.

But then, who wouldn't have been nervous under the circumstances? I had just sued Smith Barney, my employer of the last eleven years, for sexual harassment, gender discrimination, and retaliation, but I hadn't quit my job and still worked in the same Beverly Hills branch. That morning I was waiting to hear the outcome of my lawsuit. I had put many years of hard work into my job as a stockbroker and had endured years of humiliation to keep it. After a decade of struggle, did I win or lose? My lawyer, Maxwell, had told me that most women lose their sexual harassment lawsuits, so, statistically speaking, I most likely would lose mine. I had given it my best shot, and hoped and prayed I'd win while simultaneously preparing psychologically in case I lost. If I lost, I told myself, I was going to march right back into my office with my head held high and manage my business as I always had. But without question, losing would be a very difficult blow to take and the emotional limbo in waiting that morning was agony.

Maxwell had checked his fax machine Thursday night for the judges' fax but failed to notice that it had fallen on the floor. He didn't see it until the next morning and then he called me at my apartment. I had taken the week off for the trial, but I wasn't about to go back to work until I knew the judges' answer one way or another. I picked up the phone on the first ring. It was Maxwell, but he didn't come out with the news right away. He was teasingly stalling.

"Well, did I win or not?" I asked, slightly agitated.

"I'm going to take you to lunch to celebrate," he answered. The tension in my chest melted and that rock on my heart disappeared. I breathed deeply. Then he said, "Do you want the total number or the individual numbers first?"

"The individual numbers," I said. The justice of it was more important to me than the total monetary amount of the win. I wanted to know what the panel of judges thought; I wanted vindication. Maxwell read to me as I scribbled the information down: "Economic Losses (past and future), $1,521,080; Emotional Distress, $150,000; Punitive Damages, $1,521,080." The total amount was $3,192,160 plus my lawyer's fee. I had won.

Although I felt immediately relieved and very grateful, I wasn't elated as one might expect. It was more like numb relief. It felt like I was taking business notes as I wrote down the numbers. Even after I hung up the phone, I didn't scream with joy, jump up and down with excitement or roll around on the floor laughing. I just sat there, alone, for a few moments. The whole horrible experience had lasted too long and had been way too painful for me to be suddenly happy. And corporations piss and moan about being victims of conniving, manipulative women who cry sexual harassment for greed or vengeance? It's more like women get their arms and legs ripped off and their torsos thrown into a ditch.

Certainly, I felt relief but it was that slight subtle relief one feels a second after a shockingly unbearable pain begins to subside. Deep down it was like something inside of my soul was numb. Nobody intentionally goes through what I went through because they are conniving or manipulative.

The first person I called was my dad; parents are always the first to hear big news. Then I called my best friend Eva, an investment banker in London. She understood what I went through and rooted for me because she had experienced sexual discrimination herself. She thanked me on behalf of all women for winning my case. I didn't want to get all official and didn't feel like a hero, so strangely I didn't want to hear her thanks. Next I called Mitchell, my buddy and the first to help me by encouraging me to call an 800 number for human resources. He had also been an enormous support for me during my whole career. Mitchell was extremely happy for me, but still my emotions felt flat. After Mitchell I called Mat, another friend who had provided strategic and emotional support. Claire, the sales assistant from the downtown branch and a class representative of the class action lawsuit, was next on my list. I sued Smith Barney as an individual but within the confines of a class action— but I'll explain that later. She had been kind and very helpful to me. She didn't answer the phone, so I left a message on her machine. I talked to a few other people, and then my brother called me at my apartment.

"You know, Tameron," he said, "I just tried to call you in your office. Your phone rang twenty times and nobody picked it up."

"Really!" I answered. My anger came roaring to the surface. Wow, I was still in warrior mode. "I'll call you back in a little bit; I have to take care of it."

"Those bastards are already counting me out," I thought to myself, "We'll see about that." I lived in Beverly Hills only a half-block from my office, so I stomped back to work fuming at the thought that someone over there assumed that I was down for the count and was not respectable enough anymore to have my telephone answered. Answering the phone is critical to my livelihood, so I wasn't going to let it slide. After calmly speaking to the receptionist, I turned around and saw that my manager and his assistant had walked into the lobby. They were standing in front of the staircase discussing something. I didn't intend to get into his face, but believing that my phone wasn't being answered on purpose— and after my pretending for so long that the harassment and lawsuit wasn't actually happening— it just came out of my mouth, and I didn't care who heard me.

I walked up to my manager and interrupted his conversation. I leaned toward him and said, "I WON 3.2 million dollars, and somebody isn't answering my phones."

He backed-up against the wall, held up his hands as if I was sticking him up, and said, "I had nothing to do with it."

He was my new and third manager by that time. His assistant just stood there with a blank look on her face. They asked the receptionist about the phones. She denied not answering them, so I said I would go up and talk to my assistant. My assistant had not been supportive of me. He also worked for another female broker in the office who had stupidly agreed to testify for Smith Barney. Between the two of them, I lived with weeks of whispers, snide cryptic remarks, and the cold shoulder. I may have been angry, but I controlled myself and didn't show it. I walked up to him and politely told him that I had won, which was the first time I ever said anything to him about the lawsuit, and that I won 3.2 million dollars. I'd be in my office for a couple hours, I told him, and then was leaving for the rest of the day to have lunch with my lawyer. Initially, he had that deer in the headlights look; a second later, he tried not to show how stunned he was. That was enough satisfaction for me, so I didn't bother to ask him about the telephone.

—⚬—

"Why did they do this to me?" was the question that wouldn't go away. "Why did this happen to me of all people? Why didn't they just nicely transfer me after I complained, as I requested, and then leave me alone in the new office to build my business? This is America. Honesty is the best policy, isn't it? And justice is supposed to prevail. They knew all along that I was telling the truth. Why did they retaliate?"

Growing up, it was implied that I could do anything or be anything I wanted as long as I put my mind to it and that being a girl didn't have any bearing on my success. I have learned the hard way that this is not true. There are people out there, both men and women, who resent women who go after and achieve the traditionally male goal of economic independence, along with the power over their own lives and the respect it brings to them. These same people, more often men, actively and consciously obstruct women from obtaining economic power, and Wall Street is one of the industries in which such men are prevalent. I know this may be shocking to some, but I was naïve enough not to know this. At the least, I didn't believe such people could deter me from my goals. I thought I could just ignore them, walk away, and get on with my business. I thought I was a tough girl.

Although I believe women are and should be treated as equal to men, my attitude toward women who complained about equality issues was, "Shut up and quit whining." I thought those women were just babies and not competent enough to compete with the boys. But I was wrong. When people who don't believe women are equal are in positions of power (and it turns out that there secretly are a lot of them) and are actively working against you with the goal to defeat you, you can't ignore them, and you can't get away, unless, of course, you quit, which I absolutely refused to do.

Is it right that women are forced out or maneuvered out of potentially lucrative positions? I wanted to stay with the best retail investment firm on the street. And at that early point in my career, it would not have been a prudent business decision for me to change firms. I feared I would lose my clientele because there hadn't been enough time to build loyalty. The real issue, anyway, was that I was a "girl" and, therefore, didn't deserve to be a stockbroker. I wasn't going to change firms because of that, and I resented the attitude that I should.

Why did I endure eleven years of discrimination, retaliation, and harassment, which started from my first day on the job? I had to ask myself, "Why did I put up with it and what kind of person could put up with it as I did? Why did I win my case when so many others don't win theirs, even when their situations are equally unjust?" I had a lot of questions and a lot of anger. In time, I accepted the fact that winning the lawsuit wasn't going to make me whole and that not dealing with the pain and anger this ordeal had caused me would eventually eat me up. It took a while, but I've pretty much dealt with it now. And in the process, I have discovered that there are lots of angry, discouraged, and wounded women out there who were also thwarted in their careers and ambitions. I am certainly not alone in my feelings.

A lot of harassing and discriminatory behavior is covert and sneaky. Sneaky or not, it is extremely damaging, but many pretend that it's not happening. Nobody seems to talk about the nitty-gritty details of how women are thwarted in their efforts to succeed in their careers. Isn't it strange that after forty years of the women's movement there are still relatively few women in positions of real power, especially in the business world? And most of the women who are in positions of power have attained those positions only since the mid-to-late nineties after the rash of discrimination lawsuits on Wall Street. It is about time we move beyond a state of female tokenism in important positions. The first step is to recognize sneaky sexual discrimination as what it is.

I realize now that from a very early age I wanted something and wanted it badly. Nothing was more important to me than the ability to protect myself by attaining personal independence, and for me— as for many men— that meant money. Additionally, I am a very determined person, which I have belatedly discovered, is not a characteristic often encouraged or admired in women. I am also competitive, ambitious, tenacious, very hard working, smart, and naïve enough to be courageous. I attribute all these characteristics mostly to the influence of my father. The ironic part is that these are the attributes brokerage firms look for in a new recruit, and, if Smith Barney had just left me alone and allowed me to build my business as they did for the guys, none of this would have happened. Although I initially complained of sexual harassment and discrimination, I probably would have let that go if they had left me alone, but they didn't; they retaliated and kept retaliating. That hurt my career significantly and was the deal-breaker for me. When I was given the chance to fight back through the class action lawsuit, I took it.

The lawsuit and the events that gave rise to it occurred during the course of my fourteen-year career at Smith Barney, from 1991 to 2005. I began working for the firm in one of its downtown Los Angeles branches in 1991, then called Shearson Lehman Brothers, where the sexual harassment and discrimination took place. Two-and-a-half years later, I transferred to a Beverly Hills branch in December 1993 while the firm was called Smith Barney Shearson. This is where continued discrimination and retaliation occurred. My second manager who retaliated against me was "retired" in 2000. The trial took place in 2002 when the firm was called Smith Barney; by that time, I was working for a third manager. I stayed with the firm until 2005 then quit under a fourth manager in order to publish this book.

II

GETTING THE JOB

But first you need to know how I ended up working at Smith Barney in the first place. I have many insightful memories of my childhood and my dad's influence on my life. "Pennies! Pennies! Daddy, can I have your pennies?" I squealed, as I jumped up and down with excitement in my family's marble floored entry hall. Every night, I was so happy to see my dad that I would run outside as soon as he pulled his Cadillac into the driveway of our California home. I would race to open the car door for him as if he were the king of England. I missed him all day and couldn't wait to see him. If I didn't catch him in the driveway, I'd catch him in the entry hall. He'd take the change out of his pocket and give me his pennies. Sometimes he'd have to tell me, "Sorry pumpkin, I don't have any pennies tonight."

It was our little ritual. But I wondered why he didn't give me nickels, dimes, or quarters. Why just pennies? After that, he'd go into his bedroom, put down his briefcase on what I called his "man's chair," take off his coat, then go into the kitchen where my mom was making dinner, and talk about his day with her. At the dinner table, most of the conversation was about my dad's business, and I just listened. When it was time to go to bed, I preferred that he tuck me in over my mother. He would give me a kiss and tickle my neck with his stubbly beard, making me giggle.

I admired him immensely, wanted his attention, and was very happy to be his little personal valet. In the mornings, I would stand next to him in the bathroom and watch him shave in his boxer shorts and undershirt. He always finished his shaving routine with a pat of aftershave on his face and neck. I thought my dad's clothes were so impressive and masculine.

I loved to see him all dressed up and ready to go out and do his thing. After putting on his cologne, he'd go into his dressing room and put on his socks, pants, a long-sleeve white starched shirt, and tie. Lastly, he'd go to his "man's chair" in the bedroom to collect his male accouterments. I loved that chair. It wasn't a real chair, in the sense that there wasn't a place to sit and it had no arms. It had a small hard surface on which he set his briefcase. The back had a hanger for his coat and hooks to hang his tie and there was a wooden dish on the top where he could temporarily and safely place his cuff links, change. He had the accouterments any good salesman would have: breath mints, nasal inhaler, and cigars. He wasn't just any old salesman; he owned the company, which at times had more than one-hundred employees.

In the morning, right before he was ready to leave, he would say, "Tameron, help me fix my collar." At six or seven years old, I would stand up on the end of my parents' enormous bed so I could see his thick neck and adjust his collar, making sure it was straight and that it covered his tie. As he left the house, I would prance out in front of him in my nightgown, down our front stairs, and try to open the car door for him again. I was very proud of him. He always looked so nice and professional, smelled so good, and seemed so powerful. I wanted whatever that seemingly inexplicable something was that he had.

—ᴍ—

My dad also was an aggressive and tough go-getter, and he almost always seemed distracted and angry. Aside from our evening greetings or morning good-byes, I don't remember getting much attention from him. I have no memory of him playing with me, sitting me on his lap to talk about my day, or asking about my school or my friends.

Regardless, I followed him around during the weekends as well. When he did yard work— which also seemed to make him angry— I watched him from a few feet away. We lived in a big house, but my dad— being a self-employed entrepreneur— was always juggling financial balls, so for most of the time, we didn't have a gardener. I would stand back so he couldn't reach out and smack me if I said something that annoyed him. But even at an early age, my tenacity was evident. I wouldn't give up and kept following him around, trying to get him to be nice, pay attention to me, and include me in his life. I stood there chattering away while he picked weeds, watered the yard, or cleaned our swimming pool. Every once in a while he'd say, "Tameron, go get me a towel" so he could wipe the sweat off his face or "Tameron, go get me some ice water." I happily complied. I loved to do things for him and wanted to make him happy.

In spite of his propensity toward frequent visible anger, he has been described as being "genetically optimistic," meaning he is incapable of seeing anything he doesn't want to see. He sees reality as he wants to see it, and as a salesman that is a positive reality, period. Anything negative or unpleasant he ignores, a very productive attitude for an entrepreneur in a cutthroat sales environment. But as a child, I didn't understand why he was angry or distracted, or why he ignored me. His behavior produced a deep niggling, nebulous, and uncomfortable feeling that I annoyed him, but children adjust, and I learned to live emotionally with his attitude.

My subconscious training, however, didn't stop there. Neither parent gave much support to any of my endeavors. We— meaning my siblings and I— were expected to figure things out ourselves, to make our own plans, and to execute them without much parental input. If we failed, it was our fault and our problem, and complaining generated no sympathy and maybe brought derision.

My dad is a self-made man. He went to community college for only a semester or two while my mother began community college classes when I, the youngest, was five and had started kindergarten. However, my education was not a priority for my parents during my childhood. As far as they were concerned, as long as I passed my classes, stayed out of trouble, and didn't embarrass them or burden them more than they thought necessary, things were fine. They would say things like, "The world doesn't owe you a living," and told me that that was the way it was in our house as well. They also reminded me that I was lucky and should be grateful for the life I had. Self-pity or complaining wasn't tolerated. Looking back, I think this family environment fueled my tenacity and intense desire to succeed. Without the preparation of my upbringing, I don't think I could or would have endured what I did while at Smith Barney. Because of it, I was the perfect candidate to go through the career ordeal I endured to the very end.

———

There wasn't much serious talk about going to college while I was in elementary and junior high schools so good grades, college preparation and goal setting was not an issue. However, after ten or eleven years of community college, my mother eventually transferred to a university and became serious about her own studies. Seeing her succeed, I believe, is what made me decide, at the end of my sophomore year of high school, to get my academic act together and try to go to college myself.

By the time that I decided that I did want to do well in high school and take college preparation classes, it was too late. I hadn't developed any real study skills. During my last two years in high school, I tried to learn on my own how to study and make up for all that I had missed; however, by the time I graduated, I still wasn't ready for a university and had to go to community college first. My mother's attitude was I'm doing my thing and you do your thing, but she made it clear that she respected doctors and would be happy if I became one. I guess I wanted to please her too and figured that if I were a doctor I could practice medicine anywhere in the world and earn enough money to take care of myself wherever I ended up. Consequently, while in community college, I took mostly math and science courses. But I think she wanted me to be a doctor because that is what she had fantasized for herself. So, during those early college years, living my mother's dream made me feel as if I had a big block in my life and I struggled. My motivation wasn't good, I wasn't cut out to be a doctor and I wasn't happy or successful trying to live my mother's dream.

Eventually I realized that in order to help myself I needed to gain self-confidence and get some success under my belt. I also realized that in order to gain that self-confidence and success, I had to follow my heart and study something I felt passionate about, regardless of what anybody else thought— without fear of the future and without fear of how I was going to take care of myself financially.

I changed direction completely. I had always been attracted to the Middle East as far back as I can remember, starting with old Steve Reeves movies from the early 1960's, like the Thief of Baghdad, and Morgan the Pirate. Also, while I was in high school, I fell in love with Cat Stevens and his music. His conversion to Islam contributed to my becoming enchanted with most everything Middle Eastern. I decided to study Arabic and transferred to UCLA as a junior. I graduated two years later with a Bachelor of Arts in Arabic Language and Culture. The summer of my graduation, I went through an intensive summer Arabic program at Middlebury College in Vermont. Then, the following September I started my first semester in the graduate program at Columbia University in Middle Eastern Languages and Culture. During my master's program, I also spent one summer at the American University in Cairo, Egypt, and another summer at the Bourgiba Institute in Tunisia.

I had grown up a lot during those four years at UCLA and Columbia. Moving to the East coast from California was a life-changing experience, and, because I had managed to get myself into such prestigious universities, my father took care of me financially very well for those years with very few questions or complaints. That four-year experience was what I needed. I felt successful after graduating from UCLA and Columbia and no longer felt that block in my life. The educational experience and world travels gave me self-confidence.

—ɯ—

In the spring of 1989, about four months before I finished the course work for my master's, I started thinking about getting a job. I wanted to make money and be independent. I knew that I would go into some type of business, like my dad; however, I wasn't sure of what kind. At that point, I narrowed it down to two possibilities: an importer or a stockbroker. I told myself these two paths essentially required the same skill set and personality traits and that they would suit me well. I thought long, hard, and honestly about what success in each choice would require and then investigated each possibility.

I did my own little feasibility study on starting an importing business by traveling to Turkey, looking for products and writing to the U.S. government about import regulations and procedures. Although I came up with good ideas, I concluded that I needed more start-up capital than I had and that I was too green to start out and succeed alone. I recognized that I needed other experiences first. It would not have been a good choice at the time, and I didn't want to set myself up to fail, so I nixed the importing possibility and turned my attention to the stock market world.

Every year at Columbia, many high-powered investment firms would come and host fancy recruiting dinners. The students would dress up and schmooze with the big shots from large investment companies like Solomon Brothers, Goldman Sachs, Paine Webber, and several others. The invitations were announced at school, so I put on my nice black wool suit and started making my rounds at these dinners. Each company gave a self-promotional spiel and laid out a buffet of fancy food for us students. I tried to mingle and chat with the firm representatives, but there was an uncomfortable feeling in the air. We students were supposed to be there to talk to our possible future employers, yet all those dark suits mostly kept to themselves with stone faces and weren't social at all. It seemed as if the investment firm representatives were being snooty. I thought to myself, "Why did they invite us if they are going to act like that?" It was the spring of 1989, and every single company that year got up and said, in a polite manner, something to the effect that they weren't hiring. The second or third time I heard that, I looked around to see if anyone else was surprised, "Have I been misunderstanding these people because I'm an Arabic major, or did they also just say that they weren't hiring?" The same thing happened one dinner after another. It was confusing because it seemed as if all the other students, the economics and mathematics majors, just sat there with placid, robot-like faces. Nobody seemed to react. I especially remember a woman from one firm that was a little more straight-forward and told us directly that, out of all the Ivy League schools, they were hiring one person. With that clear admission, I stopped wasting my time. That was the last dinner I attended.

By February 1990, I had completed all the requirements for my degree. Unfortunately, I had given up my Columbia University-issued apartment, and my boyfriend and I had broken up, so I had no place to stay. I moved back to California to find a job there. Nowadays, a degree in Arabic looks like a smart choice; however, in 1990, it was considered much more esoteric and bizarre. Those with liberal arts degrees usually have a harder time finding jobs, but in 1990 it was especially difficult. The United States was in a full-fledged recession, and California had been hit hard. I had a very difficult time finding a job, to say the least.

I was living with my brother in Orange County, but I wanted to move back to my old neighborhood in Los Angeles. I drove an hour to the library at UCLA and copied the yellow pages under "investments." I called and sent a resume to every manager in every office of every investment company in the West L.A. area that I recognized. I didn't get a single response, and nobody would take my phone calls. L.A. was as bad a place to find a job as New York, or maybe even worse. My ideas of getting into importing and sales or becoming a stockbroker went out the window. I became desperate to find a job, and I was soon looking for anything, anywhere. At that point in life, I was on my own financially, as far as my dad was concerned, and he meant it.

My job search turned into a one-and-a-half-year nightmare come true. I had a long series of weird interviews and job hunting experiences. Early on, I interviewed with a man who owned a small real estate company on Brookhurst Boulevard in Orange County. The office was devoid of people, a bit dumpy, and filled with empty desks. In the back of my mind, I thought that it was odd, but I just let it go. On the other hand, the real estate company owner was very intrigued by me.

"You look like Brooke Shields," he marveled, "and you're so impressive; you're a real renaissance woman." He paused to see how I'd react; I didn't. I just sat there looking at him, starting to feel ever so slightly uneasy. "I never thought I'd meet one (he meant a renaissance woman) in my lifetime," he continued, a little more softly, hoping he'd get a flattered response out of me.

I smiled nervously and thought to myself, "I just want a job, buddy."

Our interview was over, so he walked me to the door, but he walked behind me, putting both his hands on my shoulders. He leaned forward and whispered in my ear like a boyfriend might do, "I am so glad to meet you and we will definitely talk again soon; I'll call you." While it made me uncomfortable, I focused more on being hired. I drove down the street and pulled over to call my dad from my cell phone to see what he thought. I was happy about a potential job, yet the guy did creep me out a little and I wanted a second opinion. I told my dad about the interview.

"I'd stay away from that," he responded, in an alarmed voice. "That's not normal!" My dad's response made me take more careful notice of the whole meeting, and I decided to forget about Mr. Slimy Real Estate Guy. If I had any doubts about whether I was doing the right thing, they quickly dissolved when the guy called back to offer me the job. Of course, there was no salary, hourly wage, or draw. It was a 100% commission job. When I told him I was going to pass, he went into this manipulation routine in a jilted and wounded boyfriend voice.

"How can you do this to me?" he whined. "You are letting me down. I didn't expect this from you. I thought you were better than this. We had a DEAL." I hung up on him. Creeepppy. A few months later I happened to be driving down Brookhurst Boulevard and noticed that the real estate company had gone out of business and the office was for lease again.

Every day, I would get into my Honda and make the one-hour drive to Los Angeles from Orange County to look for a job at the UCLA Career Center. I sent my resume to any job that even remotely sounded as if it didn't require a technical degree. I would follow up my resume with a phone call and make as many appointments for job interviews as I could. The first year that I owned my car, I put more than 40,000 miles on it looking for a job.

I did get one job, after looking for a year, with a clothing manufacturer. He was a Middle Eastern man who seemed to be impressed with my educational background.

"I want to learn how to run a business," I told him, "especially one that deals with importing or exporting in any way."

"Good," he told me, "because I really need someone to learn to run my business for me and run it well. I'm tired of this business. It's difficult and a pain in the neck, and, honestly, if I had it to do all over again, I would have chosen something else. Are you sure you really want to try this?" he asked.

"Absolutely," I responded enthusiastically. "Taking on something difficult is fine with me. I really want to learn. Give me a chance and a little time. I am able and willing to run it for you."

There were, however, a couple of little problems. He never told me about his son and brothers. His brothers didn't own the company, but they did own another company that did business with him, and they all occupied the same space. When his son was told why I was hired, he got very upset. The Playboy bunny-type girlfriend of the business owner also didn't seem to appreciate my presence there.

"All his girlfriend ever wants to do is fuck my dad," the owner's son complained. Why he thought I needed to know that little tidbit of information is beyond me. My presence there was upsetting an already weird and unhealthy family and business dynamic, and it turned out that there were also several ambitious employees who were also upset at the reason why I was hired. That job lasted exactly one week. The following Friday, during the company Christmas party, the owner sent the controller over to tell me that I was fired. He gave me a crystal bowl as a Christmas gift, as all the employees were given, and sent me on my way. A Middle Eastern man with his son working for him and a couple of brothers (regardless of how lazy and incompetent) working with him isn't going to hire an American woman to teach her to run the business for him. Well, duhhh. Apparently, it all worked out though. After that episode, the son became more motivated and took things over from his father. I know because I ran into the son at a Beverly Hills restaurant several years later and he told me so.

Everybody I interviewed with was impressed with my resume, with the interview, and with me— or so they said— but no one would hire me. Several potential employers said flat out that I was over-qualified for the job and that, after they would train me, I would get bored and find something better. I would deny it and tell them what a hard worker and good salesperson I was. I'd tell them how I started working for my parents at thirteen years old selling cheese. My parents had a couple of gourmet cheese shops as side businesses. It was very good training for me. I had to go out into the mall, smile, and hand out samples of cheese to entice customers into our shop, or face the wrath of my father. If you knew my father at the time, you would understand why I quickly got over my fear and inhibition and was handing out cheese samples like nobody's business. I became good at it, and asking for business— which would turn out is absolutely essential to becoming a stockbroker— became easy for me.

The job search became so desperate that I was practically begging people for a job. When it became obvious that I wasn't going to get a real job quickly, I looked for anything to pay my bills, in addition to looking for a career-type job. Initially, I looked mostly in L.A. but couldn't even get a job in a restaurant. I tried everywhere. I had lots of experience because I had waited tables on and off through high school and college. It's a great way of making money working short shifts, perfect for a student. I applied to so many restaurants I lost count. I would go to interviews where fifty out-of-work actors would be sitting around filling out job applications. Decent restaurants didn't want to hire me either because, again, I was over-qualified. They wanted so-called actors who they knew would be around for a long time. Things got really scary. While in school, I never dreamed that I would have such a problem finding a job. I was an Ivy League graduate with a master's degree, smart, ambitious, traveled, and hard-working. The difficulty I was having was beyond my imagination. I was so sure I would get a job that I had rented a one-bedroom apartment and bought a Honda. That was about February 1990. By October of that year, I had to give up the apartment and move back in with my brother, who lived alone in a three-bedroom house in Orange County. The stock market had crashed in October of 1987, and I was looking for a job twenty-seven months later during a serious recession with degrees in Arabic. The prognosis was not good.

I finally did land a job when I wasn't expecting it. It wasn't much, but it paid my bills, and I was very grateful to have a job, any job. I went to a restaurant in Orange County where the owner, who was almost never there, happened to stop by at the moment I showed up to ask for a job. It was my lucky day, and he hired me on the spot. The restaurant was a twelve-table dive at the beach with cockroaches, mice, and no on-site managerial supervision. The waitresses took the money for the bills and gave change back to the customers. We then put the nightly tabs into plastic baggies along with the order tickets and dropped the baggies into a locked wooden box.

While waiting tables at night, I continued looking for a real day job. UCLA Career Center had several places within it where one could look for job postings. There were various note posting boards, posting books, and a computer posting board. One day I was on the computer and saw a very short advertisement for an assistant stockbroker. I called and sent my resume in right away. Lo and behold, I actually got a call back from a Mr. Errol Planet. We made an appointment for an interview for about two o'clock in the afternoon sometime in May 1991. I dressed in my best suit and drove to the downtown Los Angeles branch of Shearson Lehman Brothers. I went into the reception area and told the receptionist that I was there for an appointment with Mr. Planet. This was my first and only appointment with an investment firm.

—∞—

I was very excited about this interview because it all looked so corporate and respectable. A guy walked out and introduced himself as Mr. Planet. He was nice enough and polite, but he just didn't have that corporate feel on first impression. I followed him into a huge room that took up a quarter of the entire floor of one of those tall high-rise buildings in downtown Los Angeles. The entire center of the room was filled with cubicles partitioned by six-inch cherry wood colored half-walls that came up to about my chest. The perimeter of the room consisted of glassed-in private offices. The corner offices were larger, and there were a few big offices that weren't on the building corners— but during that initial meeting, I could only see this large room, which I would later find out was called the Bull Pen. The branch office encompassed the entire floor of the building and a part of the floor above it. High on the wall was a big electronic ticker tape with that day's closing price of stocks flashing by. "Wow," I thought, "Wall Street." I was impressed.

Mr. Planet and I sat down in one of those cubicles and talked about all the normal stuff, including my employment history, experience, and educational background. He seemed to be impressed, especially with the Arabic, and talked about what the job entailed. I nodded my head and kept saying, "That sounds good," "I can do that," or "That sounds interesting." And it did sound interesting.

"Shearson Lehman Brothers," Mr. Planet explained to me, "has an extensive research department that does research on hundreds of stocks. Brokers then call their clients and tell them what stocks to buy based on the research. The clients buy the stock and that's it. It's better for the broker," he continued, "to have other people calling for them instead of just calling for themselves, because that way, they are contacting more people to whom they can sell stocks to in a shorter period of time. It's like leveraging yourself and your time. So, to help them get more clients, brokers have cold callers that help them find potential clients by calling all over the country asking those potential clients if they want to buy stocks. That is what your job will be. Wouldn't you like to be a cold caller for a big broker in the office?" He asked me, as if he was offering me the prize behind door number one.

"Yes, I would," I said, with a smile on my face. "Oh my god," I was thinking, "I want it, I want it, I want it, please god I want it."

"OK," he continued, "being a cold caller would entail proving that you can get good leads. If you can do that, then maybe you can get your license, and if you get your license, you have to open thirty accounts for your broker, who gets to keep those accounts. The trade-off is that your broker gets the thirty new clients, and, in the meantime, you are taught how to do it, how to be a broker. Then you can go out on your own, meaning you don't have to work for another broker anymore; you can work on your own, and you get to keep all your commissions and maybe even get cold callers of your own." I could make several hundred thousand dollars a year, Mr. Planet told me, and he bragged about the twenty-six-year-olds in the office making a half million dollars a year.

"Yahoo!" I thought to myself, "I could do that." I thought the interview was going very well.

There was just one little problem. Once the interview began, it was obvious that I was not talking to someone with much position. He didn't have much confidence, he wasn't well spoken, and he had a hole in his shoe. "Oh, no, another weird interview," I thought. "But this is Shearson Lehman Brothers. They are a reputable firm, and I am sitting in their office," I rationalized. "It has got to be legitimate, so I'll just go with the flow."

Then Mr. Planet asked me if I had any questions. I briefly reiterated what he said to make sure that I understood. I said something about reading the research and choosing stocks and making sales over the phone.

He freaked out. "What!" he said in a loud voice. "You are going to pick stocks! Who do you think you are? You're not going to pick stocks," he said, indignantly.

Oops. I didn't know what was going on, but I understood that whatever it was I had said, it was the wrong thing to say to him. I backpedaled big time as obsequiously as I could. I just wanted the job. He calmed down.

"Do you want the job or not?" he asked.

"Absolutely," I said enthusiastically, "No question about it. When do I start?" I was as happy as I could be. Finally, I was getting a job with a real firm.

"Good," he said, and then he dropped the bomb, "You know the job pays five dollars an hour?" My jaw dropped, I couldn't believe my ears. Mr. Planet was irritated again. "Do you want the job or not?" he said with annoyance.

Without hesitating, I said, "Yes, yes, when do I start?" Again, I didn't understand what was going on at that moment, but I thought I'd figure it out later. This was a real company, and I was really desperate to have a job with a real company with prospects. I wanted to get my foot in the door, and I did.

"Good," he said, "be here at 6:30 a.m. on Monday morning. You'll work from 6:30 a.m. to 1:00 p.m. when the market closes."

It had been a year and a half since I had graduated, but now I had my foot in a door that I really wanted it to be in. As we walked toward the elevator, I noticed Mr. Planet had another hole in his back pants pocket. Something wasn't quite right, but that was OK. I was too happy to be bothered by it. At least I was in and could still wait tables at night to support myself until I was trained and promoted. I would come to find out that Mr. Planet was basically an office flunky. His job was to hire some of the cold callers for five dollars an hour and to collect their time cards for management. I wondered if he had initially mistaken me as male. One can't tell by my name automatically if I am male or female and by the time I called him back for the appointment, he couldn't back out. I always felt that he was overly impressed with the Arabic and I also wondered if it had something to do with an admiration of Black Muslims, and, if together, that had something to do with his hiring me. He was let go about a year and a half later. I would come to conclude that, from the company's point of view, I was hired by accident, by an office flunky that management didn't pay attention to until it was too late.

III

COLD CALLING: EARLY BROKER TRAINING MONEY FLOWS THROUGH THE TELEPHONE

My first day on the job was June 3, 1991. "I'm going to put you with a very big broker with a corner office," Errol Planet told me first thing that morning. "Wait here for a minute. I'll be right back."

I thought it was a little odd that he would make me wait in the hallway, but I did what he said and used the moment to take in the scene around me. The room was huge and filled with cherry wood-colored cubicles. There was a long hallway, which I would later discover led to another section of offices and cubicles. It seemed like I stood there awkwardly for ten minutes. The place was loud and buzzing with activity and noise. I noticed there were about forty guys just in the open area cold-calling and pitching stocks over the phone. The electronic ticker tape was flashing, and there were little white cards all over the floor that the guys had launched into the air. I would learn that those cards were used lead cards that no longer had any value. It was exciting, and I was very happy to be there. However, I didn't expect what would happen next from such a reputable company. Errol came back to where I was standing in the hallway.

"Ah, well, when I told the big broker you were here, he said, 'A girl, get her out of here.'"

Without even thinking, I blurted out, "Whaaat!" in a shocked voice. I couldn't believe my ears.

Errol tried to placate me by making a motion with his hands to keep it down— even in that loud place. He answered, "It's Ok, it's Ok. There is another big broker to put you with, a woman, don't worry, she's big, really, she's a big broker too. Just wait here for another minute."

He walked into another office almost directly in front of where I was standing. A few minutes later, he came back out into the hallway and invited me into her office. Her name was Annie Talbot, and she looked to be only a little older than I. She smiled and said hello. Errol introduced us, told her a little about me, and left. Annie was a disarming person. She was about 5'7" and in good physical shape, with a sweet, pretty face and long, dark, strawberry-blond hair. She seemed to be kind, understanding, and sympathetic, but when she opened her mouth, she had the vocabulary of a longshoreman with a thick New York accent and a cynical, deadpan sense of humor. The mix was unexpectedly funny.

She already had a little place set up for a cold caller with a chair, a small desk, and a telephone. Her office was one of the glassed-in offices that surrounded almost all the eighth floor and all those cubicles in the middle. You could look down to the street below from her office or see out into that large, loud room. I sat down, we chatted a bit, and she explained what I was to do. Annie gave me a script so I could read what I was supposed to say to potential customers until I got the hang of it. She also gave me another sheet to keep track of my calls by scratch marks. I was to make three hundred phone calls or dials a day. I was to indicate on the blank sheet whether someone picked up the phone or not and, if they did, whether they were interested in receiving another call about investment advice. If they were interested in another call, I would take down some information about them on an index card, and that was called a warm lead.

"Do you have any questions?" she asked. I didn't. "OK, then start dialing," she ordered.

I looked at the phone. "OK Tameron," I said to myself, "this is it, your big chance; pick up the phone and start dialing for dollars." I just sat there,

I couldn't make my hand move; I couldn't pick up the receiver. "Pick up the phone!" I screamed inside my head. But I couldn't do it; I just sat there staring at the phone for several minutes.

Finally, I turned to Annie. "I'm scared," I told her. She had a look of supreme understanding on her face and said, "I know, honey," she called lots of people honey, "just do it." So I did it, just like that. After the first handful of calls it wasn't so bad, and the second day wasn't nearly as bad as the first day. After that, each day of cold-calling got easier and easier. It wasn't long before I was fearless. I worked from 6:30 a.m. until 1:00 p.m. Pacific Standard Time, Monday through Friday. When I'd get a warm lead, Annie would send out her card and a letter. A week later she was supposed to call them back to make a pitch to sell them a stock over the phone.

By June 1991, the downtown Los Angeles office of Shearson Lehman Brothers was an amalgamation of several other offices and companies through the various mergers between Shearson and Lehman Brothers, E.F. Hutton, and other firms. The brokers and the way they ran their own book of business or clientele reflected this amalgamation. Established brokers were left alone to do their own thing in their own way as long as they were making a living, and, in many instances, if they had been in the business for a while, they were left alone even if they weren't making money. However, the predominant culture and method of doing business among most brokers on the eighth floor and all young brokers or newer hires was working the "Lehman System," as they called it. What made it the "Lehman System" was the level of aggression in cold-calling, sales tactics, and sales pitches as well as, honesty, and consulting in basically sound investment behavior. Some of the brokers who were originally from predecessor firms other than Lehman Brothers continued doing business the way they always had, but many chose to take on that aggressive style of cold-calling.

Most of the brokers participating in the cold-calling program had at least one cold caller sitting with them; many had several. The big broker in the corner I was supposed to work for that first day of work had five or six cold callers sitting around him at any given time.

A typical cold call might go something like this: "Hello… Mr. Smith… Yes… This is Joe Blow Hard calling from Shearson Lehman Brothers in Los Angeles, I trust you're familiar with the firm?"

"Yes."

"Is that by reputation or have you done business with us?"

"Reputation."

"The reason I'm calling is to introduce myself and to let you know about a program we have available to private investors… Two or three times a year we make recommendations to our top corporate accounts, and I'm offering to make these recommendations available to you in the future. Does that sound reasonable?" Regardless of whether the prospect answered yes or no, there was a comeback response to determine if this was a person who had money and whom the cold caller wanted to call back, or if the prospect was a "piker" and not worthy of calling back. The goal was to find the money. If the cold caller determined the prospect didn't really have any money and was therefore a waste of time, he would end the call. If he wasn't sure, he kept talking until the prospect gave the impression that he had some serious money and agreed to be contacted in the future, until the conversation came to an impasse, or, until the prospect hung up on him. If the potential client said he[1] was not interested, the cold caller would probe more deeply. "Is that because you have had a bad experience in the market or because you're not in the position to do any investing at the moment?"

"Not in the position at the moment."

"So, you do invest in the market from time to time, is that right?"

"Yes."

"OK, I don't have anything for you today, but when I do have something in the future on which we expect to make a 30% return and if it fits your

---

[1] Most of us didn't cold-call women and we didn't talk to wives except to leave a message.

investment parameters, would you be interested in hearing about it?"

"Sure."

"Great." The cold caller would then get as much information out of the prospect as possible. "So I can get an idea of what kind of investor you are can you give me three names of stock you hold in your portfolio that would typify your investment parameters?"

"Microsoft, IBM, and Cisco."

"Oh, so you only invest in tech stocks?"

"No, not exclusively."

"Do you own any consumer staples like Johnson & Johnson, or Proctor & Gamble?"

"Yes, I own Kimberly Clark."

"And how about financials? Do you own any financials?

"Yes, Bank of America and American Express."

"So you only own large cap stocks?"

"No, I have Chiron."

"And any other biotechs or pharmaceuticals?… And how much do you usually put into a single idea? $50,000, $60,000?"

"No, I wouldn't say that much."

"OK, so what is a ball park range of the size of your portfolio?"

"300,000."

"OK, and how many issues do you hold?" (By this time, the prospect would be getting impatient.) "OK, if I bring you a good idea, can you put $20,000 into it?"

"I could, but I don't know if I want to though."

"OK, is your address blah, blah, blah?" and the caller would confirm the prospect's address and the best time to call him in the future. Then the caller would say," "I will send you my card, and when something comes up that I think will interest you, I'll let you know. Have a good day," and hang up.

All this information was written down on a 5"x10" card and stapled to the original lead card, where the prospect's name and number came from in the first place. The broker's business card and brief letter were mailed to the prospect and the 5"x10" card was put into a small file box. Inside that box were index dividers representing the twelve months of the year and sub-dividers representing the days of the week. The index card with all of that prospect's information on it was now a qualified lead and was filed away according to when the cold caller was going to call the prospect back. The second call was supposed to occur ten days later, regardless of whether there was some special advice. There was always advice; it was, "Mr. Smith, buy this stock now."

We did a lot of IPOs[2] in that office, so the second call might go something like this: "Mr. Smith, this is Joe Blowhard getting back to you from Shearson Lehman Brothers in Los Angeles. We have a new issue coming out that I believe you would be very interested in. Do you have a pencil ready, and I'll tell you about it?"

"I have a pencil."

"Good. XYZ stock is blah, blah, blah. Are you following me? Yes, good, blah, blah, blah. Can I put you down for 1,000 shares? At the IPO price of $20 a share, that's an investment of $20,000 are you comfortable with that?"

"No."

"Can you do 500 shares?"

"Yeah, I could do that."

"Good, I know you're going to be happy with it. This is how it works. I need to take down some basic information in order to open an account. You send the check in for such and such amount, and when the stock is allocated on such and such date, the stock is yours. Or if it wasn't an IPO, I'd say I need to take down some basic information in order to open an account. Once I have that information, I'll open the account and buy the stock. I'll call you back and tell you what you bought the stock at and for

---

[2] Initial Public Offerings

how much to write the check. You send the check in and you own the stock; that's it. What is your Social Security number?"

The prospect would give his Social Security number and all the other information we needed to open an account— just like that, over the phone and on the spot. It was amazing how much information people gave us over the phone and how much money they sent in without ever meeting the person on the other end of the line. Sometimes the money was in the six figures per security position. The cold caller would have the broker for whom he worked, and a manager sign the account and then take the paperwork to "the cage," which is what we called operations. Operations would issue an account number immediately, and the cold caller would go back to his desk and buy the stock. After the order was filled, the cold caller called the new client back and told him how much he bought the stock for and how much the client should write the check for and mail in and then confirmed our address so that we would receive the check right away. IPOs were a little different in that clients had to wait to have stock allocated to them.

Ten days later, the broker usually took over and placed the second call. The broker would go through the same routine and sell the client another stock. The client was technically the broker's client, even though the cold caller opened the account and made the first sale. The broker would continue to call the client every ten days or so to sell him another issue of stock. After the client held the first stock for a month or so, the broker would often call back and tell him to sell it. The broker did this until he built a "relationship" with the client or until he "blew the client up." As you might surmise, getting blown up was not a good thing. It meant the client would no longer work with the broker, due to some sort of negative experience. The cold caller who originally opened the account moved on to make other leads and open more accounts.

—m—

There were two stages of "cold caller-hood." The first stage was the beginning stage when a cold caller was not yet series 7 licensed and therefore not legally permitted to sell securities. A new cold caller could only make calls to get qualified leads for the broker to call back and pitch a stock. This period of time would be as short as possible. A new cold caller had to decide whether he wanted to be a broker quickly, and a broker had to decide if he wanted to sponsor a cold caller quickly, because it did nobody any good to have an unlicensed cold caller who couldn't open accounts or make sales. The second stage was when a cold caller was series 7 licensed. A series 7 license is the basic license one must have in order to sell stocks or bonds. When a cold caller was to be licensed, there was a money outlay on the part of the firm and a time and possible opportunity outlay on the part of a broker. The advantage for the cold caller in this system was that he got licensed and theoretically trained by the broker. The rule was that once the cold caller was licensed, he needed to open thirty accounts for the broker and then the firm would allow him to become a full-fledged broker himself. The advantage for the broker obviously was that he got thirty new accounts. Once the cold caller became a broker in his own right, he would, in turn, get cold callers for himself, and the cycle continued. That was our training in the "Lehman System."

I worked for Annie from June until sometime the following October or November. While I worked for her, she never opened a single account from a lead I had gotten over the phone. She wasn't a Lehman-style broker, wasn't into the groove of the office, and either wasn't able or willing to train me in that way, but she did help me. From the beginning, she repeatedly tried to persuade me not to pursue a career as a stockbroker because it was a "shitty" job. "Why would you want to do this? Do you really want to do this?" she asked over and over. Sometimes she would see something going on outside her office. Nothing necessarily terrible — it could have been something as mundane as young guys within sight range talking, bragging, or laughing, and she'd say, "Look at those little shits." The attitude in that office bothered her, too.

I got tired of hearing her gripe when there was an obvious benefit to the job. One day, I turned the question back on her. "Well then, why do you do it?" I asked. "Why don't you go get another job?"

"I can't," she answered, "there is no other job out there that would pay me what I make here." She told me that she also had some kind of liberal arts degree in like political science or english. I asked her if she made $100,000 a year. This was in 1991. She hesitated, because most people don't like to divulge how much they make, and then she responded, "A little more than that." Not only did she make a decent living in 1991, but also did it working, at that point in her career, from 6:30 a.m. to 1:00 p.m., every day. She could go home after the market closed at 1:00 p.m. to be with her two-year-old, and nobody bothered her about it. That sounded good to me.

After about a month and a half, when Annie was convinced she wasn't going to talk me out of being a broker, she told me I had to go ask David the sales manager for permission from the firm to sponsor me to get my series 7 license. In order to get a license, you had to 1) be sponsored by a firm 2) study for the series 7 test through a one-week crash course and 3) pass the test. David Greenblatt, the sales manager, had come into Annie's office to say hello and chat for a bit a handful of times. Part of his job description was to keep his brokers— i.e. revenue producers— happy, and his visits were a way to do that. In the course of those visits, he never once said hello to me, introduced himself, or asked who I was. He completely and totally ignored me as if I were a piece of furniture in that small office of maybe 10'x 10'.

"Tameron," Annie said to me in her heavy New York accent, "get your butt into David's office and ask if he'll sponsor you for the series 7." She wasn't mean about it. It was her way of telling me what was required if I really wanted this job, and she encouraged me to bug David enough so that he would give in and sponsor me.

It took me a few minutes to collect my courage. I got up and walked out of her office, turned right, and walked two offices down. It was difficult at first to get up and go ask because David behaved like such an ill-mannered and abusive heel, not just to me but to others as well. I must have gone into his office at least ten times all together asking if the company would sponsor me to get my series 7 license. After a few nasty rejections, I numbed my emotions and kept asking on automatic pilot.

One day, I got up to ask David again. As I was walking past the inside glass window to get to the door of his office, he yelled at me through the window with this vicious look on his face, "NO!" I didn't miss a beat. Without even reaching his office door, I just turned around and walked back to Annie's office. Out of the corner of my eye I could see him laughing through the window. The next day, I got up again and went to his office and asked him if he'd sponsor me. This time he said something to the effect of, "You just don't stop." I agreed with him and told him I probably wouldn't.

David did have a heart, somewhat. He finally gave his permission for the company to sponsor me to take the exam. Errol came in to Annie's office to congratulate me and to say he would schedule me into the next available class at a certain school that the branch used to help its cold callers pass the series 7 exam. I was enrolled and took a week off, unpaid, to take the crash course. The rule was that you could only take the exam once, and if you failed it, you were fired. Sometimes they enforced it; sometimes they didn't.

During that time in that office, getting licensed through the crash course was the only option available. I was told the formal training program had been suspended. Each day, after my shift of cold calling from 6:30 a.m. to 1:00 p.m., I would jump into my Honda and jet down to Orange County to wait tables at night. I was very tired, often working thirteen or fourteen hours a day, driving for two hours and studying in between. I studied in my car in the restaurant parking lot or across a little street at the beach parking and fall asleep in my car with my book on my chest. We were allowed to go back to the class and audit for a second week before we took the test, and I decided that was the right thing to do. I took the class once to see what I was in for. I did all the work and all the studying required during that week. I then reread the whole thick study book and did the practice exams again, after which I retook the class and scheduled the test. In December 1991, I passed on the first try, thank goodness.

—⁓—

Approximately two months before I took the test, Annie had gone on disability. She was pregnant with twins and was ordered to bed where she continued to do her business. The problem was that I was left to sit in her office alone getting leads, although for what I didn't know. If a warm lead isn't called shortly after one gets it, it is no longer warm. It is effectively "dead." Also, I had nobody to observe, nobody to listen to, and nobody to train me.

As I already mentioned, I surmised that my getting the job was a fluke. Errol's job was to hire five-dollar-an-hour cold callers like me and assign them to brokers. Cold callers were in and out as if the company was a revolving door. Because management didn't want to be bothered, it was Errol's job to hire the colds callers, keep track of our time cards, pass out our paychecks, and hand out the lead cards that we used to make that first cold call. Lead cards were little 3"-x-5" cards that were purchased from various companies like Dunn & Bradstreet. Each card contained somebody's name, address, phone number, type of business, professional title, often a dollar amount that reflected how much money that individual probably made, and the income of the company and its total sales. The downtown branch received these leads by the dolly load, and Errol put them into stacks and passed them out to brokers participating in the cold calling program.

During the few months between the time Annie went on disability in the fall and before I passed the series 7 test in December, I felt very vulnerable. I had felt safer being protected by Annie so to speak, but now I had nobody to protect me, and I had no value to the company because I was not yet licensed. I did, however, already feel, see, and experience the gender hostility there. My response was to keep my head down and to be as inconspicuous as possible. I had already gotten permission to get licensed but hadn't yet passed the exam so I didn't want to rock the boat by demanding my sales manager put me with someone else. As far as I knew they could have fired me because they had no place to put me. No broker was obligated to work with me. Even so, David, my sales manager, should have done his job by encouraging one of the guys to train me. I don't think he did because, even though he allowed me to study, I still didn't really count. I believe I was allowed to stay to keep Annie happy and so that she could play big broker too. It felt to me as if my presence was allowed there because I had gotten in under the radar and they let me stay as long as I had lain low. I believe they patted themselves on the backs for that "charitable generosity." They pointed to my hiring to say, "See, we're not sexist." Female brokers were unusual, and almost all the female brokers in that office had a special story of being protected and helped by a man in the business.

In 1991, there were five female brokers in the downtown branch that I remember out of close to a total of ninety brokers in total. The first was a big broker named Hope, whose office was on the ninth floor. She started out as a secretary for a very wealthy broker (I'll talk more about her later). The second woman was Annie, who also started as a secretary. Her boyfriend, who had become her husband by the time I met her, was a broker. Eventually he quit to take a government job with a stable paycheck, and she took over his book of clients as well as manage the business she had already built on her own. I don't know any more about how Annie built her business. Under the "Lehman System," she should have been pitching, hard core pitching the Lehman way, for a good part of the work day, but Annie didn't do that. During the six hours a day I was there, she spent a good four hours talking to various relatives spread out over the United States, or patching them through to each other, on Shearson Lehman's dime. It was so disheartening for me. She was also very paranoid that I'd take her clients. Instead of teaching me the ropes, she'd say over and over again, "You're gonna take my clients." I was so clueless at the time and so happy to have a job that I wouldn't dream that one broker could take another broker's client away even if he or she wanted to. I didn't even know how to get a client or what to do with a client if I got one. Her suspicions were ridiculous. Still, she went on and on about how she knew I was watching and gathering information about her clients and how she knew I was going to try to steal them. It was weird, and although I was grateful to have a job, and she did help me get licensed, I wasn't in a mutually productive situation with her as other cold callers were with their brokers.

The third woman was a Chinese woman named Amelia, who worked with two very successful Chinese brokers named Thomas Chang and Paul Wong. Their offices were in the back corner. They almost never interacted with the rest of the branch as far as I could see. I know nothing about her. People in the branch called that back corner Chinatown, and all I know about them was that they were hugely successful. Thomas Chang's clients were institutional clients acquired and handled by him, a retail broker. The gossip was that at some point Shearson Lehman Brothers met with some of his clients behind his back in Europe. They wanted to take them away from him. He found out and ended up cutting a deal to jump to another firm. Reportedly, he was paid several million dollars to do so, and the new firm gave him his own office in Shanghai. Paul and Amelia did not jump firms with Thomas. They stayed with Shearson Lehman for a while, but they also did end up leaving, at some point, to go to another firm.

The fourth female broker in the branch when I arrived was Victoria. Victoria was a piece of work. She was one tough cookie but could also be very kind. In some ways she was my hero. She is several years younger than I but would cruise to work in a beautiful Jaguar. We didn't talk much when I was in the downtown office but became friendlier and went out together a handful of times after I moved to the Beverly Hills branch. She was my hero because of how she got into the business and the environment in which she built her clientele. She seemed to be fearless and absolutely imperturbable.

She told me that one of her early jobs in the industry was working for a small firm owned by a Middle Eastern man. He took the whole office out to dinner for their Christmas party one year. She was sitting next to him in a large booth. In order for her to get out, everybody on one side would have to slide out. The Middle Eastern boss came on to her by touching her in an unacceptable manner, right there in the booth in front of everybody, while she was trapped next to him. She hauled off and punched him in the face and then made a fast getaway by sliding under the table and escaping. She quit the firm and never went back. That, in a nutshell, was Victoria. She convinced the notorious David Greenblatt to hire her at the Lehman branch before it was merged with Shearson. She built her business cold calling the "Lehman Way." She has wild stories that make my stories sound like tales from a child's birthday party. However, it is not my place to tell about her experiences. Suffice it to say, the branch in which she built her business seemed to be a very sexually hostile branch, to say the least. She had to have been an unusual woman to withstand what she did and to function and succeed for the time that she did. Victoria also ended up suing Shearson Lehman Brothers for sexual harassment. She sued separately, not in the class action through which I won my case. I know it must have been a terrible experience for her and I don't think she got much in monetary damages. Sexual harassment and gender discrimination are very difficult to prove. She signed a confidentiality agreement preventing her from telling her story and she is no longer a stockbroker.

I don't know much about how the fifth female broker, Sherry, built her business. I do know that she was established and making a good enough living that James Ayala, the downtown branch manager, found it in his interest to recruit her to his branch from another firm. Sherry was terribly unhappy in that downtown branch and told me she had made a mistake by moving there. She eventually would also sue the firm for sexual harassment and gender discrimination and is no longer a broker.

Shortly before I was scheduled to take the exam in December, David finally stuck his head in Annie's office door. "What are you doing in here?" he asked, in an irritated voice.

"Getting leads," I said lamely.

He got this look on his face as if to say, "How stupid," and walked away. It was stupid; I should not have been sitting there by myself. There was absolutely no reason for me to do so and no benefit to anyone for me to do so. It was actually a waste of the firm's money, even if it was only five dollars an hour. Obviously, I wasn't worth any effort from him. I passed the exam, and David once again stuck his head in the door.

"Congratulations and hold tight; I'm going to put you with another broker in a few days," he told me.

"Great," I thought to myself, "Now maybe I'll learn something." A few days later he came back with a broker named Jacob Rosenthal, an older man, in his early sixties, with a very established business. David introduced us and told me I would be working with Jacob but that I would not sit in his office as other cold callers did; I would have my own cubicle. That was not the way the system worked and I wondered how I would learn, but I wasn't going to argue. At least this broker had specifically asked for me, as David said. I didn't know why Jacob had asked for me, but he did, and sitting in a cubicle alone was better than being fired because nobody else wanted to work with me. We agreed to the arrangement, and David told me to wait in Annie's office until January, another three weeks away.

IV

HARASSER'S HEAVEN AND THE FORMAL TRAINING PROGRAM

I started working as a cold caller for Jacob in January 1992. Over the next six months, I was moved several times, but to begin with I was assigned a cubicle in front of Jacob's office. He called himself a consultative broker as opposed to a cold-calling broker. He was also a well-established and big broker, so I have no idea why he wanted a cold caller. I have always wondered if getting a cold caller for both Annie and Jacob had just been an office status thing for them— because neither one of them was interested in cold-calling or training me. I also have no idea what he did in terms of business for the entire period I worked with him. I never listened to one single conversation he had with a client. In fact, if I was in his office to get his signature for a new account I had opened and the phone rang, he would excuse himself and wait until I left his office to talk. Even though I opened a number of accounts for him, twenty- five to be exact, he couldn't have cared less about them. I don't know that he ever talked to a client whose account I brought in and opened. He never told me. I worked for him technically from January 1992 to June 1992. In reality, I was almost completely independent of him. I opened twenty-five accounts in six months, which meant, on average, I was opening one account a week. I needed his signature on each account, so I interacted with him about once a week besides saying good morning. I got no training whatsoever from Jacob. But at least I felt a little protected by working with as respected a broker as he was.

Jacob was always polite and gentlemanly with me unlike some of the guys I encountered in the hallway.

One day, early in my employment at Shearson Lehman, another cold caller was standing in the hallway talking to a couple of guys as I passed by. "Hello," he said, inviting me to stop and chat for minute. I didn't realize it, but he wasn't intending to be social and personable. "So how are you today Tameron?" he inquired in a flirtatious voice.

"Fine, thanks, how are you?" I answered normally.

"Well then, how about having some sex with me," he sneered contemptuously. The other guys did their "What a macho man, can you believe this guy?" laugh routine.

"Yeah, me too," another added.

I turned around and walked away. "That will never happen," I called out.

There is no way that comment could have been construed in any way other than to humiliate. I didn't even know those guys. On another occasion, in the same hallway, another guy body slammed me after someone mumbled, "What's she doing here: I want to get me some of that."

Being body slammed as if I were at a punk rock concert while standing in a Shearson Lehman office in a business suit? I steadied myself and then walked away again. It was all so bizarre. I didn't say anything that time. It was so shocking. It was one of those moments where you're not sure that what happened to you just happened. It was incredibly aggressive and meant to be threatening. These kinds of incidents happened all the time and came out of nowhere. Some guys were just nice guys doing their business, so you felt everything was normal, and then something like this would jump out of nowhere to humiliate you. The inconsistency of the environment made me feel off-kilter, and I began to get very nervous. I never knew when walking to the bathroom, elevator, or operations area was going to be an ordeal and when it was not.

—w—

I was in my chair every morning at 6:30 a.m. and was registered to sell stocks in all fifty states, so I called the East Coast in the morning and worked my way across the country during the day. Once I'd get a lead, I'd send out a follow-up form letter and Jacob's card, even though I was talking on the phone. Amazingly, it didn't even matter to the client on the other end. I still made three hundred phone calls a day, and every day I got at least one lead. After a short time, I had accumulated enough leads to start "pitching." Pitching was calling a prospect and making a sales pitch. Other cold callers sat with a broker literally one or two feet away from them. They would observe how their broker pitched over the phone, how he handled objections, and listened to the questions of clients or potential clients. Most brokers had mute buttons on their headsets so they could press mute and say something instructive to their cold caller, make funny comments, or make fun of or cuss out the client/prospect without the person knowing. Some brokers, as part of the training process, would sit right next to their cold caller while the caller was trying to make a pitch of his own. The broker would literally give the pitch into one ear of the cold caller and then the cold caller would repeat the pitch to the client, like simultaneous translation. The broker could hear what the client was saying to the cold caller, and the broker would answer the client back in the cold caller's ear. Then the cold caller would repeat what the broker was saying to the client over the phone. All this was hands-on training for the cold caller to become a broker within that branch system.

We had what were called "pitch books." The firm didn't give us an actual book that I know of, but predecessor firms did. Old scripts from these pitch books floated around the office. If you were on the ball, you bought a special kind of notebook that was kind of like a picture album. I bought one and collected all the scripts I could get my hands on. If you opened the notebook, you would find vertical rows of cellophane envelopes attached to the binder where one could slide in a script. At the bottom of each script, there would be a one-line tab identifying the objection it represented, which stuck out from beneath the cellophane envelope. During the course of a telephone exchange, if the client said for example, "I have to ask my wife," you would flip to the tab that said, "I have to ask my wife" and flip that cellophane envelope over. In a picture album, there would be a picture to look at, but in this case there would be an "ask my wife" objection response.

"Mr. Jones, you're the president of your company, aren't you?"

"Yes."

"And your success is the result of your making the right business decisions over the years, correct?"

"Yes."

"Let's be candid. You built that company yourself didn't you?"

"Yes."

"You are the decision maker, right?"

"Yes I am."

"Then why would you leave such an important decision like this to your wife? I'm sure she respects your business decisions."

The goal was to make a sell right then and there. You never wanted to let a live one off the phone without selling him a stock if you could help it.

"Let's start this relationship with five hundred shares. Are you comfortable with that?"

"Yeah, I could do that."

"Good, what's your Social Security number?" Then the cold caller got all the personal information he needed to open the account over the phone as I previously described.

There were hundreds of scripts floating around that various brokers had acquired, accumulated, and/or hoarded. If I found out somebody had a script that was particularly successful for him or was a script in an area I didn't have, I would ask that person if I could make a copy. Many of the guys wouldn't have much to do with me. Some would have absolutely nothing to do with me and told me to get lost. Some were openly nice and some were nice on the sly. They would give me copies of a script or tell me something important that would help me in my cold-calling but tell me not to tell anyone that they told me or gave me a script.

Years ago, I threw away the outrageous scripts that were actually written on paper.

The most obnoxious pitches were impromptu and the spontaneous creations of the most obnoxious pitchers. When a guy like that was on a roll, other guys ran over, surrounded him, and listened. It was a learning opportunity. The more cantankerous and obnoxious an exchange was without losing a sale, the more of a hero the pitcher was. He had "hammered" the client. Exchanges like that were pathetic and offensive, and looking back after building my own clientele during a fourteen-year career, even I am shocked not only at the abuse people put up with from these brokers but also by the fact that the clients sent the brokers their money at all.

The abusive behavior and obnoxious bravado was encouraged by management and was directly responsible for the hostile environment. Management loved it. One time when I was sitting close to the branch manager's office, he walked out, surveyed the scene, and said to me in a pleased voice, "Look at these guys; throw 'em raw meat," and walked back into his office. David Greenblatt, our sales manager, bragged about the good ol'e days when he used to use lines like, "You have to ask your wife!— pause— Mr. Jones, reach deep into your wife's purse, pull out your balls, and buy this stock."

—⚬—

Why would Shearson Lehman Brothers allow such a branch to exist? Because it made them money, lots of money, for several years. James Ayala, the branch manager, had come from the E. F. Hutton merger. He came across as a nice, polite, and mild-mannered type of guy. Many of his brokers, and even his sales manager, made fun him behind his back because he seemed like such a nice guy. He wasn't; actually, he just played the game well. I think the big numbers of the Lehman branch impressed and seduced James. Instead of cleaning house right away after the merger, he converted to the dark side. He couldn't argue with money. David was the real know-how guy with respect to that "Lehman System" in the branch and had been a manager with Lehman Brothers. David and James actively played a version of good cop/bad cop, except in this case it was smart manager/stupid manager. David was the badass— i.e. smart manager— who managed the animals while James played the dumb, nice guy from the Hutton side who sat in the corner removed from it all. I was amazed to observe David, the badass, assume a downright subservient demeanor when talking to James on the floor. James was the boss, and David showed extreme deference. It seemed to be another manifestation of the abusive corporate culture.

They went out to lunch together a lot. It was during these lunches that the pornographic movies were shown in David's office. At the time of the movies, I sat about twenty feet away, almost directly in front of David's office. The first movie was not what would technically be a pornographic movie, I don't think. I'm not sure because I didn't see most of it. It was called, somebody told me, *Howard Stern's Lesbian Butt Bongo.* All I remember is everybody crowding into David's office trying to look at the VHS playing on his TV. There must have been twenty to thirty guys stuffed into that office and spilling out into the hallway. They were kneeling and standing on the credenza that sat outside the inside window that looked into his office. There was no way one could see what was going on without being part of the inside crowd. Of course, just like with pitching scripts, I was always trying to figure out what was going on and if I was missing something that would help me in my business or hurt me if I didn't know about it. After a few minutes the guys started to filter away. By the time there was enough room to see what was going on in the office, all I saw were scantily-clad women in a limousine. They may have been kissing; I don't remember now. It was stupid. I walked away.

The second movie was full-on porn. The same scene happened, except this time there seemed to be more guys, and they were more tightly packed in, if that were possible. After it was all over, the guys started piling out of the office, pushing and shoving. Some were clearly grossed out, and many were arguing. Again, I asked several people to tell me what was going on. Finally, after most of the guys had left the vicinity, one guy told me what happened after I had pressed him and he had refused several times. He was the same guy who gave me many of the cold-calling scripts but asked me not to tell anybody he gave them to me. He said it was a movie of a woman masturbating. She orgasmed, and gooey stuff squirted out of her vagina in copious amounts. The guys were arguing about whether it was real or not and about whether it was possible for a woman to naturally have gooey stuff squirt out of her as it would from a man. Apparently, some of the guys were arguing about whether she had some kind of device inside of her that would make it squirt out like that for entertainment value.

One morning, around 8:00 a.m., two guys sitting in cubicles close to me greeted each other way too loudly for me to ignore. It was all part of that "badass" bravado that pervaded the environment.

Sammy called out to Walter over the cubicle wall, "Hey Walter, Ja do any fudge packin' last night?"

"SHUT UP, Sammy," I shouted.

John, the guy sitting next to me, turned to me and said, "If you can't take it, get out."

"Shut up, John," I said.

These types of comments and conversations went on all the time. Language such as "STUPID FUCKING WHORE" referring to a wife screening her husband's call from one of the brokers or a guy shouting out "YOUR WIFE WAS FUCKING GOOD LAST NIGHT" was common. What do you do in an environment like that? I really wanted my job. I ignored it or told them to shut up. Running and crying to the manager would have been ridiculous. Not only did management know and understand what was going on, they encouraged it and personally participated in it.

One day, another new female broker who had also come in as a secretary, a male broker, and I were leaving the office for the day. The three of us were standing in the hall between the four elevators for that floor. Chad, a new sales manager, came through the double doors and passed through the hallway between the elevators. As he walked through, out of nowhere, in a loud "manly" voice, he called out to the male broker, "Ya gonna nail 'em both tonight." He was referring to me and the other female broker. None of us even flinched. It was as normal as saying, "Have a good evening."

Mick, the male broker in the hall waiting with me for the elevator that night, was another piece of work. He was a very smart guy and at times amusing; however, he also had a serious disrespect for women and harbored a serious level of misogyny. Many of the guys I worked with were nice guys who enjoyed and respected women. That is one of the reasons why I believe gender discrimination is so difficult to prove. The good and the bad coexisted together. Mick, on several occasions, would be so excited after he made a sale that he got down on all fours in the middle of an isle between desks and pretended he was beating a woman. Can you imagine a guy in a suit, on all fours, in the middle of a professional office, pretending he was straddling a woman while holding her down with one arm, cocking back his other arm, and punching the air toward the carpet? All the while he was yelling, "Take that bitch fucking bitch, take that," as he punched the imaginary woman, again and again. Then he'd jump up like some kind of boxing champion. What would make a guy like him believe that he could carry out this kind of behavior in a professional office, let alone not get into some kind of trouble for it? Yet it was normal, and nobody even said anything to him.

One day, I was walking down a hall going back to my desk when it just so happened that Andrew, another broker and a relatively big broker at that, stepped out of someone else's office and into the hallway. We walked together just chatting as people do when they find themselves walking the same direction at the same time. There was a wall to our left. To our right were several offices. Instead of being glassed in, there were open walls, and the desks were placed in front of each other. So, there were two rows of three desks in each row. Brokers and cold callers were sitting there making calls and conducting business like any normal day. Again, out of nowhere, a broker called out to me. "Hey, Tameron," I turned to look at who was calling out to me. It was Victor, one of the few I had thought, until then, had always been a really nice guy and good-looking too. "I could fuck you so hard," he continued, "you'd have to hold your guts in with a two-by-four." What do you say to something like that? How do you respond? I ignored him. I turned to Andrew with a look of disbelief and asked, "What did he say?" as if I didn't hear him correctly. Andrew, slightly embarrassed said, "Never mind, never mind," and we kept walking.

On another day, a woman walked into the office apparently coming to visit one of the brokers. I was on the phone when I heard several guys start to whistle. A few guys whistling was no big deal. The place was so loud and obnoxious that a couple of whistles would have just added to the cacophony. After several more guys joined in the whistling, I looked up to see what was going on. Instantly, it seemed the place exploded. It sounded as if every guy in the place hung up the phone and started whistling as loud as he could. I stood up to look around over those cherry wood walls to see what was going on. I didn't see anything, except a normal-looking blond woman. This woman stopped in her tracks and was also looking around to see what was going on. *She* was what was going on. When she realized it was she they were whistling at, her face showed amazement then embarrassment. I sat back down. She was pretty enough but really was just normal-looking. We are not talking about Pamela Anderson or Farrah Fawcett walking in there. Most of those guys who whistled didn't even know who she was. Someone whistled, and everybody followed behind like a mindless piranha feeding frenzy. She could have been anybody's client— one of those women that Smith Barney would eventually chase in an effort to change their image. Luckily for Smith Barney, she turned out to be somebody's wife or girlfriend coming to visit. I never did find out whose.

—∞—

One day in April 1992, James asked the entire branch in the daily morning notes, which were distributed to everybody, to welcome a new employee. He had never asked us to "welcome" a new employee before. It stated that his name was Eamon Richards and that he had graduated from Columbia University. Eamon was starting the formal training program, and we were supposed to make him feel welcome. "WHAT!" I screamed in my own mind. They hired some new guy who graduated from the very school that I had graduated from two years before and they were putting him in the real training program but making me stay working with what I thought were a bunch of knuckleheads! I got angry. It took me about ten minutes of stewing. I barely knew James. He never talked to me but I marched right into his office anyway.

With the notes in my hand, I politely said, "Ah, James, can I talk to you for a minute?" "Sure," he said, "Have a seat. What can I do for you?"

"I see from your morning notes that the formal training program has been reinstituted and since Eamon Richards, who graduated from the same school I did, has just been hired, I would like to go into the program too," I stated politely.

After a pause, James replied, "Well, you'll have to go talk to David." was his answer. I thanked him and left. David was a diehard soldier of the "Lehman system," so it was going to be another nagging-him-to-the-death episode before he'd allow me to go into the formal training program. It seemed obvious to me that the Lehman style of doing things was not the right or ethical way of doing things. Most of the guys in that system didn't know their asses from holes in the ground. They knew very little and cared very little about sound investing. They were fast-talking, slick-tongued telephone scam artists. I knew it and wanted to learn the right way to do things.

From April to June, I bugged David to put me into the formal training program the same way I bugged him to sponsor me for my series 7 license. I tried to talk him into it, and he tried to talk me out of it, but he also started paying attention to me from a distance. He passed by my cubicle many times and saw and heard me on the phone constantly. One day, he passed by and there I was dialing for dollars with twenty leads on the side of my desk. They were laid out neatly so that the bottom inch of each successive card stuck out from the card on top of it. Stuck to the bottom of each card was a piece of a little yellow Post-it note with a time written on it that indicated when I was supposed to call each person. They would say, for example, 10:00, 10:10, 10:20, etc. If I called somebody and he wasn't available at that moment but his secretary told me he'd be back in twenty minutes, I would change the sticky and put the card back in its appropriate place in the card lineup for twenty minutes later. David never stopped to chat, say hello, ask how I was doing, or help me in any way. He kept ignoring me as he had from the beginning, but that day, I could see him looking at me out of the corner of his eye. He was smiling and had a very pleased look on his face.

In the meantime, I was still acquiring new clients and opening new accounts for Jacob. I was in his office one day to get his signature. He looked at me and in a somewhat annoyed voice, said "Relax, you're such a Nervous Nelly."

I was embarrassed, but what could I say? I knew he was right. Going along with the program, thus putting up with offensive behaviors and sometimes downright misogyny, was critical to keeping my job. It is ridiculous to think that a cold caller, especially a girl cold caller, could have made waves because she didn't like the methods or attitudes of almost the entire office. I wanted my job, and I wanted to be a broker. Not only did I have my foot in the door,

I now had one leg in. The office environment and hostile culture was so prevalent and pervasive that it was just a part of daily life. You had to endure it and deal with it if you were in that office, period.

—⁓—

It's difficult to describe the emotions that one internally cultivates to be able to function and stay in a place like that. A hostile environment has a creeping effect on you that I would liken to secondhand smoke. Its insidious emotional effect is constantly in the air. You cannot protect yourself from breathing it in or from being adversely affected by it unless you leave the premises. And, even then, what has gotten into your lungs has done its damage.

Towards the end of June 1992, David finally gave in. He knew I could do it; he saw me working and heard me on the phone. He warned me that what I wanted to do was useless, but, if I insisted, he would put me into the formal training program. He said I'd have to interview with James, take the required tests and pass, as any other new hire would have to do, but if all went well, I was in. I went back to James and set up an appointment to interview with him. That interview went well and he gave the OK to take the required tests, which I passed, so I was accepted into the training program and no longer worked for Jacob.

I was officially a broker trainee and, as such, received a base salary of two thousand dollars a month for one year. After the one year of salary, my pay went to straight commissions, and the clock had started ticking immediately after being hired. The bad part was that those people who were hired straight into the formal training program were not series 7 licensed. Through the program, those hired all over the country in a particular month formed a specific class. Each new hire studied independently as well as a group through large countrywide conference calls. This study period lasted about four months before they took the series 7 test. I already had my license and had been opening accounts for

Jacob for six months, so what was I going to do for the next four months? Almost nothing. Again, it was another totally dead period and a waste of time. In October 1992, when the rest of my training class had passed their series 7 licensing test and we were all brought together for the one month of training together, I finally quit my job at the restaurant.

Because I was no longer waiting table and was earning a salary to get started, I worked late in the office every day until five or six at night. On many occasions, late in the afternoon, my phone would ring and I'd pick it up and hear a young male voice go off on a pornographic monologue. I'd hang up after a few seconds as it registered in my mind what was happening. Some guys didn't want to keep it just between the two of us. They would call a prostitute, or so they said, and have her talk dirty to them. They would put her on the speakerphone so everyone could enjoy her talents. The problem was I didn't want to hear it, especially when I was cold-calling trying to get leads. It was so loud that the person on the other end of my line would have been able to hear the prostitute over me.

Can you imagine getting a cold call from one of the premier brokerage houses of the time— "Hello, Mr. Smith, yes, this is Tameron Keyes calling from Shearson Lehman Brothers in Los Angeles. I trust you're familiar with my firm?"— and then hearing some little wench in the background say, "Oh yeah baby, I wanna suck your dick?"

I'd have to stop calling. I'd just sit at my desk for a few minutes and wait. I don't know why, but the public porno calls would start and stop over and over. Maybe the guys involved would call several times or maybe they would call more than one woman. Maybe the women would give them teasers and then hang up if they didn't pay. I don't know, but there would be quiet spots, and I'd start calling again. After a few minutes, pornographic talk would start again on a speakerphone so eventually I would just give up and go home.

Another time, someone left me a little gift on my desk. It was a bath and shower gel sample of Vita Spa. Stapled to it was a 5"x10" index card we used for qualifying leads. Written on the card were the words, "USE IT!" There was no way I was going to make myself a "problem." I knew what I wanted, and I wasn't going to blow my one chance at it. There were many more incidents that I just can't remember anymore. It was exhausting living through it, and I tried my best not to think about it or let it bother me. It still was shocking, and the cumulative effect of events like these, day after day, wore me down emotionally.

—⁓—

The experience of my training class was an encouragement and a bit of a relief. The class was split into two groups. All new hires from the western half of the country came to Century City in Los Angeles for a month of classroom training together, and those from the eastern half met at World Trade Center in New York for one month at the same time. After that one-month classroom session, trainees went back to their respective branches to start their careers. After four months on our own in our respective branches, the whole class met again for one week at the World Trade Center in New York. After eleven months if you met certain production numbers, the company flew you back to New York again for what was called "Segment 3." I heard from my fellow class members that they didn't learn anything new in Segment 3. It was just the perk of being sent to New York again for those who had made the most money during the first eleven months of their producing career. There was no way I was going to make Segment 3. Unbeknownst to me, I was about to begin nine years of retaliation, legal trauma, corporate manipulation, and personal survival strategizing that lead up to my trial/arbitration in December 2002 and several more years of emotional aftermath.

V

AN UNFORTUNATE
PROMOTION
TRIGGERS THE WAR

David Greenblatt's extreme deference worked. He was promoted to become a manager again in December 1992. He would leave our branch as sales manager and become the branch manager of an office in a suburb of Los Angeles. Sometime in January 1993, a fellow broker in the office, Chad Porter, took the sales manager position. I didn't know him at all. At some point, I sat in a cubicle directly across from his office, and I remember him coming in regularly at about 8:30 in the morning, but he never said hello or acknowledged me in any way.

His management training of the office began immediately through our branch meetings. That was the first time I really heard him talk. It was obvious to me he was in over his head. He was very insecure and tried to cover it up with his tough-guy former football player act. Bullies are essentially cowards, and Chad was a bully. Unfortunately for me, he got himself into an opportunity where he could humiliate, dominate, and show those he thought weaker than he who was boss. By this time, the company had changed names again, and, also unfortunately for Smith Barney Shearson, as we were then called, Chad's judgment was way off. His attacks on me began in the first month he was promoted. I came in one morning at about 7:00 a.m., which was unusual for me. The guys sitting in the cubicles around me immediately told me that Chad wanted to see me in his office as soon as I got in. I went into his office and asked if he wanted to see me.

He laid into me, "What time is it?" he barked.

"7:00 a.m." I said, confused and still not understanding what he wanted.

"What time does the market open?" he snapped again. Then I understood and got angry. Mr. Consistently 8:30-in-the-morning is giving me a hard time about getting into the office after the market opened?

I fought back and, defending myself, said, "I'm never late," then turned walked out of his office without waiting for a response. My business is my business; what if I'd had a breakfast appointment with a client? I wasn't going to let him get away with that by standing there like an idiot and taking it. I was angry because it was so off-the-wall and unfair. I started keeping track of when all the guys sitting around me came in the morning. I wrote the times down in my Franklin Planner each morning in Arabic so nobody would understand what I was doing. The next time he tried that bully tactic, I would be able to whip out my numbers and throw them back in his face. Lots of guys habitually came into the office an hour or more after the market opened. I, on the other hand, was always in my seat at 6:30 a.m. with rare exceptions. He had no good cause to jump on me like that.

My interactions with Chad were short and few. He called me into his office again one day, after I had politely complained to James Ayala that I was demoralized. In turn, James, I'm guessing, told him to help me. Now that he had put me through the formal training program, James must have thought he had an interest in my doing well, at least enough interest to mention something to Chad. During that interaction, Chad told me that a good stock to pitch was Orbital Sciences, stock symbol ORBI, and proceeded to show me how to write a ticket taking down a nickel or a dime. Taking down extra money was really adding a dime, nickel, or whatever to the price of the stock. The extra money went into the broker's pocket, and it was perfectly legal. It was weird because the whole office took down extra money on over-the-counter stocks; it was part of the game there. I had been doing that for months with over-the-counter or foreign stocks. Did he think I was a total moron? I was annoyed by the condescension, but he was now my boss, and I had to be polite. He seemed to be uncomfortable and annoyed with me as well. To make matters worse, I was also having a problem with my eye contacts and couldn't see his computer screen well. He looked at me as if I were an idiot. I thanked him for his tip and left his office. It wasn't a positive interaction.

Another time, I went to his office for a signature. During the course of that conversation, he said to me in a sarcastic voice, "I'm going to knock you across the room." Did he mean it literally? Combined with all my other experiences in the branch and my experiences with him specifically, I took it as a threat, and I believe he said it to intimidate me, whether he meant it literally or not. Is that how a manager is supposed to manage? The guy didn't know how to talk to people and his contempt for me was obvious.

—⚬—

One morning, I came into the office and tried to unlock my cabinet as I usually did. I stored everything in there: my client files, leads, lead cards, headset, etc. The key wasn't working right. As I played around with the cabinet and then started to struggle with it, the whole cabinet tipped forward, towards me. Then the drawer fell open, and I had to grab the cabinet by the sides before it fell on me. I realized my key didn't work because this cabinet was not my cabinet. Between the time I had left my office the day before and the time I had come in to the office the next morning, someone had stolen my whole cabinet. Apparently, someone had decided that his broken, unstable cabinet would be a good replacement for my cabinet, so he broke into my cabinet, took all my stuff out, stole my cabinet, replaced it with his broken cabinet, and put all my stuff back into the broken cabinet. It was obvious to me that whoever stole my cabinet did so because he knew there would be no consequences. It was just a girl's cabinet. I was angry again, so angry I marched to my sales manager's office. He wasn't in yet, but his secretary, Karen, was there. Karen seemed to be about fifteen years older than I, but she had been in the business for a long time. She struck me as another woman from a slightly older generation who had to learn to just put up with a lot of shit from obnoxious and bad-mannered men. She was an ordinary woman, a single parent, who to me seemed to have low self-esteem and low self-confidence. I also imagined that she probably spent her life going along to get along and had endured and justified abusive relationships. David, our previous sales manager, had habitually treated her like crap, in my opinion. She, in turn, was often cantankerous and abrasive herself but paradoxically professed to like David. She eventually even followed him by transferring to his branch.

This particular incident even pissed Karen off. When I told her what had happened so that she would tell Chad, she got so angry she did something I didn't expect. She grabbed the managerial copies of the keys and marched down the hallway to hunt for my file cabinet. She marched into a couple of sets of large brokers' offices. It was so early they hadn't arrived yet. She tried their cabinets with her keys. None worked. I was hoping that she would try Trenton's office because I suspected he took it, but he was a good friend of Chad's. She mumbled something about it but hesitated. I don't think she had the nerve to push it because Trenton and his crew of cold callers had already arrived and she didn't want to confront them. She knew there were limits to women fighting back. I never found my cabinet, and management never did anything about it.

During the course of my time in the downtown office many things were stolen from me but nothing was ever done about any of it. My qualified leads were stolen twice and my chair was stolen in August of 1993. I knew it would be and was sick of guys behaving badly towards me. I was about to go on vacation and I knew leaving anything exposed for a long period of time was dangerous, so I decided to take preemptive action. I marked the underside of my chair with a piece of tape with my name on it. The guys sitting around me thought I was leaving a day before I was actually leaving, so they were surprised to see me that morning. My chair was gone. I did what Karen had done. I went from office to office quickly and quietly checking all the chairs, whether there were men sitting in them or not. I was pissed. Three offices away, in the corner office where one of the brokers had made "the girl" comment on my first day of work, I found my chair. A cold caller was sitting in it. He wasn't just any cold caller. He was at least 6'3", a big beefy guy. I think he was an athlete of some sort from USC.

I said to him without hesitation, "Get up, you're in my chair." He looked around for a second, but his broker didn't jump in for him. After all, I was a broker by that time, and he was just a cold caller. Still, it was going to be a battle of status and nerves, at least for a few seconds. I repeated myself louder and then nailed him with his theft: "I marked my chair and put my name on it right there. You are in my chair, GET UP."

He got up slowly right in front of me. He didn't push himself back and then stand up as one normally would. He stood straight up so when he faced me it was as if we were standing eye to chest. He looked down on me with a look on his face as if he were trying to intimidate me.

I would have none of it. I looked up at him with a "just try it" expression on my face, my head bent all the way back and said, "It's my chair." He stepped back. I had prevailed. I wheeled my chair away.

As I approached my cubicle wheeling my chair in front of me, the guy who sat next to me laughed in surprise. "I thought you were going to Hungary," he said.

"I am," I answered, "tomorrow."

—⁂—

Regardless of how capable a woman is or how much she fights back or stands her ground, if that kind of behavior is allowed, men can always triumph over women if they are so inclined, in the end, by pulling the "woman" card. All a man has to do to put her in her place is to revert to social-sexual humiliation. He lowers her status by sexually ridiculing her, besmirching her honor, or sexually insulting her. The equivalent doesn't exist for men. Men can socially lower a woman by attaching something sexual to her in a derisive tone, including just pointing out that she is female. Call her a whore, or a cunt, make a lewd sexual joke, or somehow put her down in a way related to sex. The same level of outrage when sexually insulting a man doesn't exit. Often a sexual insult towards a man is accepted as an acknowledgement of his superior masculinity. Calling a man a whore is not even as remotely humiliating or shameful as calling a woman a whore. In fact, just calling attention to sex acts has the connotation of dominance and control for men and a lack of respect for and higher status over women. How many people have heard a mother or grandmother trying to remind others, within earshot, of her dominance or status by shouting out to her neighbor, "Hey Gertrude, did the milkman lick your pussy this morning?" It doesn't make any sense socially, but the opposite does.

There were strippers in the office at least three times while I worked there. The last time is the time I remember best. I was a broker and wanted a cold caller of my own. I wasn't going to get one from management, so I put out an advertisement of my own for an assistant stocker broker just like the advertisement to which I had responded originally from UCLA. A few days later, a guy named Moses called.

"The first step to becoming a stock broker," I explained to him over the phone, "is to be a cold caller first. Cold calling is pretty tough, and a lot of people can't do it. But if you can do it, and you stick with it, this can be a very lucrative job, in fact, a great job once you've built a business." He was about to graduate from UCLA with a degree in economics or finance, something to do with numbers.

"It sounds good to me," he replied enthusiastically, "I'm willing to try." We agreed he'd come in a few days later in the morning. Cold callers came and went in that office. It really wasn't a job anyone could do; it was hard. You had to be self-confident, well-spoken, and able to turn it on at will. One really has to want to be a stockbroker to do it. Many tried and then decided they didn't want to be a stockbroker so much after all.

Moses showed up at about 11:00 a.m. He was young and seemed to be a bit quiet, but that didn't matter to me. People often think I'm quiet, too, or conversely and ironically that I'm an in-your-face, intense kind of person, so I figured you never know until you try. "OK," I said to Moses, "here's the deal. I'll do a few calls so you can see what it's like. Then you can sit over there," I pointed to a phone I already had set up on a credenza, about four feet away from my chair. "I'll give you a script to use until you get the hang of it. If we both think it will work out, you're hired."

I had to pay him out of my own pocket, so I wanted to make sure he was really willing and able to do the job. He made a couple of bumbling calls. Remembering Annie's patience with me my first day on the job, and the fact that she pretty much ignored me so I wouldn't be nervous, I let Moses stumble along without paying much attention to him. I didn't want to make him nervous by listening to every word. I got on with my own calls and was engrossed in my own work when suddenly I was blasted out of my chair by disco music. Unfortunately for both of us, someone had hired a stripper for one of the guys who sat across the aisle from me. She came to a spot a little to the right of my cubicle, right in front of where Moses was sitting. Poor Moses was totally exposed. The stripper had put her boom box on full blast and started doing her strip dance. For the first few seconds, everybody was surprised by the blasting music, then guys started jumping up and running over to watch, hooting and hollering. Moses turned around with a look of disgust on his face. He tried to ignore the hoo-haa and started dialing again. You can't cold call with a boom box blaring five feet away.

"Wait till it's over," I shouted to him over the music. I was resigned to this kind of thing, so I didn't realize how much it might upset a newcomer.

Moses stayed for a few more hours then asked, "Can I leave now?"

"Sure," I said, "How do you feel?"

"It was OK," he answered, "but I have to go now."

He seemed to be OK. At least he didn't say anything about the stripper. I called his house soon afterward because I wanted to give him the job and left a message with his mother, but he never called back. That was his first and last day at Smith Barney Shearson.

While I was sitting in that same spot, several times I witnessed the broker across the aisle strip out of his suit down to his boxer shorts in the middle of the office and change into exercise clothes. He couldn't bother going to the men's restroom to change.

That vacation I mentioned earlier was actually a trip to Budapest to go to the wedding of Eva, my graduate school roommate. Unbeknownst to me, going to her wedding would trigger Chad's final move to get me out of the company. The wedding was in August, but I couldn't really afford it, so sometime in May 1993, I had gone to my branch manager's office and asked him if I could temporarily take another waitressing job at night. I explained to him that Eva was getting married and that I desperately wanted to be there but didn't have the money to go. Several new brokers had other jobs on the sly, and maybe I made a mistake by asking permission, but asking permission was in the corporate policy, so I asked. I just wanted to work for about six to eight weeks to afford the plane ticket and that when I came back I would quit. He gave me permission to get another job without hesitating, and he made no objections.

I got another job waiting tables at a restaurant in Venice Beach. My tips working four hours a night, three days a week, were enough to buy the round-trip plane ticket to Hungary. About eight weeks later, shortly before I was to leave, Chad called me into his office. He told me I had to make $10,000 a month in gross commission every month from that time until the end of my first year contract in mid-October or find another job. I had been a broker for nine months at this point. I protested and pointed out that lots of the guys in the office, many who had been in the business for years, didn't make $10,000 gross commissions per month. I also pointed out that James had explicitly stated during at least two separate and recent branch meetings that he wasn't interested in absolute numbers but that he was looking for "upward progression." Obviously, the same rules didn't apply to me— surprise, surprise. I didn't fight with Chad; I simply stated my case. He also wasn't aggressive this time. He told me how things would be in a very calm voice. The meeting was over, and I left. It upset me, but I would think about it when I got back from Hungary. I told several people in the office about Chad's ultimatum, including Annie, the first broker for whom I had worked. I tried not to think about it while I was away, but once I returned, I really started to sweat my employment situation. After putting up with and ignoring crap, trying to be a good sport and not a baby, dealing with rage, eating humble pie, and using all sorts of strategies to cope with the environment, in addition to working my butt off and jumping through ten hoops when the guys only had to jump through five, now this has-been football punk was going to fire me! I had been unemployed for one and a half years after I finished graduate school. It had been very difficult to find this five-dollar-an-hour job to start, from which I had worked my way up, scratching and kicking silently, to succeed as a broker. I moaned and groaned to several people about the ultimatum, but I was also angry, scared, and desperate.

Every day, the branch's entire commission run of every single broker in the office was posted in front of the sales manager's office. We not only knew how much money everybody made, we also knew which day they made it on. It was not right that Chad was putting this ultimatum on me especially after my branch manager had assured us that he was looking for "upward progression and not absolute numbers." On the last commission day of August, I waited until the late afternoon when most brokers were gone for the day. With paper and pencil in hand, I walked up to the commission run and wrote down every person's name who had ended the month with less than $10,000 in commission. That August, there were twenty-two people who didn't make the $10,000. At least eleven of them had been in the business for many years.

Annie had tried to be helpful. She casually tried to talk to Chad several times on my behalf. The last time she tried, she came back to me shaking her head and reported to me that he was definitely going to fire me. July and August had passed and I didn't make $10,000 in either month, which meant I had already failed the every-month ultimatum. From that point forward, Chad was just waiting until October when my contract ended to do the deed. This information was corroborated from another source. Jenny, another cold caller, told me that she had heard the same thing, several times. Jenny seemed to know a lot about office stuff. She was blond, bubbly, giggly, always smiling, and didn't take the job seriously. She was a student at USC and had other plans for her future. This was just a job on the side for her to make extra money while she was still in school. Guys didn't see her as a threat and would talk in front of her. Jenny is also the person who told me that Chad walked around the office and flat-out said on several occasions that women shouldn't be stockbrokers. That belief, to this day, is still prevalent in the industry; a lot of the guys feel that way and don't mind saying so.

—◊—

The hostile environment that was tolerated and cultivated in that office didn't affect just me and other women adversely. I believe it hurt Smith Barney clients and stockholders as well. Several of the guys I used to work with have had their licenses revoked or have been disciplined by the National Association of Securities Dealers (NASD) several times. Unfortunately you don't have to be licensed to manage money through a hedge fund, and I know that several of my former colleagues ended up doing just that. I am positive that many people could, if they were so inclined, tell story after story about events in that downtown office that would boil most people's blood. The level of arrogance and audacity of bad behavior was atrocious. As I said, I do believe there is a correlation between sexual discrimination and other unethical behavior. One of the partners in the office where it was said "a girl get her out of here" my first day of work was sentenced in 2010 to ten years in jail for securities fraud. He became a hedge fund manager and stole more than 25 million dollars or his clients' money. I'm not sure if it was he or his partner who made "the girl" comment but the same unethical audacity gets all mixed together.

One day as I stood close to the elevators, I heard a broker excitedly tell a couple others that Fritz, our compliance manager, was letting a client have it on the phone. Several guys went running toward Fritz's office. They were trying to keep it quiet, but several guys running toward a manager's office loudly whispering, "Fritz's letting that asshole have it; he's on a roll; come on," wouldn't go unnoticed. There were three or four guys running to Fritz's office. I just happened to stumble on the scene and I didn't want to miss out. I felt like I was always struggling to figure it all out. I wanted to be a successful stockbroker, and this branch was the only branch I knew. I ran after the guys. One of them tried to close the door on me. I stuck my foot in the door, pushed with my hands, and protested loudly. Fritz already had the client on speakerphone. Rather than risk having me make a ruckus, the broker let me in. Basically, the compliance manager was very skilled at these types of conversation, and was in the process of chewing the client up and spitting him out. The guys were impressed and were soaking in his technique. At one point, one of the brokers tried to be a part of the conversation, and, stupidly, partially admitted to the client's complaint. Obviously, that broker wasn't the sharpest tool in the shed and clearly didn't have Fritz's skill. He was just trying to show that he was a powerful tough guy too, so he had to add to the conversation.

Fritz looked at him with an exaggerated, "What the hell are you saying?" look and mouthed to the broker, "Shut up!"

The young broker reminded me of a little chihuahua barking furiously behind a Rottweiler. I had seen enough. I thought that it was pathetic and walked out. The conversation continued a few minutes later. Apparently, after being chewed up by our compliance manager and not getting any satisfaction, the client called the broker involved one last time. The broker put the client on speakerphone for all his buddies to hear. While the client rambled on pleading and crying, the broker literally put the receiver down and started talking to his neighbors as if the client wasn't pleading on the phone. The broker thought he was a funny tough guy. My desk was close by, so I saw and heard it all. The client was literally in tears. I heard a grown man crying on the phone. The broker had shystered and humiliated the client, yet the company stood behind him. The broker had won; the client hung up defeated. The broker laughed, high-fived his friends, and called the client a "fag." He was ecstatic and literally danced in the aisle. Lots of burned clients were called "pussies" or "fags."

Another day as some guys were talking, something they said triggered my curiosity, so I asked what was going on. It involved Sammy, the "fudge-packing" broker. Sammy had shown the guys around him a letter he had received. I wanted to see it too, so after I cajoled him for a minute or so, he handed me the letter so I could read it for myself. It was a handwritten letter from one of his older retired clients from the Midwest. Sammy had burned through the retired client's entire retirement savings over a three-or-four month period. The client was very polite and overly kind in writing to tell Sammy that his money was all gone, that he didn't know what to do, and that he "guessed he would have to go back to work." He also "wanted to know what Sammy thought about that." Sammy had a heart and did feel awfully bad... for about ten minutes.

There was another guy, Keith, who habitually called himself a Senior Vice President during his cold-calling pitches. Just for the record, broker titles like Vice President, First Vice President, Second Vice President, and Senior Vice President do not denote authority. A broker with a Senior Vice President title has no authority over any other broker, even a rookie.

Titles are awarded— mostly, but not always— based on production. Therefore, if you do $300,000 in annual gross commission, you most likely will be awarded Second Vice President. If you do $350,000, in annual commission you most likely will be awarded First Vice President. However, this is within the manager's discretion. If a manager brings a new broker into the office and sees fit that the broker be given a title of Vice President, even if he has never actually produced, it can be done. Regardless, it was against company policy to misrepresent ourselves over the phone. That didn't stop many of the guys of my level from presenting themselves over the phone with erroneous titles. Keith sticks out in my mind because even ten minutes after James had held a meeting telling us not to misrepresent ourselves by using titles we didn't have, Keith was back on the phone loudly saying, "Mr. Jones, this is Keith Sargensky, Senior Vice President at Smith Barney Shearson. I trust you're familiar with our firm."

We were taught not to ask people how they were because we didn't really care. Being out of line was a way of life in that branch, and going too far only meant causing the company to get caught. Getting caught was what seemed to upset management, not the fact that brokers were dishonest or unethical.

—⁂—

At the end of September, I surreptitiously went back to the commission run and again wrote down the names of everybody who had made less than $10,000 that month. There were twenty three people on the list that month, including me. It was October and very close to the end of my contract. I was very stressed out and had nightmares about being homeless. Several people in the office knew about the situation, were afraid for me, and kept telling me to get another job because Chad kept saying he was going to fire me. Then my colleague Mitchell gave me an idea.

"Tameron," he said, "do not run away from these guys with your tail between your legs. Call human resources about this stuff. This is sexual harassment, and you have to tell them about it. Report that you're being sexually harassed."

It never occurred to me on my own to call HR because I am not a whiner or a complainer. I was taught that if you want something, you go out and get it. You work hard and persist, and you will succeed. But Chad had made success in that office impossible for me. I was about to be fired.

Fortunately, there are men like Mitchell. "Are you sure I should do that Mitchell?" I asked, resisting the idea of telling on someone.

"Oh YEESSS," he said. "Call HR and tell them you're being sexually harassed. Companies don't like that at all. Oh nooooo… They will be very worried," he said in a mock scary voice. "Yes, Tameron," he continued emphatically, "Get a pen and write this number down. You can call them and report that stuff *anonymously*."

VI

PULLING THE PLUG: CONFRONTING THE GOOD OLD BOYS

Anonymously! What was I thinking? I couldn't have been thinking clearly. But, as Mitchell had suggested, I wanted somebody in the organization who wasn't involved with the branch to know what was going on. My job was in jeopardy, so I especially didn't want to leave the office early and New York is two time zones away. That meant that I had to call from somewhere in the office, but just the thought of it was unimaginably scary. The consequences of getting caught, I believed, were fatal to my career, but Chad was trying to fire me anyway. Still, I wanted my job, so I had to do it. The lessons of my upbringing— of "no complaining," "suck it up," "don't be a baby," or "difficult, uncooperative, ungrateful, little girls shouldn't be telling on powerful men"— were in mortal combat with my desire to tell on the branch and expose them for what they really were. What they were doing wasn't right and I had to make a last-ditch effort to fight for my job. I was so scared that I felt like hiding under my bed to make the call. It took me a few days to get up my courage. I scoped out a safe place within the branch office to make the call and prepared to do it. I worked through the logistics in my mind. When would I make the call so nobody else would hear? Where would I make the call so nobody would see me or walk up behind me when I was talking?

The 662 Branch of Smith Barney Shearson occupied the entire eighth floor of the building and part of the ninth floor. The ninth floor was much quieter and more private, so I went up there to look around. One hallway was almost completely empty. It seemed as if there were only two guys who occupied private offices there. I made reconnaissance test runs during the day to see if I could figure out when those two brokers would most likely be in their offices and when they left in the afternoon. The remaining offices in that hallway were used mostly to store extra furniture and files. An empty office closer to the opposite end of that hallway had a phone in it. It was perfect, because I wanted to be far away from the offices that did have occupants, just in case one of them came back in the afternoon. I didn't want them to hear noises and come down the hallway to investigate. I chose my time and place. Late one afternoon, I went to the ninth floor as casually as I could. If I ran into anybody, I was going to pretend I was going up to chat with someone I knew. On the day of the actual call, nobody had seen me walk into that hallway so far as I could tell; I was in without a hitch. I walked into my chosen private office, closed the door behind me, and sat in the chair. I moved the phone so I could talk with my back facing the door and the large glass window next to it. I didn't want anyone to see my face or intrude on the phone call. Putting my back to the window and door was a "Do Not Disturb" gesture.

I dialed the number. A woman named Rebecca Eaton in New York picked up the line. The conversation did not go as I thought it would. She listened to me for a minute and then wanted to know who I was and from which branch I was calling. I resisted giving this information for a while, but she was persistent and then became nasty about it. The conversation ended up taking me by surprise. Mitchell had told me I could make this call anonymously, but he was absolutely wrong. Rebecca became so aggressive with me that I started to doubt whether I had called the right number. I made her clarify that I had indeed called the correct HR hotline and that she was the HR manager, the person one should contact with a complaint such as mine. The last two years had been very difficult, and I was emotionally exhausted. The attitude of this woman on the other end of the line quickly overwhelmed me and I started crying. I felt completely exposed, but there was no backing out. I gave her my name, branch number, and the name of my manager. "James Ayala," she repeated with a touch of wonderment in her voice, as if she knew him.

The call did not go well as far as I was concerned. Instead of having a feeling of relief, I felt an even more desperate sense of alarm. Despite what Mitchell had told me, this HR woman spoke with me as if her role was to ferret out the enemy within the organization rather than to be an impartial arbitrator and protector of employees.

The result of the call prompted me into additional action. My instincts told me to act fast if I had any hope of protecting my job and myself. Over the next several days, I had no choice but to go home early to make phone calls from the privacy of my home phone. I started calling organizations I thought might be able to help me. I called Women Helping Women, California Women's Law Center, Equal Rights Advocate, National Association of Working Women, and the Association for American University Women, among others. I spoke to several people, all who were supportive and sympathetic. They gave me the advice they could or referral numbers of people they thought could help me better. I picked everybody's brain who talked to me. Someone at one of these organizations told me to sit down and make notes of everything that I could remember up to that time. It was good advice, because the notes would eventually be the basis of refreshing my memory many years later during the legal part of my ordeal.

Another person, I can't remember who, told me to ask for a meeting with my manager James Ayala and to call HR back and ask for a copy of Smith Barney's sexual harassment policy and all information pertaining to the rights of employees.

One advisor at one of these women's advocacy groups also suggested I tell James that I didn't feel I'd had an adequate opportunity to grow my business as a result of the hostile environment I had worked in and that I thought it would be fair to start again, in a different environment, with my salary reinstated. I was also told to send a copy of the meeting to Rebecca Eaton, the nasty HR person on the phone in New York.

I did call HR again to ask for a copy of the sexual harassment policy and for the meeting with James Ayala. Again, Smith Barney's HR person was sharp on the phone with me, which made me definitively conclude that HR was no friend of an employee with a real labor problem. I was such a naïve person that it was difficult to believe that what was happening to me was really happening. That first meeting with James was arranged. I had asked for a third person to be there as a witness on the advice of one of the organizations that I had talked to. HR and James asked me if Cynthia, a woman older than I who worked in our branch operations, would suffice. I said yes, and the date, time, and place in the office were agreed upon.

A female lawyer from Equal Rights Advocacy gave me even better advice.

"Ask for a meeting with your branch manager," she advised me. "But you can do it by yourself without a witness; that way it is less confrontational and threatening for them. Don't hold anything back; be calm; convey in your demeanor that you know your rights and have talked to lawyers. Be non-threatening; you don't want a battle," she continued, and "be confident."

I called HR back and asked that Cynthia not be there. I had changed my mind and wanted to meet with James alone, I told them. Smith Barney agreed, and James and I met alone on the ninth floor on Wednesday, October 6, 1993.

A lawyer friend of my mother's named Brad was nice enough to prepare and coach me about how to conduct the meeting. Preparation is always very important, so I wrote and rewrote the notes I intended to use until I memorized them. Brad had a different opinion from the other lawyer and told me to tell my manager James just enough to make him understand that he had a serious problem and that he had to deal with me. In my anxiety, I kept asking Brad "what if" questions, so he practiced with me how to stand firm.

"Tameron, in the end," he said, "after you have given him enough information, you just say, "'I'll be back.'"

"Well what if he says...?"

Brad cut me off. "I'll be back," he answered.

"But what if he then says...?" I tried to protest.

"Just think of Arnold[3]," he repeated. "I'll be back. It will be OK; you can do it. Just keep repeating 'I'll be back,'" he said.

—⁂—

I gave a lot of information to James, but the discussion did come to an impasse, so I followed Brad's suggestion and kept repeating a variation of "I'll be back." Several times, I said either, "I'll get back to you" or "That's enough," and smiled when he pressed me for more. It was a game of self-confidence and nerves.

I played it and got through the first round. As politely and calmly as I could, I began the conversation. "The reason I asked for this meeting," I told James, "is to ask you if you'd help me transfer to another branch and reinstate my beginning salary for another year so that I may start over in a different environment." At that time, new brokers who went through the formal training program received a small base salary for one year and then went to straight commissions.

"Why do you want to transfer?" he asked, even though I am sure HR had already filled him in as to my reasons.

"The environment in this branch is intolerable. The behavior that is tolerated in this branch is wrong by any standards, and it's progressively getting worse." Of course he pretended that he didn't know what I was talking about. It was hard for me to follow Brad's advice, so I relayed to him almost all of the stories I have already told you. "This environment has prevented me from functioning as I should have been allowed to function; therefore, I think it is only right that you help me to transfer to another

---

[3] He meant Arnold Schwarzenegger in the film *The Terminator*

branch, preferably in Beverly Hills, which is closer to my apartment," I continued.

At that time, it was almost unheard of to be allowed to transfer within the same division. It just wasn't done. If you moved far away, then of course you could try and transfer, but brokers could not generally move to another branch if that branch was within driving distance from the branch where the broker was originally located. The lawyer I had spoken with at the women's organization wasn't the only person who helped me strategize. A black broker had transferred to the downtown branch from another branch close by. Nobody knew why he was allowed to transfer, and it was highly unusual. People noticed and whispered about it in the branch, so I knew local transfers were possible.

"I consider this matter very serious, Tameron, and I will be on top of it," James responded. He ended our meeting in a disingenuous way. "Have I personally ever offended you?" he queried.

"No," I answered. As I mentioned previously, he was a soft-spoken, well-mannered man, which played so well into that stupid manager/smart manager gig with our earlier sales manager David and made the branch what it was.

James put his hand to his heart and, in a slightly indignant voice, said, "I have a wife and daughters." As if that fact would make it impossible for him to be associated with bad or inappropriate behavior. This was his first covert denial. Wow, what a cover! He was implying that, because he had a wife and daughters, he could not possibly discriminate against or behave badly toward a woman. Using that logic, it would mean that no man who had a wife or daughters could behave badly toward women, which is obviously ridiculous.

On Monday, James left a note on my desk stating that he had some ideas to share with me and asked me to meet him on the ninth floor. This time he was prepared. When I walked into the room, there was another woman there. She handed me her card. Her name was Carol Farmer. She was Rebecca's Los Angeles HR counterpart; however, I don't believe she said anything during that meeting. She sat there silently, and it seemed to me that she was there to be a witness, just like the one I had originally been counseled to get for that first meeting with James but had decided against getting at the last minute.

During the second meeting, James, ever-so-politely and diplomatically, said, "Your complaints don't have any validity, but I am going to hold some branch meetings and seminars. And I can't help you transfer Tameron."

"Why not?" I asked.

"Because your production is too low," he told me. Then in an even more polite way, he said that he didn't believe me and didn't care about what I had to say! "But," he threw in, "we have got to get you out of there, so I want you to move to the ninth floor."

For a moment I couldn't believe what I was hearing, but I wasn't going to back down so easily. I answered him back, also ever so very politely, "What I had to endure was wrong by anyone's definition, James. This situation is far beyond moving me upstairs as a solution."

He had already said that he thought I was a liar without using that word and that he didn't care about anything I had to say. I looked him right in the eyes and calmly said, "James, the problem in this branch is from management on down. The environment in this office is unacceptable, and your solution is unacceptable. And what you're telling me doesn't make any logical sense. I am telling you that because the environment in this office is so bad that it has prevented me from succeeding, and now you are telling me that you are not going to help me transfer because my production is too low! My level of production should not have anything to do with your decision to help me, James, and it doesn't make logical sense. Again, because of the harassment and hostile environment in this office, I have not been able to function. You are cultivating this environment, so you are not allowing me to function as I should have been allowed; therefore, my low production is exactly the reason why I need to leave the environment and why you should help me.

To say that you can't help me transfer because my production is too low makes no logical sense whatsoever."

There was no beating around the bush; I was very direct with James. Sitting there telling these things to my boss's face felt so weird at first. But, on the other hand, he had basically told me that he thought I was a liar and that he wasn't interested in what I had to say. Once he told me that, there could be no holding back on my part. He and I repeated our respective arguments over and over and argued in this circular way until it became ridiculous. We were definitely at an impasse. All the while the HR representative present never said one word. She apparently had no opinion about my details of the behavior in the office and no input into the conversation I was having with James. She sat there like a pathetic little lump.

Finally after I repeated my argument yet again, he responded, "It depends on whose standpoint."

Well, I guess it did depend on whose "standpoint" it was.

There was no point in going around and around as we were. "James," I said, "I am not going to defy my manager. If you want me to move upstairs, I will move upstairs, but this situation is way too far gone to consider moving upstairs as a solution, and I do not see it as a solution."

"Fine," he said, "you can move today and I am going to call New York."

I got up and left the room. Ding, ding, ding. That was round two.

—∞—

That meeting was not productive at all. It was obvious that both James and I had been counseled. He refused to acknowledge that anything was wrong. Just for the record, it was rumored that at least eighteen women from that branch alone joined what would become a firm-wide class action lawsuit against harassment, gender discrimination, and retaliation. Among those women, I am told, was the woman who almost became my witness to that first meeting with James. At least one woman I personally know about sued on her own, independent of the class action. I say "rumored" because eighteen women did not tell me personally that they were in the suit. I will talk more about the actual lawsuit later, but, for now, you need to understand that joining the lawsuit was absolutely confidential. Therefore, any claimant's colleagues would not have known that she was in the suit unless she herself told somebody, and the word got out. Many did personally tell me that they were in the lawsuit, and we claimants talked amongst ourselves and passed that information amongst ourselves. There could have been more, but we don't know. It is very possible that many more than eighteen joined, but if individuals didn't tell any of their former or current colleagues that they had joined, nobody else would have had the opportunity to know.

My situation was getting as serious as it possibly could get. The next morning at my new desk, I noticed that about 15 seconds after I picked up my phone I heard three clicks. If I picked up my phone, heard the clicks, waited a few seconds, hung up, and then picked up the phone again, I would not hear the clicks, as if the recording device was still engaged. If I hung up and waited a minute or two and then picked up the receiver, I would hear the clicks, as if the recording device had disengaged because I had been off the phone too long and then re-engaged when I picked the phone up again. I knew Smith Barney had the right to listen in on our phone calls. I specifically remember signing an employment contract, when I was accepted into the formal training program that stated in small print that the corporation had the right to listen to our phone calls. James's assistant had also confirmed to me personally that they did indeed have equipment in the branch set up to listen to our phone calls. She told me that she handled the equipment and how easy it was to operate. She said she just "popped in" the tapes.

It seems that sexual harassment, as it is defined by law, is commonly misunderstood. There are two types of sexual harassment. A quid pro quo is basically demanding sexual favors or acts to keep one's job or get paid— blatant stuff like, "Come on baby, suck my dick or I'm not giving you your paycheck." The other is hostile environment, which is when the working environment is so hostile that it effectively changes the terms of employment. Telling dirty jokes or having a stripper in the office is not enough to constitute a hostile environment. It is not illegal, in and of itself, to say to a woman, "Hey baby come sit on my face." It may be contrary to a corporation's policy, and a corporation may fire someone for unprofessional conduct contrary to its policy, but a few incidents would not constitute a hostile environment. As I listen to popular talk shows and to common conversation, it seems as if many people believe any comment can be construed as sexual harassment worthy of a winnable lawsuit; yet in fact, most women lose the sexual harassment lawsuits they file. It is also law in California that once someone makes a complaint, of the type and scope I was making to James, a company must investigate the allegations. Alleged perpetrators and witnesses must be interviewed, and the results of the investigation must be reported back to the accuser. If the allegations prove to have merit, companies must remedy the situation. They have to fix it: it's the law.

Rebecca, the HR person in New York, and I spoke again. "How did it go?" she asked me.

"I don't think James understands the severity of this situation. He has told me to move upstairs, but that is not an acceptable solution to me Rebecca," I told her. "Do you have any thought s on the matter?" I asked.

All she could come up with was, "James had the decision." Once again, she was very sharp with me on the phone and seemed firmly on James's side.

Then I called Carol Farmer, the HR woman who was brought in as a witness during the second meeting and who had given me her card. I made an appointment to see her the next day in her office in Beverly Hills.

"Carol," I told her, "the meeting with James was completely unproductive, and I don't see moving to the ninth floor as a solution. I want to know from you, as a representative of Smith Barney, if you consider it a solution." Carol, once she actually spoke, confirmed to me that she was a spineless wimp with no thoughts of her own. She had nothing to say except to repeat James's stance. I ended up totally losing it during that meeting with her alone and cried. Through my sobs, I asked, "How can you, as a woman, go along with those guys?"

Of course, she had no answer. All she could muster up was, "I'll be back to you." She said she was going to Houston to see her boss the next day and that she'd get back to me a few days after that with an answer. She never did relay to me any answer or comment her boss had about the matter. Handling these types of situations, it would turn out, was the complete responsibility of the branch manager as Rebecca had previously said, even if he and his management team were implicated in the complaint. HR was window dressing.

I didn't want to sue. I wanted my job, but I did have a strong sexual harassment case in 1993 when I moved to the Beverly Hills branch, so while negotiating with the three managers to make the move, I was also strategizing for plan B, in case the negotiations didn't go well. I would have sued in 1993 if they hadn't allowed me to move, but I was having difficulty finding a lawyer in whom I felt confident. I met with a well-known man/woman law team in Los Angeles who specialized in sexual harassment. The problem was that I didn't feel comfortable with them. This law firm definitely wanted to take my case, but something told me not to hand my life over to them. It didn't feel right, and I didn't like their attitude. While I was still in the downtown branch and in the middle of the negotiation to move, this law firm had their secretary, Loretta, call me in my office. That was the very morning I first heard the clicks on my telephone. I had already told them not to call me in my office but to call me at home instead. I answered my office phone, "Hello this is Tameron."

It seemed it happened in nanoseconds. I heard "Hi Tameron, this is Loretta from..." I cut her off in a desperate voice. I didn't want the law firm's name revealed.

"Loretta," I snapped, "they are tapping my phone; call me at home," and I hung up on her. I did call her back from home and told her that I hadn't made a decision as to what I was going to do and that I was negotiating to move to another branch.

About two weeks later, I received a big manila envelope in the mail from that law firm. It was addressed to me, so I opened it up. It was another woman's entire file. Apparently this person had asked the firm to represent her. They were turning her down and sending her documents back to her. I called Loretta and explained to her that someone's documents had been mailed to me. She totally copped an attitude with me and started getting nasty! This was the last thing I needed with all I was going through to have a secretary cop an attitude because she had made a mistake. She wanted me to bring the package back to the office.

"No," I said, "I'm going to leave it at the mailbox where it was delivered, and if you want it, you have someone pick it up; otherwise it will stay out there," and I hung up. I didn't have the time or the energy to fix her mistakes, especially with the tone of voice she used with me. "Thank God I didn't go with those people," I thought. In late December, after I had already moved to Beverly Hills, I received another letter from that law firm. They were just reminding me of how they could help me— hint, hint. "Forget it," I thought, "if this is the way they run their business, they won't be able to help me."

I had also contacted Gloria Allred's office for the first time during this time period. They wanted a $200 fee and a written explanation of the experience that caused me to seek their help. I didn't have $200, and I didn't have the energy to write an essay, so that eliminated that office. I would call Allred, Maroko & Goldberg three times during different stages of my ordeal seeking help. I spoke to two different lawyers at that firm years later. They were neither helpful nor polite. It made me feel that much more vulnerable and alone in my ordeal.

James left another note on my desk. He said he had some prospecting (i.e., cold calling) ideas that he wanted to share with me and another female broker he had invited. The meeting was completely weird. Why would he call a meeting in his private office about what he did to prospect when he first got into the business with just two brokers and female brokers at that? It was so bizarre, after all the branch sales meetings, the months of making phone calls like a machine, all the tally sheets I had racked up, the scripted book I had already compiled and used every day, and the organized lead box I already had. My God, I had been time-blocking phone calls in five-minute blocks for more than a year, and then this guy, all of a sudden, calls me into his office to show me a one-sheet blank page on which to mark and keep track of the calls I make? He had recruited Sherry, the other female broker in the meeting, from another major firm to join his office. She already had a decent-enough business to motivate him to ask her to jump firms. As I said, she would also eventually sue the company.

Later that day, I went to Fritz, our compliance manager, to ask a question. His door was open, as usual. I stood there for a few seconds, waiting to get his attention to let him know I had a question, as one normally would. He was on the speakerphone, which he used a lot. In just those few seconds, I clearly heard him say, "We should get rid of her before she hurts us." Then he looked up and saw I was waiting for him. There was, just for a split second, a flicker of alarm on his face, but he quickly composed himself and picked up the phone. He was definitely good at his job. Compliance managers are the branch legal guys. They are not lawyers, but they wrestle with bothersome clients and are the point men in complying with laws and regulations.

—⁊⁊—

It turned out that a lot of little changes occurred in the following days and weeks after my second meeting with James. I had been counseled to take notes by the women's groups I had talked to, and I continued to make notes while I was downtown. I made a note about the beginning of a change in tone. As pathetic as it was, I wrote, "Chad and James are both smiling and saying hello and good-bye now, which is a 100% turnaround, especially for Chad."

James walked by and heard Sammy cussing in a loud voice and stopped and told Sammy to stop it. Sammy looked confused. They also started cracking down on some trading practices. A meeting had been called, and they reminded us of the rules that we were supposed to follow for opening option accounts. In the past, if management gave us a managerial reminder, the guys would just ignore it— and management seemed to let them ignore it. It was an obvious game. I imagine that management had to at least pretend they were somewhat ethical and following corporate rules, but the guys knew they could get away with anything. As long as management could say they made an announcement, it seemed that they thought they covered themselves, and business went on as usual. Management called a meeting and announced that we were not to trade options without a client and options agreement in hand. Options had a next-day settlement as opposed to a five-day stock settlement at that time. Therefore, with options, you couldn't make a pitch over the phone, make the sale, open the account, do the trade, and mail the paperwork out to be returned by the client later, as we usually did, if you were following the rules.

The very next day, Sammy, sitting in close proximity to me, did exactly as management had just told us not to do. Chad, our sales manager, came over to Sammy's cubicle and chewed him up.

"I'm busting your trade Sammy," Chad barked loudly. "Which part of yesterday's meeting didn't you understand?"

Sammy was confused again. I wrote in my notes that the look on Sammy's face was "like a dog that has been allowed to shit and piss all over the house and then suddenly has his nose rubbed in it as a means to finally housebreak it. The dog looks up at its owner with big brown eyes that seem to say, 'I don't understand. What's going on? You never did that before.'"

Shortly after I made the very first phone call to human resources, James called an impromptu meeting over the PA system: "At 11:00 there will be a brokers meeting in the conference room. All brokers to the conference room at 11:00." As before most meetings, there was a buzz in the room, and everybody was talking. While sitting there waiting for the meeting to start, I heard several people wondering out loud and asking around what the meeting was about. I heard another guy sitting behind me say something about sexual harassment, and I felt myself stiffen up. After James walked in and called everybody's attention, he announced that he had called a meeting to tell us not to engage in sexual harassment. Pretty much just like that. It felt so weird.

The guy sitting behind me just about jumped out of his seat. "I knew it!" he whispered loudly. Then there was an awkward silence. It was like a collective *Scooby Doo*, "Huh?" The meeting lasted literally for two minutes. I thought to myself, "Oh no, the word is already getting out," and I knew that, very soon, everybody would know I had complained.

James handed out a one-page sheet that stated Smith Barney's sexual harassment policy. Then, he told us, "Don't do it." He didn't define or describe what sexual harassment might be. It was me and a couple of other women in a room full to the brim with men. The secretaries and other support staff were not invited to the meeting. That was it; the meeting was adjourned.

After my chats with James, other odd things happened. Chad was talking to someone as he normally would, and Karen, his assistant, butted in saying not to say such and such because it could be construed as sexual harassment. She said it in the tone of voice of a protector, like a secretary who runs after her forgetful boss to hand him his briefcase on his way to an important meeting. Chad looked at her as if to say, "Oh…right, thanks."

Another day, I heard James talking to someone, in the hallway out in the open. He was telling this person that he questioned who determines the definition of sexual harassment. In other words, what one woman feels is harassment is not necessarily harassment. The answer, he had been given, that he told this person was the "lowest common denominator." I took that to mean that the highest standard would be pegged at whatever would offend the most sensitive women. At the time, I had no idea what the definition of sexual harassment was, and I wouldn't learn what it was until my lawyer told me eight or nine years later. I still don't understand what "lowest common denominator" would mean in any given situation. What I did know and what I told them was what they were doing was very wrong. They knew it, and I knew it. It was so extreme and pervasive that it even made many of the guys uncomfortable, but how would a guy have complained? A guy complaining would have been even more strange than a woman complaining, given the circumstances, and he would have been running the risk of being targeted himself and being called a "fag," like some of the clients and prospects were called.

—⁂—

My branch management's attempts to backtrack and cover for themselves were pathetic. I am sure that the individuals in management at that time were, and probably still are, angry that I rained on their money-making parade. What an uppity, audacious bitch I am. They had charitably hired me, and I showed my gratitude by doing this to them. The stress of working two and one half years in that office was piling up. It is not fun to go to your place of employment and hear your managers plotting and maneuvering to fire you. Come hell or high water, I wanted my job, and I wanted to be a successful stockbroker. There was no reason why I couldn't or shouldn't become one. I also didn't want to be punished when I had done nothing wrong. Although the environment was incredibly hostile, I still endured. I was doing much better than some of the guys and definitely held my own with the newer brokers even under those horrendous circumstances. As I have mentioned, most branch managers would have loved to have had a rookie like me. I was exactly what brokerage firms looked for. I had worked since I was thirteen years old. I worked harder than most. I am competitive and ambitious, and I obviously have a very strong will to succeed. I refuse to give up, am very independent, don't need to be baby-sat, am a self starter, and I am confident. This is exactly what Smith Barney and all the big brokerage firms looked for back then and even to this day.

—⁓—

Emotionally, it was very intense throughout the day. Every couple of hours or so I couldn't stand it anymore and needed to talk somebody. I needed an ally, somebody I could trust and use as a sounding board. I was trying my best not to let that management team out-maneuver me or intimidate me into leaving without a fight, but in that stressful situation, I needed a friend's support. I knew they were listening to my phone, so when I really needed to talk, I would run across Figueroa Street to the mall and call Mitchell, who worked at another branch, from a pay phone. Mitchell was, and still is, my friend from my training class who had given me the HR phone number. I can't describe in words what the emotions felt like when I needed to run across the street to call a friend from a pay phone. I literally panted on the phone with stress while I talked to him. He listened to every word I said, kindly and patiently.

So, again, why did they do it? They could have made money from me, as I would prove later. Economic reasons are not the answer. I believe it was motivated and fueled from that very deep-seated mentality of male prerogative and dominance and a heavy dose of good-old-boy instinct to protect their own. Chad decided, very quickly after he was promoted, that I was out. As stupid as I am sure it sounds to a lot of people, the guy openly stated several times in the office that girls shouldn't be stockbrokers.

Therefore, when Chad thought that he had his chance, I was "canned," to use his word. His superiors, the ones who had promoted him in the first place and who had a vested interest in his success and reputation, took that male prerogative so seriously that they wholeheartedly supported, and protected, and fought for him by plotting, scheming and maneuvering to get rid of me. It makes no logical sense to me, and I'm sure it doesn't make sense to many others. People often do stupid things. The ironic part is that it turned out Chad wasn't even management material after all. I heard that Smith Barney eventually fired him. Prudential hired him as a manager but eventually fired him as well. Before I quit my job to write this book, he was back to being a broker at a mediocre brokerage firm just a few floors below me in the same building where Smith Barney's Beverly Hills office is located.

I grew up believing that truth always prevails. Tell the truth, and everything will work out judiciously. I was so naïve. My dad still tells me that justice prevails in the end. Now I believe that he is naïve too. At least twice during the negotiations, I offered to take a lie detector test. I still couldn't shake the belief that if management knew the truth, they would do the right thing. Silly me, the truth was beside the point. A week or so later, I just happened to ride up to our eighth floor office with James. He told me that his boss, Aaron Weisswasser, was coming to the office the next day and wanted to talk to me.

Aaron did come to my desk the next morning at about 7:00 a.m. We went into the conference room to talk. "I am a fair, hands-on guy," he started out by saying. "I also did not talk to James or Chad yet because I want to hear your side of the story first."

Immediately, I believed he was lying. Just fifteen or twenty minutes earlier, I had seen him, with my own eyes, in McDonald's with Chad. I went to McDonald's every morning for coffee after I logged on to my computer. As soon as I saw them through the window, I kept walking and bought my coffee someplace else that morning. I will concede that

I don't know what they were talking about, but I do know I saw Aaron Weisswasser standing in line at McDonald's with Chad at about 6:40 that morning. Chad is a big, tall guy— I'd guess about 6'2"— and Aaron is a short little guy of about 5'6". I saw Chad bent over toward Aaron looking angry and talking very animatedly with both hands. I don't think they were talking about sales numbers. Besides, Chad reports to James. It is James's responsibility to train Chad. James reports to Aaron. Any problem or concern with the branch such as sales numbers or business issues would be James's responsibility. I think Aaron took Chad to McDonald's to have a quick chat about my accusations and that Aaron was lying to me, right off the bat.

However, it is not wise to accuse your boss's boss of lying when you're trying to get him to grant you permission to move to another branch. Instead, I made my case to him.

"I've worked my ass off and put up with all the garbage in this branch because I want to be a broker so badly," I told him. "I heard Fritz and James discussing getting rid of me. I am not a whistle-blower or a baby, and I can handle guys. I'm a loyal employee, and I cannot understand why the firm wants to get rid of me. I am not an undesirable, so why don't you just transfer me?" I pleaded. I was very upset, but I was still composed. "Nobody cares what is happening, and Carol Farmer is not on my side."

"That is not true," he said very kindly. "Just relax," he continued and handed me my cup of coffee, which I had set on the carpet next to my chair.

Just that little bit of empathy, even from someone I believed to be lying to me, made me lose it. I started to cry. God, I felt stupid for crying. Boys don't cry, and girls aren't supposed to cry either, especially if they want to be like the boys.

"I feel so stupid," I sobbed, "it has just been too much. Several of the guys have told me that they would not have put up with what I had gone through. I did it because I wanted to be a broker so badly. Why doesn't James want to understand that? James wanted to know why I hadn't complained earlier. I did tell him I was demoralized, but it is ridiculous of him to think that someone in my position and a 'girl,' would have complained especially in that environment." I told Aaron that it was a systemic problem, and, given my position and the pervasively hostile environment, I felt I did what I could.

—ᴍ—

Aaron told me he would talk to some people and get back to me. He did get back to me that same afternoon. He told me he had spoken to a branch manager in Beverly Hills. There were, at that time, three branches in Beverly Hills. The manager he wanted me to talk to was Lyndsey Shanahan, and I was to call him. I called Lyndsey right away and made an appointment to meet with him on November 10, 1993.

I sat in the lobby of the Beverly Hills branch waiting for my appointment and soaked in the scene for a few minutes. I heard talking, and three people came out into the lobby. One person kept walking down the hall to another part of the office, and the two others stopped for a second to talk. One was tall, about 6'1", had white hair, and wore a suit. He talked in an authoritative voice that made me think he was Lyndsey, but the conversation between the two ended, and he walked away. For a split second, I thought, "OK, that's not him," but then he stopped before he got out of eyesight, turned around, pointed at me, and, in a very uninviting voice, asked "Are you Tameron?"

"Yes," I said, and he motioned with his hand to follow him. Right off the bat, the guy was being intentionally rude and intimidating.

I followed him a few steps down the hall to his corner office when he stopped again, turned around and looked at my bag, and in his— I would soon learn to be famous— quick-witted and sarcastic tongue said, "What do ya have in there, an AK47?" Then he turned back around and kept walking toward his office.

I was not told that this move was a done deal. I was told to go talk to Lyndsey, and that is what I was doing, but we weren't having a conversation as people normally would in a job interview. I don't remember the conversation, except that I thought it was very weird. About five minutes into our discussion, Ben Perti walked in and sat down. Ben was the sales manager of that Beverly Hills office at the time. Lyndsey introduced him, and Ben apologized for being late. I didn't know anyone else was going to be there and felt a stab of uneasiness. There was nothing that I could do about it, so I ignored it and continued. Lyndsey and I talked for a minute, and then Ben jumped in and asked a perfectly reasonable question, given that what I was asking for was not normal, as transfers like this were usually not allowed. He asked me basically why they should move me from one office to another. It seemed to me that he didn't know why I was there. There was another split-second of fear that I'd have to go over my experience and whole argument again with these two managers, but Lyndsey shut him down. Ben got a weird look on his face as if to say, "What is going on here?" He waited for about another minute, excused himself, and got up and left. I was relieved; the fewer people who knew, the better.

At the end of the interview, Lyndsey had his arms folded on his desk, and, in a very sarcastic, ridiculing voice and with an intimidating look on his face, he leaned forward and said, "Is there anything else you want?" He was very deliberate and practiced in intimidation. He was good at it and seemed to revel in it.

I didn't expect it, and I absolutely didn't want a war. I felt I was no match for these guys. I slunk back into my chair. "No," I said and that was it.

"I'll get back to you," Lyndsey told me. It was becoming the standard answer.

Carol Farmer called a day or so later. "How'd it go?" she asked.

"Not smooth," I answered.

Several phone calls went back and forth between me and Lyndsey and me and Carol. I was trying to get an answer. Carol finally called on November 17 and told me the move had been approved but that they were still working on the money. Remember, I had asked for my one-year salary to be reinstated. A few days later, she called me back, this time with a hostile edge to her voice. I felt again that her attitude and comments showed she was just a mouthpiece for those guys. She had no real power or pull. She told me the money was a no-go but, "They are going to keep you," as if they scripted her words for her. I balked. "They knew you weren't going to like that," she added, referring to the part about no-continued-salary.

"Who specifically made the decision Carol, I'd like to know?"

"It was James, Lyndsey , and Aaron together," she answered.

"Can you please give me Aaron's phone number?" I asked. She gave it to me, and I left him a message.

I ended up going up to Aaron's office and having another talk with him, basically repeating what I had been saying repeatedly about starting over and needing that salary to survive in order to start over. I also didn't like the "They're going to keep you" comment. It was unnecessary, and I thought it was manipulatively threatening, so I wanted to address it.

"Are you guys thinking of firing me?" I asked.

"That is one of our options," Aaron calmly replied. "I have heard your arguments Tameron; I'll get back to you." He did call the next day and told me over the phone that they would give me $800 a month for six months and that was it. I made an audible noise that indicated I wasn't happy about it.

"I'd thought you'd be happy with that," Aaron responded in what I now recognize to have been another manipulation tactic. They were much better and infinitely more experienced at this than I was. Basically, their offer was a continuation of what our training salaries had diminished to, so instead of starting over, they continued that diminished salary for six more months. I felt it was the best that I could do with them, so I accepted it and moved to the Beverly Hills office on December 1, 1993.

VII

THE BRANCH KING

Perhaps after what I had experienced in my first two and a half years at Smith Barney Shearson I should have known that moving wasn't going to be a solution with this company, but I didn't. Entrenched beliefs and habits are difficult to change. I persisted in my habit of ignoring obstacles together with my belief that people, in the end, do the right thing allow justice to prevail. A large part of my mind believed they would let me move, leave me alone, and sincerely allow me to start over, even if I didn't get my starting pay. The initial interview with Lyndsey was my first clue that moving peaceably wasn't going to happen, but I knew this was my one shot at trying again, no matter how disadvantaged I was. I took what I could get. I wasn't in a position to make any more demands, and the thought that they would try to get me to leave by other means once I had moved didn't even occur to me. As I have said, I am an optimist by nature, so again once I put my eye on the ball I tried to ignore everything else.

I moved myself. I packed my boxes of client files and all my desk stuff, put them in my Honda Civic hatchback, and drove to Beverly Hills. I told Annie that I had gotten the approval to move but told her nothing about the complaint I made or the negotiations I had with management. I saw no benefit in telling her but did see possible negative consequences, so I kept my mouth shut. She seemed surprised that I was able to get the transfer but was happy for me. I don't think I actually went down to her office to say good-bye the day I left, and I'm sure I didn't say good-bye to anyone else. I called all my clients, told them that I was moving branches and that their account numbers would change but nothing else. There were no papers to sign; it would just happen. They had no idea about what had been happening in the downtown branch, the negotiations, or why I was moving. I told them I was moving branches to be closer to my apartment.

Unlike the downtown branch, Beverly Hills had only two of those cherry wood cubicles at the time. They were located against an inside wall on the northeast side of the floor across the hall from the branch compliance manager's office. The rest of the branch was composed of private offices. Most Beverly Hills brokers were much more mature, both chronologically and behaviorally, and seemingly more ethical than the downtown brokers. The branch was quiet. It had the same sound and feel as a bank, exactly the opposite of downtown. I was assigned to one of the two cubicles. There was a guy about ten years older than I sitting in the other cubicle. He introduced himself as Raymond Gregory and told me he had been a successful executive recruiter earning a six-figure income for ten or so years. He had gotten tired of it and wanted a change, so he became a stockbroker.

Looking back, I think it was a blessing that I got to sit next to Raymond. He was always up, positive, and supportive— a nice guy who probably could have been successful as a motivational coach. We often talked to each other over the cubicle wall and could hear each other's telephone conversations. To this day, I can repeat Raymond's self-introductory cold call. Many years later, Raymond told me that when I first transferred to the Beverly Hills branch, I was bouncing off the walls with nervous energy. He said I was very high-strung, talked fast, and was generally nervous. What he didn't know at the time was that I had good reason to be nervous. Anybody who had gone through what I had gone through would have been nervous too. I was really looking forward to beginning my career again in peace and be given a fair shot to start over. Even if they had just left me alone and not tried to undermine me or defeat me, it would have been enough.

—◊—

Lyndsey, my new manager at the Beverly Hills branch, was what I would call a player. It appeared that he took his identity from his pride and power. He was very smart, a graduate of Dartmouth, tall, white, fit, single man with thick white hair who seemed to be in his late fifties or early sixties. He was a wealthy resident of Bel Air who has been in with the "good old boys" for a very long time. I wouldn't call him handsome, more like leaning toward handsome, as if he hadn't aged well and had been better looking when he was younger. It seemed to me that he had ruined his face a bit by his earlier heavy drinking. He had stopped drinking and smoking by the time I met him, but he had been known to have been a party animal. Colleagues told me that he used to drink with them after work and I heard him brag that he used to "run with models." He had a square-ish face with blue eyes and his bottom eyes lids drooped slightly as if they were in the very early stage of alcoholic droop. I'm not trying to be unkind but his face reminded me of a boxer. Not a boxer like Joe Lewis, but like Oscar, a white boxer dog one of my friends used to own.

I think most people who knew Lyndsey would agree that his most memorable characteristic was his quick-as-lightning incendiary verbal skills. He could cut Genghis Khan to shreds with words. He behaved as if his life had been permeated with that old-fashioned male prerogative: "I am the man; I say this is the way it is going to be, and it is so." A woman who did not play her proper subordinate role was an insult to his God-given masculinity and dominance. It seemed as if he was very uncomfortable with independent women. They didn't fit his worldview; therefore, they deserved to be taught a lesson, crushed, and put in their place. He was a very crafty guy and smart with regard to those endeavors as well.

They were allegedly going to allow me to start over, and there was no way I had it in me to complain about Lyndsey under the circumstances. It would have been ridiculous and would have made me look like a psycho.

What could I have said, "Eeweh, I don't want to work for him; he's too sharp tongued for me?" They were ostensibly giving me a chance, and I was going to hang in there; however, it wasn't an auspicious start.

I settled into my cubicle just fine for the first few days or so, until one day when Lyndsey was standing in the hallway close to my cubicle. I was about to drop a ticket and needed what was called a time stamp. A time stamp is a machine that stamps the time on stock or bond order tickets. Nowadays, most trades are done by computer, so the time is recorded automatically, but back in the early '90s all the way up to the 2000s this was not the case at Smith Barney, and it certainly wasn't the case in late 1993. All tickets in the downtown branch had to be time-stamped by the broker in addition to being time-stamped by the wire operator. I believe now that this was the case because of all the compliance problems and all of the lawsuits in the downtown branch. It was not the case in the Beverly Hills branch, but I didn't know that. I simply asked Lyndsey where the time stamp was.

"You want a time stamp, why don't you go back downtown for a time stamp," he growled at me with an unbelievably nasty sneer on his face.

"Whoa, where did that come from?" I thought. His response shocked me; even the manager downtown didn't talk to me like that. I didn't expect overt hostility from him. This was straight out of the branch manager's mouth unprovoked. Why did he take me into his branch if he felt such hostility toward me? I was speechless for a few seconds.

"Well, ah," I stuttered, "I'm dropping a ticket, and I need to stamp it." I realized that something was wrong with this picture, but I didn't know what. I instinctively understood it was not the time to get to the bottom of my confusion but to just back down and leave the scene. Later I asked somebody else and subsequently found out that we didn't need to time stamp every ticket in that office.

Lyndsey had lots of reasons to come to my corner of the world. My cubicle was across the hall from the compliance manager with whom

Lyndsey often interacted. More importantly, on one side of the compliance manager's office was the biggest broker in our branch, and two offices over on the other side was a corner office, meaning another big broker and another big producer. That area of the branch meant lots of money to Lyndsey. Not long after the time stamp incident, I needed to approach Lyndsey again and did so in about the same place in the hallway. I don't remember what I needed from him, whether I asked him a question or needed a signature. Whatever it was I said, his response was totally off the wall and, again, unexpected. Picture a 6'1" branch manager— i.e., branch king— getting that menacing sneer on his face, and in a totally hostile and loud voice, saying, "I'm sick of you." "How could you be sick of me?" I remember thinking, "I just got here." These early events quickly let me know where I stood with Lyndsey and set the tone for all of our future interactions. His nasty behavior toward me came out of nowhere, was uncalled for, unprofessional, out of line, unsupportive, and blatantly obstructionist for most of the next four years.

—⁓—

We got paid once a month on the tenth, but when I opened my paycheck for that first pay period in Beverly Hills, the additional $800 was not there. I was alarmed. "Oh, god," I thought, "I went through all this and now they're going to screw me. They got me over here, and now they aren't going to pay me."

Even though I had it in writing that they were extending my salary and all three managers— Aaron, James, and Lyndsey— had signed the document, a wave of fear rushed over me that they would renege. Aaron was the two branch managers' boss, and he ultimately made the decision to move me. I really saw the agreement as between him and me. And when I noticed that the additional $800 had not been included in my paycheck, I called Aaron right away. He wasn't in, so I left a message on his voice mail saying that the extra $800 wasn't in my paycheck.

Apparently, Aaron didn't like that because he called Lyndsey and, it seems, had a very unpleasant conversation. Lyndsey, instead of calling me directly, called Pete, the Beverly Hills compliance manager whose office was across the hall from my cubicle. Pete called me into his office and was definitely agitated.

"Lyndsey just called me from his car phone," Pete said to me in a very annoyed voice. "He told me to tell you that he got a call from Aaron and that he, Lyndsey, will handle it."

"OK," I said and was about to walk back to my cubicle across the hall, but Pete wasn't finished with me. He tried to get me to tell him what was going on, but I wasn't talking. It seemed that he wasn't in the loop, and I wanted to keep it that way; the fewer people who knew, the better. I played innocent as if I didn't notice that Pete himself was now angry and trying to get information out of me. Once he understood he wasn't going to intimidate me into talking, I left. I did get my money a few days later and every month after that for the full six months. It wouldn't really matter that Pete hadn't been in the formal loop. He, along with many others, would figure out that I was on Lyndsey's shitlist soon enough.

I was hoping that nobody in the branch would know about the problem downtown because I just wanted to get on with my career and forget about the unfortunate beginning. I behaved as if most people didn't know. I still don't know who knew or when they found out, with a few exceptions. About two weeks after I moved into the Beverly Hills branch, the branch Christmas party was held at Tatou's, a discothèque located a couple blocks over on Beverly Drive. My new assistant, Lisa, whom, of course, I had just met a few weeks prior, couldn't help herself. She asked me as nonchalantly as someone could, yelling over the music and trying not to come across as nosey, "I heard you had a problem downtown."

"Huh?" I said as innocently as I could and denied it. She had been friends with Lyndsey's assistant, Penny, and I think that is how she knew. I prayed that she and Penny kept their mouths shut.

Smith Barney and Lyndsey knew I had a strong case, and, I believe, knew I had talked to lawyers. Lyndsey, as many people who have worked with him have articulated to me, was a lazy manager and also a bully. I surmised that his strategy was not to fire me straight out, because he couldn't do that; it would have been more of a hassle for him. He was doing his own boss a favor— "nudge, nudge"— by taking me into his branch to begin with. His strategy was not to overtly provoke me into suing but to wear me out, grind me down, belittle me, humiliate me, obstruct my efforts, and demoralize me to the point where I would eventually quit. He blocked me at every turn, and all interactions were a battle with him. Years later, I would find out, definitively, that Aaron had given an order to get me out. Unfortunately for Lyndsey, Aaron, and Smith Barney, I refused to fail. As Raymond, the guy in the cubicle next to mine used to tell me, "Tameron, you burned the ships," and he was right.

But the disadvantage to me was huge. Social scientists call career perks a cumulative advantage and have identified several stimulus factors for them. I had a cumulative disadvantage because of the obstructionist and humiliating manner in which Lyndsey treated me.

I rarely had a normal conversation with him. He wouldn't allow me to finish sentences. He was constantly cutting me off, insinuating I was lying, and accusing me of stupid things such as reading the papers on his desk upside down. He was always short with me and snapped often. Getting a required signature from him in order to drop a specific kind of ticket was a nightmare. He acted as if I were an idiot and not doing things correctly when I approached him, even before he knew what I wanted. He would make snide comments as he passed me in the hallway and say, "I don't know how you live" or "Do you know you're getting minimum wage?" or "Why don't you take a secretary's position?" It was obvious Lyndsey treated me like absolute trash.

—m—

My first sales assistant who had asked if I had a problem downtown became pregnant and quit her job to be a stay-at-home mom. I was assigned another assistant named March. March was a smart enough woman but reminded me of one of those bratty kids in grammar school, who was always a discipline problem. She was a "problem assistant," as Lyndsey called her, but she was especially bad with me because she knew she could get away with it. She disliked her job and hated the fact that she worked for me. She would deliberately try to sabotage my work. I had opened a large account, and I asked her to send the paperwork to the new client. She never did. The client called and asked for the paperwork, so I asked March to send it again. Sometimes mail does get lost, so I gave her the benefit of the doubt. We went around like this at least three times. She told me to my face that she had sent it, but she never really had. I lost the client, which, in the early time in my career, was a big loss. It turned out that she would use this tactic on me several times. I would have done things myself if I had known and, in retrospect, I should have. I can only chalk it up to a learning experience, but she should not have been allowed to get away with it. I also asked her to send out a weekly flier that was a municipal bond teaser showing a sample of the various municipal bonds we had available. I had a list of people interested in municipal bonds who wanted to receive this weekly inventory teaser, and it was a productive marketing tool. It took me months to figure out she wasn't mailing it. March did many things like this. I complained many times to Lyndsey. March just refused to work for me as her job description required, and she knew Lyndsey would do nothing about it. Instead he would use the opportunity to humiliate me.

One morning as I was walking down the hallway, Lyndsey was standing there chatting with another broker. I walked by them and kept walking down the hall to my cubicle. In a loud voice he called out after me, "What assistant problem? Do it yourself; I did." I ignored him and kept walking, then he shouted out, "Not enough gross!" He meant that I wasn't generating enough gross commissions for him to act like a decent manager or a decent human being toward me.

—∞—

Within the first year of moving to Beverly Hills, I started getting sharp pains all over my body. I couldn't understand it. I rarely get sick, and, in fact, I wasn't actually sick. I didn't have a cold and I didn't have the flu, but I kept getting sharp pains all over. It lasted for months, but I couldn't figure out any kind of pattern to the pain that would help me identify what was wrong. I couldn't go to a doctor and just say that I had sharp pains all over and that it hurt so badly. A doctor wouldn't know what to do with that. The pains bothered me so much that I started complaining to my cubicle neighbor Raymond. He tried to help me figure out what type of doctor to visit by writing some thoughts down along with a few doctors' names that he thought might be able to help me. It was sweet of him, and I still have that note. The strange pains didn't make any sense, so to figure out a pattern to determine what kind of doctor to go to, I started to write them down. I wrote:

When I sneeze it hurts deep in my chest

Deep growing pain like pain in right arm on underside above wrist

The farthest bone out hurts, applying pressure alleviates the pain

Severe pain in my left elbow, sometimes it wakes me up.

Pressure in my calves in the flesh part

Pain in flesh on my hips from backside

Pain in my wrist when I woke up

Ring and middle finger go numb in left hand

Shoulder bone on left side feels like somebody punched me

Ankle bones hurt

Blood vessels feel like they are popping out

Back of my knees the tendon on back side most outer part 4 inches up.

In another entry in my Franklin daily planner, I wrote: "My blood feels thin." How does one describe pain and other strange bodily feelings? I never did figure out what was happening to me. At one point, I had red lines on my fingers that would get redder and redder and then split open and bleed. It was obvious that I should go to a dermatologist for the bleeding cracks on my fingers, so I went to one up the street from my office. She knew immediately what it was. She said that it was stress-induced. Because it was just stress-induced, I ignored it. Eventually, all the symptoms stopped, and I forgot all about them.

—ɷ—

Lyndsey gave me every reason to believe he wanted me out of there, so I was vigilant about making sure I didn't give him an excuse to get rid of me. For years, the first thing I did every morning when I arrived in my office was to pick up the phone and call time to document when I came in. I was never rude, abrasive, combative, or insubordinate in any way to him. He was the alpha dog, and I understood that. I followed every rule and regulation, crossed every "t" and dotted every "i," believing he was just waiting for good cause to fire me. I was constantly worried and afraid of being fired. Periodically, I would copy my book of clients so I would have their contact information and take it home just in case he fired me. At least four times during my career at Smith Barney, I investigated and/or interviewed with other firms. After a few years, it didn't do me any good because my numbers showed that something was wrong. I wasn't producing at the level someone in the business four or five years should have been producing. When a firm hires a broker away from another company, they want proof of your production numbers— i.e., the commission you generate. If a broker is not making decent money, other firms don't want you either.

It was very difficult to function under these circumstances. Self-confidence is the most important ingredient in being a successful broker, and I believe clients and prospective clients could smell that something was wrong without being able to put their finger on it. There were also business considerations. Brokers always lose some clients when they jump to other firms, and, given my circumstances, I felt that if I left, it would be the *coup de grace* to my career. I had seen several younger brokers jump firms too early in their careers only to lose their whole business. I decided it wouldn't benefit me to leave and that the best chance I had at succeeding in my career was to stay with Smith Barney and slug it out. Besides, I still hadn't done anything wrong, and I wouldn't accept that they could penalize me.

—m—

Lyndsey's accusing me of lying and spying behavior, like reading the papers on his desk upside down, would have been comical if it had not been so painful and threatening. His accusations were ironic because that is exactly what he used to do to me. Sometime in 1994 or 1995, Victoria (the one who punched her former boss in the nose) called me in the office. During the conversation she told me she was suing Smith Barney. She started to say things that I didn't think she would want Smith Barney to hear, so I cut in and said, "Victoria, I have to warn you that Smith Barney could still be listening to my phone calls, so you should know that before you say anymore." I have to admit, I thought she was foolishly arrogant to keep talking as she did.

In her classic Victoria bravado she said, "I don't care; I'm getting on the gravy train." She did seem to have a very strong case. I surmised from her description of the events that had occurred after I left the downtown branch that she had a quid pro quo case of harassment. Unfortunately, I don't believe she handled herself very well. She settled with Smith Barney, and rumor has it that she didn't get much. She is also no longer a stockbroker.

That's the prelude. The weird part of this story is that the very next day after that telephone conversation, Lyndsey came over to my cubicle and asked in a nasty voice, "Are you still talking to those people downtown?" The question totally took me by surprise. How could he have known I was talking to Victoria a day earlier? Before I had a chance to answer him, he barked, "Well don't!" and walked away.

That was a tad scary. I froze in my chair for a few minutes. "How the hell did he know that I had talked to Victoria?" I sat there wondering. And he had obviously also known we were talking about something unflattering to Smith Barney management. "Oh God, what do I do?" I thought to myself. There was nothing I could do. I was petrified, but I just kept working my business. I never figured out how he knew I had spoken with Victoria that day. He could have been lurking around my cubicle, but I was speaking circumspectly and in a low voice, or he could have been told of a recording. I suspect that Victoria was being recorded downtown and somebody called and told him about the conversation. Who the hell was he anyway, to tell me whom I could talk to and not talk to? It's a free country, isn't it?

Lyndsey was a slippery character. He had a special skill of shitting on people in front of others and then covering it up by making a funny quip. Everybody would laugh and forget that he had just shat on somebody. But he wasn't always funny. He also loved to remind those under him who was boss and seemed to derive sadistic pleasure from hurting people in the process of showing his power and dominance. That outward sense of respect was extremely important to Lyndsey. I imagine that being exposed as the type of man he really was had to have been a source of anxiety for him so he played the power and dominance game vigilantly. I doubt that anyone working for Lyndsey in a management capacity actually enjoyed it. During my early years in Beverly Hills, the compliance manager complained bitterly in private about Lyndsey's treatment of him. Pete was eventually given permanent disability. He told me that his problems, according to the doctor, were brought on by stress. I have also been told that our operations manager used to go into the women's bathroom and cry over Lyndsey's treatment of her.

The corporate game is to flatter with alleged respect and admiration. But what people said in public was one thing and what they really felt was another. Victoria was a racehorse lover and owned several of them. Gambling doesn't interest me in the least, but I did go to the track with her a couple times. Several guys from the downtown office used to go. Chad had left Smith Barney, and the new sales manager, Jess, from the downtown branch was at the racetrack one night. He didn't know me, but we started chatting as people do. He knew I worked for Smith Barney, and somehow we started talking about Ben Pertie, my sales manager. Jess told me that Ben Pertie was his "best friend." Lyndsey Shanahan's name came up and Jess expressed extreme disapproval. "That's an interesting reaction. Why would Jess respond like that?" I thought to myself and took the opportunity to ask, "Well, does Ben like working for Lyndsey Shanahan?" "Would you like working for Lyndsey? He can't stand Lyndsey!" Jess answered. His response was intense, as if I had asked the most offensive question he had ever heard. "Whoa, alrighty then," I thought again, "this is a sore spot," so I didn't say anything more. But I understood the feeling because, of course, I did work for Lyndsey; just not in the same capacity as Ben. Years later a magazine article came out in which Ben publicly praised Lyndsey and his leadership. He had been promoted and had left our branch about a year after I arrived in Beverly Hills. Maybe time and distance away from Lyndsey made Ben forget how painful it was working for him. Or, more likely, Ben was just stroking the powers that be in order to climb the corporate ladder, and get where he wanted to go. I knew Ben hadn't always felt that way and he is now in Aaron's old position.

—∞—

What Lyndsey did to me was illegal, but he was unpleasant with many people, unless they were big brokers. Big brokers were his bread and butter and the ones who really paid his bills. To lose one of them because of his mouth would have meant taking a big, unnecessary financial hit. He was strategic in the way he decided to treat each person he dealt with, so some people really liked him, especially sales assistants. Sales assistants had no power and weren't likely to get any; therefore he wasn't even remotely intimidated by them and, at times, was downright kind to them. There were also lots of people who privately thought he was an asshole, even some big brokers, but they had no reason to make a big deal out it.

One day, I was walking around the northwest corner of the office passed the operations area, so the two people there who were talking didn't see me at first. A corner-office broker, one of the biggest and most respected in the branch, was standing next to Lyndsey's secretary's desk talking to her. The broker wasn't talking angrily. I believe they were just having a chat, and he was talking in a calm voice as if he were being plainly honest. He told Penny that Lyndsey Shanahan was really just a "prick."

Penny responded with resignation: "I know…he is a prick." I just kept walking. "Wow," I thought to myself. "Even people who he thinks respect him don't respect him." The dynamic was amazing to me. Lyndsey would go into this big broker's office every day to kiss ass because the broker was an important profit producer, but this mature and unthreatened broker's honest opinion was that Lyndsey was a prick. I know other brokers, who were friendly and professional with Lyndsey to his face and called themselves his "friends," felt the same way. If Aaron wanted to get me out of the organization, Lyndsey was the right manager to do it.

As I mentioned, Lyndsey did have his admirers. They were usually, but not always, people who owed a large part of their success to him. I'll never forget another scene I witnessed between Lyndsey and a relatively big broker named Bettina, who was one of three other female brokers in the Beverly Hills office when I first transferred there. She was also in her late fifties or early sixties and had been a secretary to a big broker for many years. When that broker was about to retire, he and Lyndsey, as Lyndsey would later explain in his sworn testimony, tried to find someone suitable to take over the broker's business. Lyndsey said they couldn't find anyone, so they gave the business to Bettina, a series 7 registered secretary who already knew all the clients. She always seemed to get along well with Lyndsey.

I think I remember this event because it amazed and disgusted me at the same time. Bettina needed something from Lyndsey, I think something like a signature. She waited outside his door for a few seconds. When he was available, she walked in as anyone normally would. Then she showed him her appropriate deference. I thought it was almost like a dog that rolls over to show a dominant dog its belly and neck as a gesture of submission. She walked in front of his desk, put her head down, and then rubbed one foot on the carpet and then the other in a mock shuffling of her feet. She made some comment about making a supplication in front of his highness and laughed; it was all in fun and jest. Or was it? I was disgusted because I couldn't and still can't understand why a woman in the mid-1990's would not expect that she be accepted as an adult and a professional like all the male brokers in the office without having to behave like that. I have seen that kind of submissive, deferential behavior often with the sales assistants toward the men with whom they worked. As far as I am concerned, it is humiliating behavior, and it irks me. Women should not have to act like that in order to stay in the good graces or their superiors or colleagues.

I noticed there was one particular broker, a tall, dark-haired, handsome man who was gone for long periods of time. Sometime around the end of 1994 or early 1995, I casually asked his secretary about him. His name was Georges. He had a big office and was obviously successful. She told me he had a lot of overseas clients and specifically a lot of Middle Eastern clients which is why he was out of the office so much. The next time he was in I approached him after the market closed. He was on his way out, so he asked me to walk with him to his car if I wanted to talk to him. He was another broker who had a beautiful Jaguar. I was a bit nervous because I didn't know him at all, but I quickly told him I wanted to make a proposal to collaborate. I thought we might have some synergies in our experience and background. He was Greek-American, and I had my education and travel experience in Europe and the Mediterranean. He was away a lot, and I would be happy to work the clients he didn't have time for or who were too small for him to bother with. That way, he would have more time to spend with bigger fish and he could be assured that the other clients were getting the necessary attention they probably weren't getting as it was. Also, because of my international experience, I understood other cultures' sensibilities and would be comfortable with his foreign clients, and they would be comfortable with me. It was an arrangement by which we could both benefit. He was open about it and told me to come to his office the next day and say what I had to say in more detail.

At 11:00 a.m. the next morning, I did just that. I sat in his office and made my pitch.

"I like it," he said. "It's a good idea, and I think it will work. Let me talk to Lyndsey about it."

I never talked to Georges about it again. A day or two later, my phone rang. I answered, "Hello, this is Tameron."

I heard a deep, angry, growling voice that I easily recognized as Lyndsey's. "I know what you're trying to do; FORGET IT! Don't go to another broker like this again. You come to me first," and he hung up. I couldn't contribute even one word to the conversation.

"Go to Lyndsey?" I thought to myself? "What a joke... for what? Help? Didn't he just nix a deal I had already set up?" In this business, brokers are entrepreneurs. They build their own businesses and are the asset gatherers for the firm. They alone are responsible for bringing in their own clients and generating commissions from which Smith Barney takes a cut. It's almost unheard of that a manager would nix a partnership/collaboration. He would usually have no reason to do that, except Lyndsey had other motives toward me.

It burned even more years later when two executives in the firm each separately put it in writing that instigating partnerships/collaborations is the responsibility of the individual brokers. Of course it is! I knew that very well, but, remember, Lyndsey was a man who could, if he wanted, fire me at any moment, and he made it clear during almost every interaction I had with him, that he wanted me to quit. One doesn't cross Lyndsey, so I didn't. Georges left Smith Barney within a year of that conversation. An argument about whether a partnership between us would have been profitable or not is beside the point; we will never know. The point is that Lyndsey blocked me at every turn. He deliberately took away the opportunities for me to succeed.

Often partnerships/collaborations between an older broker and a younger broker can end up catapulting the younger broker up to a new level and resuscitating an older floundering broker by bump-starting his career again, which is what happened with Raymond. Raymond approached an older broker named Jack. Jack agreed to the partnership, and they both ended up doing very well. Partnerships/collaborations, working together, whatever you want to call it, is very common in the brokerage industry. I would say just about every newer broker in our office had some type of partnership with an older broker, except me.

What really stuck in my craw was that the next day, after that phone call from Lyndsey, I heard Harold, a tall, young guy who had just gotten his license and was floating around the office cold-calling for various brokers, brag that he was now in a partnership with Georges. The copy machine was in the hallway, between my cubicle and the compliance manager's office. Harold was standing there waiting to make copies, bragging away. He was using the exact vocabulary I had used during my pitch with Georges. I couldn't believe my ears. This guy was new and had not gone through any training program whatsoever. For the record, I don't begrudge anybody who succeeds in their career or any help or advantage management might give them, so I don't blame Harold, or Georges, for that matter. What was happening to me wasn't their fault, but I do hold Lyndsey Shanahan and Smith Barney responsible for breaking the law. One cannot treat a female broker differently than a male broker; yet that is exactly what Lyndsey was doing.

Lyndsey did many other things to publicly humiliate me in front of my coworkers and colleagues in an effort to demoralize me and to try and get me to leave. For the purposes of this book and for telling my story, I wish I had written it all down, but I didn't. It would have taken up more time, energy, and emotion than I had. Focusing on succeeding, not dwelling on the obstacles to success, took everything I had in me. I also had no idea at the time I would ever need to tell my story.

—⁂—

My social life from 1991 to 1998 was subdued to say the least. I didn't have the time, money, or emotions to devote to it, so it suffered tremendously. Most of my socializing was for business networking. It also didn't help that I am a proud and competitive person. My situation made me feel like such a loser that I didn't want anyone to see my life as it really was or to share it with anyone. I didn't talk much about what was going on, if at all, with my family or friends. My family would not have been sympathetic or supportive; that is just the way they are. I didn't want to hear any negativity, so I didn't bring it up. I coped as best as I could and took crumbs of support where I could find them. From 1992 when my brother's first child was born until she was three in 1995, I spent two to three weekends a month at my brother's house. His baby was my rescuer during that time period. She took my mind off my work situation most Sundays. Baby-sitting and playing with her assuaged my stress and put joy into my life. She had a palliative effect on me.

As for my friends, I didn't share much, but I know now that I did talk a little. Years later, after my trial, friends that I hadn't seen in years relayed to me little things I had told them about my work life in the '90s. My dating life was so sparse that, at one point, my brother even asked me if I was gay. That remark just poured salt into the wound of my nun-like existence. I wanted to strangle him. During those years, I socialized by sailing through the UCLA aquatic center, bicycling at the beach, and every once in a while I went out dancing or to restaurants with friends. Dates with men I was interested in were few and far between. Most of my life was to work, back home, and then to work again.

—⚏—

During my first few years at Beverly Hills, between 1994 through 1996, I had become associated with at least three organizations that I intended to use as a means of professional networking and to market my financial advisory services. I had asked Lyndsey for a little help, which was completely reasonable and customary in the business. The answer was always no!

The first situation was being invited on a team of financial consultants who gave financial education seminars for a major HMO in Southern California on an ongoing basis. Each one of us was assigned a hospital. The HMO was going through a wave of downsizing, so it was a fabulous opportunity to meet people as they were about to retire.

The second situation was when I became the co-chairperson of a group called the Ivy League Business Breakfast. It operated under the auspices of the Ivy League Alumni Association of Southern California, an organization that hosted events that brought together the Southern California chapters of all seven Ivy League Alumni organizations. My co-chairperson and I would scare up well-known people in the business world to speak at our monthly meetings. We had speakers like Linda Greigo, CEO of Rebuild LA, after the Rodney King riots; JD Powers of JD Powers & Associates; Gil Garcetti, Los Angeles District Attorney; Brad Jones, founding partner of Brentwood Associates, one of the most respected private equity firms in Los Angeles; Bill Simon, Jr., of William

E. Simon & Sons, Private Equity Partners; and Joan Payden, founder and CEO of Payden & Rygel, the largest-privately held fixed income money manager in the country at that time. It wasn't ladies tea, it was a serious networking opportunity. The speakers were the movers and shakers of Los Angeles's business community. I co-chaired for two years. Not long after I resigned, the business breakfast stopped functioning and, as far as I know, was never resurrected.

Not only would Lyndsey not chip in for any costs, he specifically told me not to associate Smith Barney's name with anything I did in conjunction with the Ivy League Business Breakfast. "Don't even use our letterhead," he told me. All of the speaker invitations and thank you letters I wrote were on plain paper. I couldn't even use my professional title when contacting potential speakers. Lyndsey's demands were completely counter-productive to my building my clientele and didn't make any sense in the context of our business. In fact, they were downright outrageous. I politely argued with him about his unfair treatment of me every chance I could. His demands defeated the whole purpose of my involvement in these organizations. But, in the end, the king's edicts were law, regardless of how unfair or ridiculous they were. He was always waiting for a reason to fire me, so I never defied him. I kept plugging along regardless of his severely handicapping me.

I also belonged to the International Visitors Council of Los Angeles. It is a non-profit organization attached to the State Department that sponsors up-and-coming diplomats as well as political and business people from around the world to visit the United States. When I first joined, I offered to put together a social mixer at The Gate, another well-known Los Angeles disco. I wanted to meet everybody. The organization agreed, and I put the mixer together but again received no help from Lyndsey. His answer to me as always was "No." He not only would not let me use the office stamp machine for the invitations, but again there was no associating Smith Barney's name with my endeavors.

About the same time I had professional brochures made. I designed them, had them approved by the compliance department in New York, and had them printed in Los Angeles. Nowadays, Smith Barney has a whole program devoted to approved brochures that brokers can put together for themselves, but, in this time period, that program didn't exist. I did it myself, with no help from Lyndsey, even though he regularly and habitually helped the guys in the office who were similarly situated as I.

Sometime in the mid-'90's, I took a brochure to Lyndsey about the California governor- sponsored Call to Action, a convention dedicated to women empowering themselves. It has now become a large and important annual conference in California. I asked him if he would help me get a booth there. He made fun of me. "NO," he said, "it's a waste of time." I left his office feeling stupid and demoralized as usual. I went to the conference anyway just as a participant.

Ironically, the next year, or it could have been two years later, the Los Angeles regional division of Smith Barney sponsored a booth, just as I had asked Lyndsey to help me do. The Los Angeles divisional boss invited many financial consultants from several branches to attend Smith Barney's booth in shifts. Smith Barney had a $100 drawing as a way to get leads and bought lunch for all of us brokers who had volunteered to attend the booth. My boss's boss's boss was there himself, all day. Waste of time, huh? I was told I got the most leads that day, which I turned into several accounts.

I want to reiterate and clarify again that every broker is completely responsible for building his or her own business. Lyndsey, or any manager for that matter, is not obligated to financially help any broker with any business-generating endeavor he or she pursues. However, brokers are the profit generators of the firm. A manager hires a broker because he, in his best estimation, believes that the broker will be able to build a business, thus bringing more revenue to the firm and to his personal pocket. Managers get a cut of what the broker produces. Although Lyndsey was never obligated to help me or any newer broker, it was in his best interest to do so, and managers usually do help brokers. It is customary managerial practice to share some business expenses with brokers, especially newer brokers. There is no reason to hire a broker if a manager doesn't want him or her to succeed.

Each branch has fixed costs for which it is responsible: leases, utilities, operations, administrative employee payroll, etc. Also every year, approximately in December, each branch manager gets a phone call from Smith Barney's corporate lawyers, who tell him how much money to "reserve." This is an estimation of how much the branch will pay out in lawsuits. What is left after a branch's fixed costs and what they are told to reserve is the branch's net profit. The average net profit, across the entire firm is about 20% of the branch gross profit.

The Beverly Hills branch, for example, did about $35 million a year—sometimes a little more, sometimes a little less. Based on $35 million the net profit was $5 million. The manager was paid from that $5 million in tranches. For example, the manager's cut from the $5 million was 13% of the first million, 14% on the second and third million, 15% on the fourth and fifth million and 16% on the sixth million and up. Therefore, in this example, the Beverly Hills branch manager received a $710,000 paycheck. After taking his $710,000 cut, he gave bonuses to his assistant and support managers as he saw fit from the remaining $4,290,000. Let's say the bonus money he paid to his three support managers and his assistant was $250,000, then, the remaining $4,040,000 went back to Smith Barney in New York. Just for accuracy's sake, the branch manager also received a base salary of $100,000 and any commission he himself generates from his own clients up to $50,000. In this example, then, my branch manager made $860,000 a year, not including stock options and pension. It's a very good business.

As one would expect, Lyndsey did help the guys who were similarly situated as I but he actively worked against me. Each time I discovered that Lyndsey had helped somebody else when he had refused me a similar request, it was by chance. I never actively pursued this information or hunted for it. I found out about most of this stuff by accident, by virtue of working in the office. The information just presented itself or fell into my lap. I am sure there are many more incidents that I never found out about. Again, I don't begrudge any of these guys for the help they received. It wasn't their fault that Lyndsey was behaving toward me the way he did.

One day, I saw a flier in the printer tray announcing that a newer broker, Rudy from Smith Barney, was teaching an investment class at a local college. Not only had he used Smith Barney's name on the flier, he also used his professional title and even charged a fee to attend the class! I asked Rudy about his class, and he told me himself that Lyndsey had approved it. This same broker told me Lyndsey had paid for a booth for him at an importing convention.

Another day, Rick, another newer broker, showed me a marketing tool, a beautiful "wedding- style" municipal bond invitation, as we called them. He had just received them from New York.

"Where did you get them?" I asked.

"I ordered them," he said, "and Lyndsey paid for them."

He gave me one as a sample, and I walked down to Lyndsey's office to ask him to buy some municipal bond invitations for me. I ran into Lyndsey in the hallway in front of his office, showed him the invitation, and asked for 500 of those invitations, just as he had bought for Rick.

"No," he answered, as usual.

I protested; this time it was just too obvious a bias against me to ignore. "You bought Rick 500 of them," I said to him, "yet you won't buy me any. That's not right."

"That's the way it is," Lyndsey answered. He and I argued for several minutes before he gave in. "OK," he said, " if I bought Rick 500, then I'll buy you 250 and that's it."

I took the deal. I did get something even though it was half of what he gave a similarly-positioned male. I was grateful that he didn't tell me to go find another job. Every interaction I had with Lyndsey was like this one, a tiring and humiliating struggle. There were many incidents like this; some big, some small, but they were constant and never let up from December 1993 until at least the end of 1998. The struggle with Lyndsey was exhausting and discouraging. Rick gave up being a stockbroker a year or two later; Rudy was no longer a broker a few more years after that. Even without Lyndsey's help and with his blatant obstructionism, I kept plugging along.

—⁊⁊—

While Lyndsey was my manager, our office went through two renovations. The first, I believe, was in 1997. My cubicle and the one next to it would remain through the first renovation; however, the whole office got a facelift. We also got new computer equipment and a new phone system. Logistically, it was a big project that took a lot of time and effort. My compliance manager, Pete, did almost all the work, as Lyndsey acknowledged. It also seemed that Lyndsey started treating Pete better after that.

The first day we came into the completed newly-renovated office and logged on to our new computers, my news wouldn't come up. Usually if we punched a stock symbol into our quotrons, the bid and ask price of that stock would appear. If we then pressed "news," news stories of that stock from various sources would come up. We could also get all kinds of news of events around the world that might affect the markets. I told the computer guys, who had installed our computers and who would be in our office for a while to help with problems, that something was wrong. I couldn't get any news and asked if someone could look at my computer. A couple of guys did look at my computer, because I'm persistent, but it was never fixed.

After a week, I started getting louder, then the computer guy in charge told me to go talk to Pete. I did, and Pete pulled out a list. As if he were a regimented inspector, he flipped through his list with exaggeration.

"You are not on the list," he said rattling his paper. "I specifically discussed it with Lyndsey and he decided that you are not to receive news. If you have a problem with it, go talk to Lyndsey about it."

"Everybody gets news," I argued," and I had it before; why wouldn't I get it now?"

"Lyndsey's call," Pete said.

"Am I the only one in the office who isn't getting news?" I asked.

"Yes," Pete answered, "and if you have a problem with it, go talk to Lyndsey."

I did. I marched down to Lyndsey's office flaming angry. I never shouted, copped an attitude, or challenged Lyndsey regardless of how angry I may have been. I always showed him the appropriate deference he wanted and expected. I felt he had been itching to fire me since the first day I walked in for my sham interview. I wasn't going to give him cause to fire me, even though he habitually tried to antagonize me. I did, however, defend myself as calmly and professionally as I could, considering the circumstances. I walked into his office and said, "Lyndsey, I can't get news on my computer, and Pete tells me it's on your orders and if I don't like it to come talk to you."

"That's right," he answered, "You don't do enough gross."

"That's ridiculous, Lyndsey; it's not right," I argued back. "You are hindering my ability to consult. How can I manage a stock if I don't even know what is going on with the company? Everybody gets news; even some of the secretaries get it. I had it before the renovation, and I should have it now."

"You don't do enough gross," he repeated again.

We went around and around like this for several minutes. Finally, he changed his mind and told me to tell Pete to give me access to news. That was it; my news was reinstated within minutes. Everything was a struggle with this guy, as if I was taking blood. As for him, again, he was just a bully, and he seemed to enjoy upsetting me and making me fight for everything.

During that same week of post-renovation orientation, we had a branch meeting with our new telephone system's representative who explained how to use the new system, program our voicemail, etc. She also mentioned that there were "phone cards" that we could get from Pete for our international clients or for when our stateside clients traveled overseas. Until then, if our clients wanted to call us when they were out of the country, they had to call collect. A few weeks later, when the phone company representative said the cards would be in the office, I went to Pete and asked him for some. He offered some bogus excuse to put me off. As the days went by, I kept asking for a few cards for my clients who traveled outside of the country a lot. It took me a couple of weeks to get them. Pete made excuses and threw out comments, as Lyndsey did, that I didn't produce enough gross commission. My commission wasn't his business. He was an operations guy; sales were not something he was involved in. It was odd that he would say something like that to me, yet he didn't say flat out that I couldn't have a phone card. I kept asking, and eventually he gave one to me. When he handed it over, I was shocked. It wasn't a specially-ordered calling card as I thought it would be. It was just a three-fold, mass-produced list of access numbers for countries around the world. For example, if the caller were in France and needed to talk to his or her broker, he or she dialed the access number for AT&T from France that clicked into the American phone system. Once the caller was into the American system, he or she simply called the branch's toll-free number noted on every broker's business card. In other words, it was no big deal. I could have gone to any colleague, borrowed one of their cards, copied it, and given the relevant number to any client of mine who needed it.

Why would Pete play a game like that? He played games like this several times over the years. He was emulating his boss. It was stupid, but

I don't really blame Pete either. He was bullied and cowed by Lyndsey like I was. Pete was usually a nice guy to me personally. During all the years I worked for Lyndsey, if I could avoid him by going to Pete, I did it every time. In fact, I went to Lyndsey only when his decision or signature was specifically necessary.

—᠊ᨓ᠊—

Ben Perti, the sales manager in the Beverly Hills office who had come to my first interview with Lyndsey and walked out, was promoted and left the branch within a year. I don't remember ever having a business review meeting with him present, but he did deliver a message from Lyndsey to me once: "Lyndsey told me to tell you that we don't make 'pitches' in Beverly Hills and to stop using that word; that is something they do downtown. We make 'presentations' here."

"OK," I answered, thinking, "Why doesn't Lyndsey talk to me himself? Is he so uncomfortable talking to a woman as an equal adult? "

The sales manager's position is an interim training position similar to the Lehman broker-training setup in the downtown branch. The office receives the benefit of having a sales manager, and the sales manager receives the benefit of getting on-the-job training from the established branch manager. Our next sales manager was Craig, who held the position from sometime in late 1994, or early 1995, to 1998. Periodically, I would have a business review meeting with Craig, and several times I met with Craig and Lyndsey. Each of those meetings over the years was, without exception, completely unproductive. They were never, in my opinion, sincere meetings in which an honest conversation took place, in which I could talk about my business and what I was doing with a supportive manager who had an invested interest and desire to see and help me succeed. They should have been. Instead, each meeting was forty-five minutes of me defending myself and Lyndsey belittling and humiliating me. I dreaded them.

During each and every meeting I ever had, without fail, I would state that I considered and calculated my progress starting from December 1993, because that is when I moved from downtown to Beverly Hills to start over, and, during each and every meeting, Lyndsey would tell me that he counted and calculated my progress from the very beginning of my career, including the time I spent downtown. He used that time period as his justification that my gross was too low and that therefore I was a loser. This point is important because it reveals another of the many bold-faced lies Lyndsey would tell under oath during both his future deposition and testimony in court.

The camaraderie with my work buddies helped me cope with Lyndsey. We tried to joke, make light of things, or envision how wonderful our futures would be. In the first couple of years in Beverly Hills, surviving became a running joke between Raymond and me. One day, he said to me over the half wall during a particularly difficult time, "Tameron, I feel like I'm wading in water up to my knees." "Your knees? If you're wading up to your knees then I'm wading through water up to my thighs," I joked. A few months later, he was wading up to his thighs, months after that his waist, then his chest, then his neck, then his chin. The water was always higher for me. "Raymond, I'm standing on my tippy toes and holding my head back so I can breathe with my lips and nose sticking out of the water." At the worst point I told him, "Raymond I'm submerged and breathing out of a straw now." We thought this visualization was funny, and laughing made us feel better. Raymond's water started to recede before mine, of course, because Lyndsey supported him.

I and several of my colleagues from my training class kept in touch with each other. It was a support network, a competition gauge, and information chain. We often shared work stories and commiserated with one another. During another difficult period, Mitchell, my best buddy, said, "Tameron, one day we are going to be sitting on the beach in the Caribbean— me and my wife, and you and whoever you bring[4]. We'll have Pina Coladas in one

---

[4] I didn't have a boyfriend.

hand and be scratching our bellies with the other." It became our positive visualization. When either one of us was down, we'd say, "I'm thinking of the beach with my Pina Colada in one hand and scratching my belly with the other." Again the visualization made us laugh, and it helped.

By 1996, Raymond was given an individual office. As I mentioned, he had been allowed to partner up and started to succeed. A new guy named Kevin was hired and assigned to Raymond's former cubicle next to mine. Kevin came across, at the time, as a very nice guy. He and I developed camaraderie of some sort and talked over the wall as Raymond and I had done, but the relationship wasn't quite the same. Although Kevin was a seemingly nice supportive guy with a good attitude, there wasn't much to say; we didn't have the same rapport. Kevin could see however, how unfairly Lyndsey treated me and how much he bothered me, so he would send me poetic e-mails of support and encouragement:

SUBJECT: This too shall pass

Things just do not happen for the best

We must make the best of what happens

Remember once a problem has been identified

It is no longer a problem

Only a situation

That needs to be dealt with...

Do what you can with what you've got

Don't worry about what you can't control...worry makes it worse-er

In spite of appearances...this too shall pass

And you'll be okay

Peace

Once when I was about to have a meeting with Lyndsey that I was really sweating, Kevin wrote to me:

SUBJECT: MEET-IN
A world to the wise is sufficient…
Just kinda bo-gart the conversation…keep your goals in the for front
Don't let'm talk too much
Tell'um what they want to hear and move on wit yo program
Peace

Eventually, I realized that my "different" relationship with Kevin was more than a lack of rapport. The fact that he never had anything substantial to say was odd. When you sit right next to someone, you do hear everything he says as he is talking to others on the phone, but you just tune it out. You have your own conversations and work to attend to. But after sitting with Kevin for a while, I began to notice how badly he sounded on the phone and would pause sometimes to specifically listen. He had the same problem on the phone with potential clients as he had with me. He had nothing substantial or interesting to say. I remember thinking that he sounded as if he were calling people all day and inviting them to a party. This is an important piece of information, but I'll return to Kevin later.

Another bone of contention I had with Lyndsey for the entire seven years that I worked for him was getting my own private office. I asked him for one, over and over and over, at least ten times, maybe even twenty. The answer was always a resounding "No," followed by belittlement and humiliation. He would repeatedly cite my low gross commission production as his reason for refusing me. When I pointed out that I had about the same gross commission as other brokers when he had given them offices, Lyndsey would dismiss it. His reply was that it took me too long; therefore, I didn't deserve an office. I sat in a cubicle until 1998, and it really pissed me off.

Regardless of how skilled I became at avoiding Lyndsey, the fact that he would never give me an office was a very public way to tell the branch office and my clients, continuously, what he thought of me and where I stood with him. A couple of my colleagues were very supportive of me and would encourage me to keep asking. One was a big broker who inquired about the results of my asking for an office on several occasions. When I'd tell him the answer was no it was obvious he was disappointed for me. This particular broker ended up casually following my office saga with Lyndsey. He could see that I was working hard, had a good attitude, didn't give up, and was progressing in my gross numbers. When I planned on asking Lyndsey for an office once again, it seemed, even to this broker, that I finally deserved an office, but Lyndsey told me no. I ran into that broker in the hallway, and he asked how my meeting with Lyndsey had gone.

"He told me 'No,'" I said, resigned. I knew there was nothing I could do to make Lyndsey treat me right.

My colleague got visibly angry. "That's chicken shit!" he blurted out.

What could I do? Challenging his authority is exactly what Lyndsey wanted me to do. I wasn't going to give him any reason, even a fig leaf of a reason, to fire me.

—ɯ—

In August 1997, I decided to go on a real vacation. I had gone to Hungary for my friend Eva's wedding in 1993, but now I wanted to go someplace just to enjoy myself.

Eva was now an investment banker living in London. She had space in her home, so I decided to go stay with her for a week. When I returned to work, I was in for more humiliation. Two rookies, who had started that year, had been given an office. It was an extra-large office that both rookies shared, but, what the heck, at least it was an office. I checked to see how much gross production each one was doing. I don't remember exactly what one had done, but I know it was less than mine. The other had done $10,000 in gross for the year thus far and we were now in September. I didn't bother asking Lyndsey why he would give such low-producing rookies an office and not me because I knew what his answer would be. I may have been making bigger numbers than the rookies, but it didn't matter to Lyndsey. In his twisted logic, I had been in the business longer so my bigger numbers didn't matter. I pointed out to him, on several occasions, that I would never get an office using his logic. If he counted the slow start, I would always be behind. There was no reasonable response to my observation, so he just shrugged his shoulders. "Who cares?" was his attitude.

"And if you don't like it, Tameron," he'd repeat over and over, "you know what you can do." He meant that I could leave.

So many times as I listened to him humiliate me, I would be thinking to myself, "He really does look like Oscar, that white boxer. I wonder if he knows he looks like a boxer? Does anybody else think he looks like a boxer?" At other times, it was hard to look at him because all I could see was that white boxer dog in his face and it disgusted me. Internally, it became a habit to steel my heart whenever I had to talk to him.

Craig, my new sales manager, was mostly an ally and a good sales manager to have. He was an educated, civil, and professional person. The company constantly told us, in many ways, that perseverance was the key to success, so I didn't give up, and Craig was very helpful to me most of the time. Usually he treated me civilly and talked to me as an adult, which I appreciated. Whenever I had a client meeting, he was kind enough to lend me his private office. I would take down all his pictures, business cards, and anything else that might give it away that the office we were sitting in wasn't mine. It was the old "fake it 'til you make it" trick. Many times he also gave me good advice: "He who gets mad first, loses, Tameron," he'd say to me.

Craig tried to help me as best as he could, and I believe he wanted me to succeed. However, I am sure there were many days when Craig felt frustrated and angry himself working for Lyndsey. Toward the end of his sales manager tenure, it wasn't going well for him there either. Lyndsey used to snicker behind Craig's back and call Craig "Boomer," short for Boomerang. Lyndsey would loudly state to anyone nearby who might laugh that he'd throw Craig a job to do and it would come right back to him hence the nickname Boomerang; ironic, coming from a lazy manager like Lyndsey.

It must have been one of Craig's bad days when I started toward his office for something. Craig was rushing out and seemed a little frazzled, probably because Lyndsey had called him down to his office on the double. Craig didn't have time to deal with me, and instead, he blurted out. "He only treats you this way. You must have done something wrong!" and continued on his way down the hall. I had never done anything wrong, and I knew I was the only one Lyndsey treated that way, but there was nothing I could do about it.

Lyndsey would often skip my business review meetings and leave them to Craig, which was a big relief for me. But it had been more than three years since I had transferred to Beverly Hills, and there was no sign that I was giving up. Therefore, it seemed, Lyndsey told Craig to tighten the screws on me. One day out of character, Craig started trying to emulate Lyndsey during one of those business review meetings. But Craig didn't have that vicious verbal skill that Lyndsey had and he couldn't carry it off. That kind of bad behavior just wasn't his style and he looked stupid trying. Other people noticed how Lyndsey treated me differently, and how hard I tried, so at this point, a few people started to intervene. It was very obvious that his treatment of me was wrong. Several male brokers, unsolicited, advised me to start making notes of events. In summary, in the fall of 1997, this is what I wrote:

> Craig came to my desk and asked if I had time on Friday for a review. I was busy doing whatever I was doing and said, "Sure," then I paused, and said, "What review?"
>
> "A review of your business, is the morning or afternoon better for you?"
>
> I told him morning so we made an appointment to sit down together

at 9:00 a.m. on Friday. Thursday, he put a form on my desk he wanted completed for the meeting. Friday morning I had a lot to do because there were only seven more commission days in the month. Still, I filled out the form as best I could. It was asking questions based on October's numbers. One question was, "how many phone calls did you make?" I wrote "Too many to count" for a couple of reasons. Firstly, I didn't realize this was going to be a formal review that would continue with Lyndsey. I thought it was my sales manager just doing his job. Secondly, October was my biggest month ever. I was slowly doing better. As far as I was concerned, based on the numbers we had agreed on back in May, I was right on target. I had no idea there was a problem until Craig came at me during our meeting with nasty comments, in a nasty voice. It's very difficult to put in chronological order what was said because the entire conversation was so convoluted, circular, and repetitive. Craig would say something to me and want an answer. I would answer him, and he would reply as if I hadn't answered him. I'm going to put down specific statements and general concepts, not necessarily in the order they were said or the number of times they were said.

Craig said I should get a job in another industry. At first I didn't know what he meant because I have been doing so well so I asked him, "What do you mean?"

He said, "Maybe you should find a job doing something else." It was obvious that he was trying to emulate Lyndsey to the extent that he was repeating derogatory comments he had heard Lyndsey say to me and was adding a few of his own.

He said, "I don't know how you live." He'd ask me many of the same questions over and over. I'd answer him, and he'd snap back, "I heard you the first, second, and third time," in a derogatory manner, insinuating there was something intellectually wrong with me.

He said whatever I was doing wasn't working and that I had to do something else. He would ask me what my day consisted of and what my other business plans and strategies were. I would tell him, but, still he would go around and around. This went on for a while. He would say that if I was doing as I just had articulated to him and if it was a good way to do things, my numbers would show it. I pointed out that October was my best month yet.

He said, "Last month doesn't matter."

Then I said, "Since May when we had our last meeting, my numbers have improved significantly," and that I was right on track with meeting my goals.

He replied, "I don't know what goals you're talking about."

I said, "The goals I wrote at the beginning of the year." He said, "I don't know where you wrote that down."

I told him, "On Smith Barney's annual goals form."

He'd move on to something else. At some point, he asked me what trades I had done the day before. I told him. Then he asked what trades I had done two days prior. I thought for a second then told him. Then he asked me what I had for dinner for the last two nights. (I should have called him on his bullshit right then and there, but I can say that now, after what has passed these many years. At the time, I was like a beaten-down dog.) I told him what I'd had for dinner the last two nights. Then he continued this bizarre conversation by saying that I couldn't remember what business I do but I could remember what I ate for dinner! I couldn't believe it. I felt as if I were in Alice's Wonderland and we were speaking in Jabberwocky. He'd ask a question; I'd answer it and then he'd pretend I didn't answer it and start hammering me in this stupid way, coming up with the dumbest stuff, like the dinner comment. He told me that my brains were scattered all over that I had too many interests, and that I wasn't focused. Why and how he came to these conclusions I have no idea. I didn't know what interests he was talking about, and I didn't ask because it was obvious the whole content of this conversation was illogical, and his goal was to humiliate and demoralize

me, on direction from Lyndsey, I assume, in an effort to get me to leave.
He was trying to talk like Lyndsey, but he just couldn't pull it off.

Craig also told me during that meeting that it was "against branch
policy" to send out mailers of any sort without following up with a phone
call. I went to a couple of brokers who I knew sent a lot of mailers and
asked if they followed them up with phone calls. They told me no. They
sent too many. It was habitual for one of the brokers I asked to send out
CD rate sheets and municipal bond rates on a daily basis. He built up
quite a successful business that way. If people were interested when they
saw the rates, they would call him. I told one broker what Craig said
during my business review, and the broker said "That's bullshit." Two
other brokers told me to document the conversation. One of those two
told me, "They want you out of here." Craig told me that we were going
to have a follow up meeting with Lyndsey the next week.

A couple of days after that horrible meeting with Craig, when I wrote
the next note, I must have seen the article in *The Wall Street Journal* about
the class action sexual harassment lawsuit against Smith Barney. I was
at my wits' end. That last meeting had snapped my resolve; I think I had
about two more weeks left in me. I couldn't take it anymore and was finally
ready to quit.

I read that a settlement had been reached and that the law firm that
had brought the suit was Stowell & Friedman located in Chicago. I don't
remember if it was that very day or a few days later, but at some point I
went home and called Chicago 411 to get Stowell & Friedman's telephone
number. I was calling just for information, I thought. I wanted to know
what was going on.

I told the receptionist at Stowell & Friedman my name and that I was a
broker with Smith Barney in Beverly Hills now but that I had previously
worked at the downtown Los Angeles 662 Branch.

"Ohh," she said in an excited voice, "I'm going to get one of the partners
to talk to you."

It would turn out that the downtown branch was notorious, and I think the receptionist understood whom she had on the phone, a broker from the downtown office who had survived. Stowell & Friedman were two female lawyers who had brought the lawsuit against Smith Barney, and I believe it was Linda Friedman who came to the phone.

"My name is Tameron Keyes," I explained. "I am a broker currently in the Beverly Hills office where I've been since December of 1993, but I started in the downtown Los Angeles Branch 662. I transferred to Beverly Hills," I told her, trying to keep my composure, but I couldn't. I totally lost it and sobbed uncontrollably almost immediately. After all my years of hard work and putting up with all that I had and believing I was, again, about to be fired, I felt deflated, defeated, and heartbroken.

Through my tears, I managed to briefly tell her my story. She was very nice and stayed on the phone with me for at least a half hour.

"Do you want me to make him stop?" she asked. "I can make him stop, Tameron. I'll put in a call to Smith Barney's lawyers in New York, and they will make him stop."

I wanted it to stop, but I was terrified by what Lyndsey might do to me if he received such a phone call. I resisted for about ten minutes. "What if it makes him worse, and he fires me?" I asked.

She was adamant: "He won't do that, Tameron. If you will allow me to call New York, it will get better."

Linda convinced me it would be OK, and that if she made the call it would get better for me, so I agreed and asked her to make the call. Still, I was petrified and was in no way convinced that I wouldn't be fired any day. However, I had to try it; I felt as if I were going to have to quit anyway if something didn't change.

The next note I wrote:

Craig was out of the office today for a managers' meeting. I heard his voice down the hall late in the afternoon and expected him to come down to my cubicle, but he didn't. About fifteen minutes later, he called me from his car. He asked me how things were going and if I had filled in the form for another meeting on Friday. Then he told me to "keep up the good work." Since when does anyone tell me to "keep up the good work!" especially Craig, who chewed me up with ridiculous comments, completely belittling and demoralizing to the point that I'm calling in sick on Friday before a Saturday meeting with a client? I believe the manager's meeting was about The Wall Street Journal article. It's interesting because he keeps telling me to "keep up the good work" after the lawsuit news came out.

A week later, I wrote again:

Craig and I had another meeting on Monday. The reason why we had it on Monday instead of the previous Friday was because I didn't go to work on Friday knowing that I'd have to have a meeting with him. I thought it would be the same old shit except worse, because Lyndsey was going to be there. I wasn't about to go into the office on Friday and have these guys completely upset and demoralize me one day before an important meeting on Saturday, with an offshore client who was in Los Angeles for a rare visit. Also, I thought I might get an order from the client, which would bring my numbers in line for November. On Monday, Craig had completely changed his attitude. He was Mr. Nice Guy this time around. He was civilized and logical and no put-downs. It was a 180-degree turnaround! I'm sure he was told to cool it, or at least figured out he should because of the managers' meeting, which I suspect was about the class action lawsuit. We talked again of my production numbers, goals, what I'm doing, etc., etc.

At some point, I said, "Cold-calling doesn't work anymore and that even the guys in the downtown office don't do it anymore."

He interrupted me, "Don't talk about the people downtown. That's bad."

We talked about some administrative things, and I made the comment that my assistant, Amelia, was great but that I didn't give her much. "I never gave any of my assistants much, but what I do give her she does a good job." Craig quickly started writing notes down about my comment, which he had never done before. He had this stupid look on his face, as if saying, "Ah ha! Intelligence info with which I can report back to headquarters."

"Craig is an idiot," I wrote.

VIII

THE LEGAL ODYSSEY BEGINS: BUT THE KING ISN'T DONE WITH ME YET

The announcement of the class action settlement was not the end of the legal action. For most of us class members, the fall of 1997, when the settlement was announced in *The Wall Street Journal*, was just the beginning. The whole suit was not wrapped up for another ten years. That November, we were sent a court-ordered notice to announce the settlement and invite members, meaning female employees of Smith Barney, to join the suit and submit individual claims. However, the deadline to join the lawsuit and submit a claim was not until June of 1999, a year-and-a-half away, and a lot would happen during that time.

I planned on joining the suit but was terrified that Lyndsey would find out and make my working life worse with more retaliation, so early on I had decided to submit my claim at the last minute. I wanted to keep plugging along and build my business with as little opposition from Lyndsey as I could maneuver. Calling Stowell & Friedman didn't make Lyndsey stop, but his behavior toward me noticeably changed and the threats from my last meeting with Craig were never made again. I don't know if Lyndsey's behavior changed because of a phone call he received from Smith Barney's lawyers or because of the managers' meeting that took place after the class action settlement was announced, but it was obvious Lyndsey had been told something. His demeanor changed somewhat as did his strategy and tactics. He became what I call "the Whisperer." Instead of keeping things relatively quiet and engaging in covert subversion of my career, he started an overt "demoralize Tameron campaign" by deliberate whispers and gossip with nearly all of my colleagues. I am sure many of them felt special that he "confided" in them and that he considered them "friends" enough to fill them in on his important managerial problems. He tried more often and more publicly to provoke ridiculous scenarios and make excuses and justifications for his behavior toward me to anyone within earshot. It was as if he was now trying to gather everybody on his side and cover for himself, which he had not done before.

I deduced he said something about "sexual harassment" and me because of the comments my colleagues started making toward me. It felt like he was trying to rally the troops and solicit help in the office from his "friends"— i.e., those dependent on him for something— in order to make me disliked and to put pressure on me. I got along with everybody in the office for the most part, so his campaign was upsetting and made me even more anxious. I was still afraid that he would fire me at any minute, so I copied my client book and started hunting around, yet again, for another firm that might hire me.

I didn't know it at the time, but there were several aspects to the class action settlement agreement in November 1997 that Smith Barney had promised to implement as a means to try and change the culture of the firm with regards to women. All of management was notified, repeatedly and in detail, of the new behavior that was now expected of them. One of the stipulations was that branch managers had to hire women as stockbrokers and cultivate their careers to success. I was told later that their monetary compensation was tied to compliance with that order for the next five years. This new corporate attitude, I imagine, alarmed Lyndsey as well as many of his male colleagues and superiors. Times were changing, but he was resentful and wasn't sure how to deal with it, so he continued to resist where he dared.

Just weeks after the settlement announcement, a woman was hired in our office. Something seemed odd about the arrangement, and I had a hunch that she was hired as a maneuver on Aaron Weisswasser's and Lyndsey's part, in an attempt to somehow make themselves look better with regards to my situation. She seemed to be such an unlikely hire, yet she told me she interviewed with Aaron first and was hired within two weeks of contacting Smith Barney. She was a Middle Eastern woman who spoke fluent Arabic. It seemed to me and to others in the office that she didn't have any real business experience. She said she had worked with her husband, but she didn't come across as an experienced businesswoman. She was nice enough, but she came across as a pampered and privileged Beverly Hills housewife. It is difficult to get a job at Smith Barney, and only one in seven applicants is hired. I was told in my training class that 80% of those who are hired fail within the first five years. No question about it, it is a very difficult job. Putting all this together, it was odd that she was hired.

I wondered at the time if Aaron and Lyndsey thought that if they could point to a successful Arabic-speaking female broker it would somehow make them look justified in their bad treatment of me and make me look like the loser that they wanted me to appear to be. I didn't have to worry though; she wasn't hungry at all and didn't come close to building a business. First-year brokers were paid twice a month. She'd open her desk drawer, and there would be five or six paychecks just lying in her drawer un-cashed. Other brokers at the time told me they thought she took the job to make her Middle Eastern husband angry. Apparently they had lots of arguments over the phone at work so that those sitting close by could hear her arguing with him. It was juvenile and silly stuff. She lived with him so they could have argued in the privacy of their own home, but some seemed to think that she was using her job as a bargaining position with him. I don't think she ever was motivated to build her own independent career. She quit and Lyndsey made a comment to me in a sarcastic tone about "what a mistake she was."

—⁂—

A month or so after I had called the class action lawyers things really started to heat up. All kinds of weird little incidents started happening that hadn't happened before. I turned to walk down the main central hall that ran the length of the office one day and there was Lyndsey standing there with two male brokers. I heard something, and, in that nanosecond in which I realized they were talking about me, my mind just clicked into concentrating on what Lyndsey was saying. I am sure that Lyndsey was talking about me and sexual harassment. When he saw me he got this weird look on his face, and the little group broke up from their circle and walked away as I walked toward them. I heard Lyndsey say, "This is a very serious situation," and Paul, one of the other brokers, agreed and repeated with emphasis, "*Very serious,*" and walked away.

The next day, Lyndsey came over to the two cubicles where Arnold, a third new guy, and I sat (Kevin had left) to use the top of the cherry-colored cubicle half-wall as a hard surface on which to write. It seemed as if he wanted to say something. I looked up, said "Hello," and went back to my work. Lyndsey was an expert at quips and quick verbal comebacks, but this time he was thinking; maybe thirty seconds went by.

I was busy with my work and not looking at him, then in an exaggerated, mock-panic voice, he said, "What's wrong!" He was trying to stir up an incident by making something up and pretending I was hysterical. What he was trying to do was so transparent.

I looked at him calmly and intentionally, as if to say, "What are you talking about?" and very casually said, "Nothing, I have a cold," giving him an out, as if maybe that was what he meant, in an effort to downplay his stunt. He had tried this stunt many times, using that exact same phrase in very strange circumstances when I wasn't even looking at him, such as when I was dropping mail in the basket or something like that. This time I had the courage to reply to him, "You always say that."

"Well you looked at me as if I shot you in the head," he answered in an irritated voice, then walked away before I could answer him.

He would also claim on several occasions that I stomped away in a "tantrum." His accusations were so far from the truth it was downright bizarre. During the same time period, I went to Lyndsey's office for a signature. Constantly trying to make me seem hysterical, Lyndsey said to me, "I am going to do this quick, so if you start screaming, it will all be out in the open." Going along with it, and pretending it was a joke, although he didn't say it in a joking manner, I answered, without missing a beat, "Sounds like a plan," refusing to let it show that he bothered me. He signed my document, and I turned around and left his office.

Since he had started his whispering campaign against me, his employees naturally followed his lead and encouragement. One afternoon, I went to the receptionist desk to have something faxed. A sales assistant, which is what secretaries were called, was filling in for the receptionist, answering the phones, and sending faxes. All outgoing correspondence including faxes were monitored and needed to be approved before sending. The fax machines were coded so that only authorized people could send approved faxes. The assistant didn't have the fax code to enable her to send a fax, so I stood there for a minute thinking about how to get the fax sent. It was a second trade notification and needed to be sent right away before the market closed. Pete, our compliance manager, happened to walk by at that moment, so I stopped him and asked if he would put the fax through for me. He did, but he was having problems with the machine and said something about the situation, which prompted the assistant to exclaim, "Mental Abuse, Mental Abuse." A male broker who was standing there laughed out loud.

I understood she was making a subtle joke about the gossip she had heard involving me, but I just acted normally. A few seconds later, she called Pete "goofy," so, without missing a beat, I played along and gave it back to her by exclaiming, "Mental Abuse, Mental Abuse," in defense of Pete. The broker standing by laughed again. I wanted to show them that I wasn't a hysterical baby as Lyndsey was trying to portray me. By itself this incident is meaningless, but when situations like this started happening over and over after I had called the lawyers, together with other things I was hearing and experiencing, then it did mean something. Her word choices were interesting and it sounded as if she was being influenced by Lyndsey and his spin campaign.

A few days later, I was walking down the hall and passed two brokers standing there chatting. One was absentmindedly pulling the dead leaves off an office plant. As I passed by, one broker changed his tone and said loudly, "That's sexual harassment," referring to the other broker pulling dead leaves off the plant, and they both looked at me accusingly. On another occasion, a guy responded to a quip I had made that if I pushed him over he'd sue me for discrimination. Out of the blue, my secretary asked me if Lyndsey's not giving me an office was a "sexual thing." I said I didn't think so, then she replied, "Yeah, he's not like that." I agreed because I was constantly trying to calm the situation down and because it wasn't sexual in the way she meant it, the "hey baby come sit on my face" kind of way. Lyndsey wasn't like that. It was sexual in the discrimination and retaliation kind of way, but that was not the time to divulge my business and get into details with her.

During the same time period, I was getting return envelopes from the storage room when an assistant walked in and said, "Stealing stuff again," in a tone that wasn't quite a joke. It was the way she said it and the fact that this was the third or fourth time she had made such a comment to me that were significant. I thought it was weird because she had always been nice and polite before.

There was one particular colleague whom I often ended up sitting next to during office meetings because we were both front row people. He would always nod off during meetings. I teased him good-naturedly about it many times as I would on one particular day. He was a funny, gregarious guy, so I said to him jokingly, "No sitting next to me if you're going to sleep and nod your head." My teasing had never been a problem for him before.

This time he loudly fake snored, then looked at me and said, "That's not sexual harassment," and laughed in an obnoxious accusatory way. After that day, he continued to make insinuating comments about sexual harassment to me. I stopped joking with him and stopped sitting next to him.

Before a meeting started on another day, I turned around to chat with another male broker, as people do before meetings start. This broker had a brown bag in his hand, so I said to him jokingly, "Did you bring us a present?"

He responded in a very nasty voice, "Why should I bring you a present?" I was taken aback for a moment at the level of hostility in his voice and face, then said, "I didn't say you should bring us a present. I asked if you did bring us a present because I saw you walk in with a little brown bag."

He responded, "Actually that was my breakfast and my lunch;" then after he thought for a minute, he continued in a nasty voice, "The only present you get is to work here." I was stunned. I had heard Lyndsey himself make that statement about me. Our sales manager was standing there, so this broker looked up at him and said, "Isn't that right?" expecting our sales manager to back him up and agree. The sales manager ignored him and walked away. I didn't say a word. I couldn't believe my colleague's meanness and audacity. We were both brokers in equal positions in the company. My employment was none of his business, just as his employment was not my business. I should have told him that, but I felt that I had to be constantly pleasant. It was a strange thing for a colleague to say to another, and I felt as if I was hearing Lyndsey's voice echoing all over the place.

Another day, I was walking down that central hallway and a colleague was walking toward me. We were about to pass each other when he plastered himself in an exaggerated way against the hallway wall and lifted his hands up to his shoulders with his palms open like one sees in the movies when someone says, "Stick 'em up." It was as if he was saying in an exaggerated and hysterical way, "I'm not touching you or even close to touching you, so don't try and accuse me of anything." It was so unbelievably stupid. I just ignored him and kept walking.

None of these strange incidents with my colleagues occurred before I had called Stowell & Freidman. Many people stopped talking to me for a while in late 1997 and early 1998, even those I thought were my buddies. It definitely hurt my feelings. Some people eventually came around and behaved normally again, but others did not. Working under those conditions was not pleasant. I smiled all the time, pretending that what was happening wasn't as if I were as thick as a brick. Living and working within this charade was terrible, and the cumulative effect of all the difficulty and having no idea how it all was going to play out was emotionally draining. I operated on a day-to-day basis as if I could be fired at any moment, and Lyndsey could have fired me. Branch managers, at the time, were like kings. They could run their little fiefdoms any way they pleased, and all decisions were ultimately theirs. Lyndsey, especially, made sure that all the others in management positions in the branch understood that. If he had fired me after the announcement it may have made it worse for himself, but then, on the other hand, maybe not. Ultimately, it didn't matter to me what could happen to Lyndsey because I still would have been out of a job, and I didn't want to take any chances. I ignored or joked and made light of all the little comments and behaviors directed at me by my colleagues.

The other managers of course followed the lead of their boss, and it made doing business that much harder for me. For a while, I felt Shannon, my operations manager, had become especially short with me and dragged her feet when I needed something from operations to be done. I was on the fearless leader's shitlist, so she acted accordingly. As a result, it took a drama and a couple days to do a simple trade correction involving a syndicate trade in February. Shannon told me to go ask Lyndsey when I needed to enroll a client in a program that was called the Fixed Income

High Net Worth Program. Another time she told me to get his OK to open an account, which is needed to use stocks and bonds in multiple accounts as collateral for loans. None of these things normally needed his approval or signature; they were just regular operational procedures, so her demands to get Lyndsey's OK were ridiculous; I knew it and she knew it. People go along to get along, to preserve themselves in any particular circumstance as well as to preserve their jobs and their own standing in their work environment, so I knew why she was all of a sudden making these unreasonable demands. However, knowing why people behaved the way they did didn't make it easier for me. I have no doubt she herself had definitely been bullied and abused by Lyndsey. She is the manager that years later, an old timer told me that she was found crying in the bathroom over Lyndsey's treatment of her at times.

I kept documentation of any kind of operational or compliance mistake or event that I thought they could come back at me with as an excuse to burn me. I didn't know exactly how they could hurt me, but I believed they could and would instigate a problem, as a method of getting rid of me. For example, I can think of two occasions, involving commodity trades, when the wire operator keyed in the wrong account numbers. The incorrect account numbers weren't discovered until several days after the fact. In one case, a client called me to ask what the item was on her statement a couple of weeks later; otherwise, I would not have known that a commodity trade had mistakenly been done in one of my accounts. I also kept documentations that I had conformed promptly to any compliance-related issues associated with accounts over which I had discretionary trading privileges. (That meant I didn't have to call the client to do a trade; I could just do what I thought was best when I thought it was best.) All of these mistakes were innocent mistakes that occur in the course of the securities business, but I was paranoid. I have seen very strange things happen in my business, and, as far as I was concerned, it was reasonable to make these experiential assumptions. If they were going to attack me, so to speak, in this way, I wasn't about to just lie down and take it, so I remained vigilant all the time.

—w—

Lyndsey was especially nasty with me because he had an agenda, but he could also be nasty to his subordinate managers. I was amazed in the early years at how badly Lyndsey treated our compliance manager, Pete, various sales managers, and Penny, his personal assistant and branch administrator. Often, when he needed Penny for something and she wasn't at her desk, he'd come over the PA system and bark "PENNY" in a nasty voice and then hang up. That meant she was to high-tail it back to her desk to see what he wanted. He treated her like a muddy doormat at as far as I was concerned. Penny's former husband was a broker in our office also. His office was next to mine at one point, and he told me that Penny dumped him to have an affair with Lyndsey, who then dumped Penny. Both of them kept working for Lyndsey anyway. Unhealthy.

Somebody in operations told me that on several occasions, after a particularly difficult episode of some sort, Lyndsey would walk by and throw down $100 bills to make some operations staff happy and, I suspect, to shut them up. Lots of people in my industry consider $100 less then lunch money, but to non-producing employees— i.e. operations and staff employees— it was enough. I don't blame my compliance manager, operations manager, or the several sales managers we had for any negative behavior they may have directed toward me on some occasions. They needed to go along to get along whether they recognized it or not; it is something almost subconscious. They took their cues from Lyndsey to whom they were solely beholden personally and individually for their annual bonuses, the calculation of which I explained in Chapter 7.

—w—

Slowly, after several months, some colleagues started to realize that I wasn't hysterical or delusional. I didn't make problems or have a bad attitude as Lyndsey tried to convince them. On the contrary, I smiled and was polite; I tried to be a good sport, regardless of what people said and did, and I worked my ass off. Attitudes are like colds; people can catch bad attitudes and, conversely, they can also catch positive attitudes. I kept plugging along and tried to be positive in spite of what Lyndsey was attempting to do. Thank God my positive attitude was effective, and eventually some people started being nicer. Most, but not all, of those who had stopped talking to me started talking to me again. It was obvious I was being severely mistreated, and many people started giving me little bits of information or subtly encouraging me to fight back. Many acknowledged that they saw and disapproved of Lyndsey's treatment of me. Several male brokers said things to me like, "Lyndsey doesn't act right toward you" or "something followed you over here." One assistant stopped me one day as I was walking by her desk and told me that a male broker, junior to me, had been given all of a departing broker's accounts. The assistant knew this wasn't fair and wanted to tell me about it. She added that it wasn't right that Lyndsey treated me badly, and that something had "followed me over" from the downtown branch. I smiled and thanked her for the information without confirming her statement. The departing broker had been another new female broker that was hired after November 1997, I assume in compliance with the settlement agreement to hire and successfully cultivate women's careers. Lyndsey had given her an office immediately. She hadn't lasted long though and quit. She told me she couldn't stand it in that branch.

During the next two years, there were many more incidents of Lyndsey's glaring bias against me. A female assistant told me that Arnold, the third guy to sit in the cubicle next to me, had been given 160 accounts as well as many leads generated from the firm's toll- free phone number. Potential clients would call that number asking investment questions and the firm would turn the call into a lead and give it to a broker. Pierre, another new rookie broker, partnered with a successful established broker. Garret, a newer broker, about three years behind me, was given all of Loretta's accounts after she quit. Loretta was yet another new female broker who was hired after 1997 and given an office immediately. She also collaborated with two other established brokers, and, of course, nobody tried to stop her. Susan and Ellen, a fifth and sixth new female brokers hired after 1997, both collaborated with established brokers. Rudy, who started as a broker about three years after me, also collaborated with an established and successful older broker. Patrick and Jules, both brokers who had started about the same time I had, were partnered up with other successful and established brokers and given many accounts. After 1997, when I was feeling more secure vis-a-vis my situation with Lyndsey, I did try again to partner or collaborate with other established brokers, even though Lyndsey had told me not to try it again, but it was too late. Lyndsey had already poisoned the water; nobody wanted to be connected to me. I would find out during the preparation for my trial that, from a legal standpoint, these factoids or bits of intelligence I was given or discovered were very important.

—※—

After things calmed down following my phone call to the lawyers, Lyndsey could see that his whispering campaign hadn't exactly worked. It was also clear that the company was trying to change its culture by insisting that women be hired as brokers. By then, I am sure that there had been several memos or re-education meetings, so that all managers in the whole organization understood that things had seriously changed. Life started to improve for me in terms of Lyndsey and his treatment of me. He still didn't treat me as any boss should have, but he got a little better. I decided to ask for an office.

As he walked by my cubicle one day, I took the opportunity. "Ahh,

Lyndsey, there are a couple offices open and I'd like to have one."

At first he had this look on his face that said, "You have to be kidding," and then the look turned to surprise. He verbally stumbled, which he had never done before, then collected himself, answering, "I'm putting Jules in that office."

There were two offices open, so I said, "What about Leslie's old office?" Leslie was a male broker who had started in the business about the same time as I had. He was another young broker who had collaborated with an older broker and had been given an office. He had recently moved to Merrill Lynch, and his old office was empty.

"I'm putting a dialer in there," Lyndsey replied.

He was putting a cold caller in an office rather than me! "I have worked hard and I deserve it," I said to him.

"Yeah," Lyndsey retorted, "how long, a hundred years?" Then he backed down— he had also never backed down before. "Ahh, I understand what you mean," he said.

"It would be a big morale boost," I continued.

"I understand," he repeated. "I'll think about it." Then he walked away.

The next day, Craig, my sales manager, asked me to come down to his office. When I walked in he gave me one corporate account lead with no contact name on it, one regular account, and one dead account. (Dead accounts were accounts whose number still showed up on our system but that the client had closed.) Later that day, Craig came over to my cubicle and gave me some call-in leads. One lead was two months old, one was one month old, and one was recent, but they all had already been pursued by one of the original three female brokers in the Beverly Hills office when I arrived. Her hand-written name and notes were already on the page, but Craig hadn't bothered to erase them before he gave the leads to me. In other words, they were worthless and his effort to give me something was a sham. But I'll never forget the look on Craig's face when he called me into his office to give me those junk leads. He was so embarrassed.

Now Lyndsey's behavior was changing and it was obvious he had given different instruction to Craig, or Craig wouldn't have all of a sudden been giving me leads or at least attempting to look like he was giving me leads. I assume he was humiliated or maybe ashamed because of his behavior at that horrible meeting we had had, but now the game plan had changed. I acted normally and said thanks, even though what he'd given me was worthless. No matter, I smiled to myself as I walked out of his office and down the hall to my cubicle. I loved the fact that now they had to behave at least a little decently toward me. After that, Craig would do little positive things such as all of a sudden invite me into his office if I happened to be walking by while another male broker was there so I could participate in the conversation.

—⁓—

As I said, Lyndsey was strategic in his decisions regarding how to treat people. He even admitted it to me one day. I was in his office for something but had to wait for him to finish a phone call. It was some sort of situation where the client was not happy. Lyndsey was very calm and smooth, but it was obvious to someone who knew him and who was sitting in front of him listening that he would have rather ripped that person on the other end of the line a new one. When he hung up, I complimented him for being so smooth and cool. "Yeah," he answered, "you gotta wait until you're sure they don't have anything, and can't come back at you before you let loose on them."

Lyndsey was a smart guy, smart enough to realize that his campaign against me wasn't working that well anymore. I imagine that he also realized that the organization was changing and that men like him, the dinosaur that he was, were not going to be able to operate as they had in the past. It was obvious that he was starting to worry, so his treatment of me became a little more civil and professional. He allowed me to finish sentences more often. I noticed that he started biting his tongue or say stupid things like he was "my savior." If I passed him in the halls, he would say out loud for no particular reason, "The devil made me do it." He was "rationalizing" his past bad behavior. A couple of times when I passed him in the hall, he started singing words to the Jim Croce song, "Don't pull on Superman's cape and don't mess around with Jim." I was beginning to feel protected by the lawsuit, and my self-confidence was coming back. I didn't feel as defeated, deflated, and demoralized. It showed, and I think it alarmed him. He didn't know how to handle it, so his singing this little song when he saw me walking by was his way of saying "I am still the boss, so don't mess with me."

However, change was especially difficult for him, a man who had been such a privileged tyrant, so he still had his limits. He would remind me not to push it and tell me what a good guy he really was! It was as if his new professional behavior toward me was unbearable for him, and he thought he should be well-rewarded and rewarded immediately for it. But he alternated his better behavior with ridiculous behavior. Once, while I was walking by him in the hall, he raised his arms up like a little kid in a Halloween ghost costume and mouthed, "Boo," at me so others wouldn't hear him. He was still trying to antagonize me but now in a different way. He repeatedly said little things here and there insinuating that I was a demanding, unreasonable woman and that he was the "poor, victimized man." If he did one civil little thing for me that would be normal managerial behavior with regard to someone else, he would comment, "This should make you happy," as if he thought he was killing himself for me and that I'd better be damn grateful for it. But the old behavior never completely went away. He continued to use the same old stuff such as trying to make me look hysterical by saying, "WHAT'S WRONG?" in that exaggerated, mock- panic voice at strange times.

Even still, the small changes in Lyndsey's behavior toward me made an enormous difference in my life. It was such a relief and made me so happy that I started laughing out loud in the office. Several people stopped me in the hallways at different times and asked me what I was laughing or smiling about. One guy told me, "Whatever it is, I want to catch it," and another told me to, "Bottle it and sell it." I wrote a note to myself that said "I literally laughed and smiled all the time and was almost giddy. So this is the way people are normally treated. I feel so much better now I can't describe it."

But, again, Lyndsey did resent the changes he had to make and had trouble with the transition. One day, Lyndsey walked out of Pete's office, which was right across the aisle from my cubicle. I had needed a signature on another second trade notification and asked him if he would sign it. "No!" he barked. Then as he was walking away, he called out, "Come to my office." Before, he wouldn't have second-guessed himself by inviting me to his office. I would have had to find another manager.

There were a couple of ways to get to his office, and he had a head start on me. I went the other way. When I got to the cage, which is the operations area located right in front of his office, he was standing there at the counter signing something for an assistant. She was smiling from ear to ear, so I asked her, in front of Lyndsey, "What are you smiling at?"

She answered, "Oh, he said he was mean to you because he had lost a document and to have Penny call you."

I was stunned. He didn't think I was going to come to his office because of the way he had barked at me, so he wanted his assistant to call me so I would come down and he could sign my document. He had never backtracked on his behavior like that before. I was so shocked that I couldn't think of a response, so I just showed Lyndsey the paper on which I needed a signature. "It's a second trade notification," I told him.

"Normal procedure?" he asked.

"Yes," I answered.

"For a DVP (delivery vs. payment) account?" he asked.

"Yes," I said. He signed it and I walked away, still speechless about the assistant's comment.

Lyndsey would have never qualified or made excuses for his behavior before, and I think the assistant was smiling because she could see the change in him as well and was happy he was trying to behave better toward me. This was his first admission of his bad behavior toward me. About a year later he actually started doing managerial things for me. I had asked him to buy a plane ticket for me to go to an appointment in Turkey. He refused, but he did say he would lend me the money, so while I was in his office getting a check from him, he asked me, "What airline are you flying, Magic Carpet Airlines?"

"No," I answered, "I already tried them and they scared the hell out of me, so I'm flying United."

Then he said, "You're not going to stay over there are you?"

"No", I answered, "You're not going to get rid of me that easily." The whole tone of the exchange was a joking banter.

"Oh, no, that was the old days," he admitted. It was his second admission that he had treated me badly or wanted to get rid of me.

—⁓—

As happy as I was with the new treatment, it was still a mixed bag, and Lyndsey's alternating good treatment with bad treatment continued. Craig was invited to be a broker. It was a demotion, and he was no longer in management. (This is the industry's way of firing management. They can still work for the firm if they want to be a broker, but if they had been a non-producing sales manager, they would have to give up most of their clients and really wouldn't have much of a business to go back to.) A few days after Craig was no longer a manager, I poked my head into Lyndsey's office at 6:30 a.m. to ask if I could use the empty office to see a client. He made a put-down comment as soon as he saw me. It was the same office he had put a cold caller in. He had realized that putting a cold caller into an office over me, especially since I wasn't letting the issue of sitting in a cubicle go, was just too much, and he had moved the cold caller back out. I made my request and he did listen to what I had to say without cutting me off and then said something like, "Sure that's great," or "That's good." Another first. His good mood wasn't to last. Having to talk to me civilly really burned him, so he had to stab back. A few days later, he growled at me, "We are getting a new sales manager and he is going to be all over you!"

Lyndsey wouldn't stop and neither would I. A few weeks after the sales manager threat, I went to Lyndsey's office again at 6:30 a.m. to ask him if I could have one of the now three open offices available. I had planned all weekend on going in and asking him. That morning, as usual, I sat down at my desk and logged on. I loathed the idea of willingly going into a situation where I knew I would be humiliated and have my ass chewed off one more time, so I got cold feet and started thinking of excuses of why I should not go into to Lyndsey's office to ask. "It's Monday," I told myself. "Mondays are always bad days for him." For years, Lyndsey made this huge deal about Monday being a bad day for him. One learned to give him a wide berth on Mondays, but, really it was ridiculous. He acted as if he had male PMS on that day. Regardless of Lyndsey's hormonal problems, I told myself, "No way. His extra nastiness on Mondays is ridiculous. No excuses, just do it, no matter what!" So I got up from my desk and went into his office and sat down. "Lyndsey, two guys are coming in to see me and to have lunch on Tuesday. I met them through a personal introduction and I'm sure they would want to see my office."

"No," he said immediately, "and if you'd like to, we can go over your numbers."

There was no point going over my numbers. My numbers had significantly improved since the settlement announcement, but that didn't matter to him. Regardless of how much I progressed, he would cite my earlier low production and slow start as the reason why he wouldn't be reasonable with me. Using his logic, I would always be behind, so his answer was always no. "Lyndsey," I continued, "these guys are your age; they like me and think I know my stuff. One is bringing the other to introduce him to me."

Of course, Lyndsey was his usual nasty self, putting me down and telling me I didn't deserve it. He repeated this stuff as if it were his mantra. The strange thing is that I didn't feel nervous or angry anymore. I just felt like I was in neutral.

"If you don't like it, Tameron," he said, "You have other options," and he waved his hand to the street below, like a game show hostess showing me door number two.

I was surprised by how calm and matter of fact my voice was. "Lyndsey," I answered, "I know what my options are; you don't have to tell me. You have given everybody else an office," I pointed out again.

"Garrett and Rudy were hired after you," he reminded me, "and they are doing a lot better than you did when you had been in the business the same amount of time they are."

"It's not just Rudy and Garrett," I answered. "You have given Trina, Jerome, Peggy, Rudy, Rick, Jules, Leslie, Raymond, and Paul offices, everybody." My reply surprised him. I could tell by the look on his face that he realized that I was right and that I was keeping track. He had given every new broker an office, regardless of their gross production, except me.

He continued with his same baloney, "Raymond and Paul have been in the business less time than you." I had about one year over them, but this didn't matter; he gave offices to new brokers with no or very little production at all. Most of them failed, but he still wouldn't give me an office, and I was making a living.

Lyndsey often accused me of arguing with him, and, when it came to the way he treated me, I did stand up for myself, politely. Any self-respecting person would have. This was the same stupid argument that he had made through the years, over and over. It directly contradicted one of the several "stories" Lyndsey would tell under oath. Again, I told him that if he used that logic I would never get an office. I would always be at a disadvantage, especially considering that a broker's business grows in a snowball effect.

Finally, finally, he conceded.

"Well," he said, "You did have a good year last year, but don't argue with me, the answer is no; I have other plans for those offices."

What could I do? I very calmly left. I wasn't freaked out. I expected it, but I had given it my best shot.

After I was already out of his office and walking down the hallway, I heard him say, "And don't stomp out of here in a tantrum."

Stomping out in a tantrum was so far from reality it was pathetic, and I wasn't going to let him get away with trying to make me look hysterical anymore, so I slowly turned around and walked back into his office. I stood behind the guest chair facing his desk and in a soft voice said, "I'm not stomping out in a tantrum. You said no and that's the way it is." He said a few more things and I left.

Later on that morning at about 10:30, Lyndsey was in the huge broker's office located close to my cubicle. I got up to do something and, as I walked by, I heard Lyndsey, kind of stumbling, say, "Ahh, ahh." I knew he wanted to talk to me so I turned around. He walked after me, indicating he wanted to talk in the hallway by the drinking fountain. I don't think he wanted anyone to hear because he was humiliated by having to give into me. Things were changing, and I believe he now felt it was in his interest to finally give me an office. A broker was in the hallway getting a drink at the water fountain. Lyndsey said to me in a hushed tone, "You have a point." It was my automatic response to try to diffuse tension with him by making light or by being sickeningly nice, so I said, "I'm not trying to be a pain." "Yeah," he responded, "but you are." The other broker finishing his drink chuckled and walked away. Lyndsey waited until that broker was out of the hallway and there was nobody else to hear, then he said, "You'll probably get an office; which one do you want?"

"The one closest to Amelia, my assistant, would be the most logical," I told him.

"I'll let you know by Friday," he answered and walked away.

He had no reason to say Friday, except to block and frustrate me because he knew I needed the office for Tuesday's meeting with those two men. The office I wanted, along with two others, was empty; we also had two conference rooms at the time, so he had plenty of room for whatever "plans" he had. Later, he called me from his car phone and told me I could have the office on Friday. He wouldn't concede defeat face to face. I know that the only reason why he finally gave me an office was because this was 1998; the lawsuit was on, and I was protected somewhat. His boss Aaron, it seemed, had recently been demoted— invited to be a broker— and Lyndsey was not sure how this newfangled corporate attitude was going to pan out.

"Fine," I said, "but I'll use the office to see the guys on Tuesday anyway," and I hung up without giving him a chance to say no. I told Pete, our compliance manager, that I was moving some stuff into the office so it would look like I already lived there for the appointment with the two guys.

"Do whatever you want," he responded, "it's your office." He picked up the phone and told Penny, Lyndsey's assistant, to change my computer over. It took one minute; it was that easy. Apparently, Lyndsey forgot to tell Pete about the Friday game until it was too late.

A couple hours later, Pete called me into his office and said there was a condition attached to my office. He said there were two times during the remodeling (our office was being remodeled for a second time) that they would need to use my office to "look at plans." There were two other offices open for their stupid plans along with two other conference rooms. Their condition made no sense whatsoever, but I went along with it happily because I knew it was bullshit and they wouldn't follow through with it. They never did need or ask to use my office after that.

Sure enough, the first thing the two guys I had the appointment with asked was, "Let's see your private office." I took them to my office, we chatted a bit, and then went out to lunch. I was back in my office at about 3:00 or

3:30 when Lyndsey walked by. I politely commented that I had gotten an office just in the nick-of-time because, sure enough, the first thing the two guys who came to see me had said was, "Let's see your office."

"Well it's not anything great," he answered with derision. My office was an inside office and didn't have a view of Beverly Hills.

"It's better than what I had before," I answered.

"Are you happy now?" he asked.

"Yes." I said.

As he walked away he loudly made the snide comment, "Who would have thought after eight years?" Yeah, thanks to him fucking bastard, I thought to myself. And it hadn't been eight years. He was making it up.

I had a networking event I had to go to that evening, so I left some papers on my desk and statement books on my chair. I was already completely moved in. The next morning at about 6:30 a.m. Lyndsey was walking by again. The first thing he said to me was, "Clean that place up. It looks like a bomb went off in there. What are you doing, seeing a terrorist?" He was completely exaggerating. The day Lyndsey finally gave me an office I had heard him say something about also moving Arnold, the new guy sitting in the other cubicle, because, "Arnold had been in the business for a long time." That was the exact reason why he'd said he wouldn't give me an office for four years! Arnold had been in the business in a different capacity, not as a broker. I know for a fact Arnold had $15,000 in commissions for the year as of the end of April.

Lyndsey was extremely irritated that I finally prevailed on the office issue, and he exacted one last payment by humiliation for it. He was so angry that it seemed to cloud his thinking and brought back that urge to put me in my place. Later that same morning, I took an insurance ticket to Lyndsey to sign. Writing insurance tickets required several steps in order to comply with the state insurance department and corporate regulations and procedures. At the time all the steps involved could take weeks and sometimes months to complete. Medical records needed to be ordered, medical exams taken, solicitation forms completed, signatures gotten from management, applications taken from the client, and preliminary signatures and stamps from New York. In this case, everything had been properly done per the firm's and my manager Lyndsey's instructions. Once everything was done, the manager made one final signature on the ticket itself, which was then sent to the wire room. The wire room credited the transaction, commission was given to the broker, and the premium was taken out of the client's account and sent to the insurance company. I was ready to send the ticket to the wire room. At that time, the procedure at Smith Barney was that the first step of an insurance transaction was that the manager had to sign a document that was then sent to Smith Barney's New York headquarters for their stamp of approval before proceeding.

Everything had been done, and I went to Lyndsey for his final signature. I didn't even get out a half sentence to remind him about what he had already signed, what had been done, and that I needed his final signature, before he handed it back and said, "I can't read this; get a better copy." He didn't need a better copy; it was an excuse to bother me. All he needed was to see that the paperwork was in order, that all proper signatures had been acquired including his, and that it had already been approved and signed by New York and by him. He was being an obstructionist because he was angry about my getting the office.

I went back to my desk for a few minutes to think what to do and then went back to his office. He freaked out and in a very nasty voice said, "You can really take your other option, Tameron." In other words, go find a job someplace else. Then he said, "Go get a form from Preston." Preston was our annuity coordinator in the office, which meant he had sold more annuities (an insurance product), than a lot of brokers and knew the procedure. I didn't need Preston. All proper steps had been taken; it was time to issue the policy. Lyndsey was telling me to start from day one and get the very first form that needed to be completed in the process. That is something I had done back in January; it was now May. "Do you have a problem with this office?" Lyndsey barked.

"No," I answered, then he jumped up to march me to Preston's office himself.

Halfway down the hallway, Lyndsey stopped. His scene was being witnessed by others. I know I looked distressed because another broker and his client had alarmed looks on their faces as they passed Lyndsey and me in the hallway. I literally whispered at Lyndsey trying to calm him down.

"Lyndsey, all the forms have been completed and approved. The transfer has already occurred; and the money is here. I just need to drop the ticket."

"Did I already sign something?" he finally asked sanely.

"Yes," I said.

He looked at the form again that I had tried to hand to him the first time. This time, he really looked at it and saw his signature and New York's stamp. He realized he had made a big mistake out of his desire to make my life difficult and had made a fool out of himself at the same time. Without a word, he signed the ticket as he should have in the beginning and walked away.

That day he succeeded in really rattling me. I went back to my office and sat down. I turned my back to the window so nobody could see my face and fought back tears. A few minutes later, I heard Lyndsey talking to someone in the hallway. He said something about how "it was a comedy of errors." I'm sure he was talking about the incident that had just happened with me. Just like he sang the song, "Don't pull on superman's cape and don't mess around with Jim," it was as if he went out into the hallway to tell somebody it was a "comedy of errors" to make excuses and justifications for his behavior. It was completely his error, and I didn't find it comedic at all.

The incident stressed me out, and it took several days to wind down. A few days later, our wire operator walked by and saw that I finally had an office. "Tameron," he said, "they gave *you* an office; what is this place coming to?" Obviously he was kidding, but his comment and others like his illustrated that Lyndsey's bad attitude toward me was evident to everybody.

I didn't talk to Lyndsey again for a week after the insurance fiasco because I had no reason to interact with him until an account transferred in. I had sold the client out of some mutual funds without fees that she didn't want and weren't appropriate for her and was then going to reinvest the money into more appropriate and safer funds using standard asset allocation. What I had done was by the book and good for the client. The interaction between Lyndsey and me should have been a one-minute-or-less exchange. If any other manager had been available it would have been, but unfortunately none were, and I had to go to Lyndsey. He started to hassle me about the trades. Obviously, he hadn't gotten over the week before and attacked at his first opportunity.

"You seem to be getting upset. Is there something wrong here? Is this bothering you?" he queried in a sarcastic voice.

"No," I said, but he was rattling me again. Technically, as the manager signing off on a mutual fund ticket, it's his job to make sure it was done correctly. However, this time he had caught me off guard because the way and the tone in which he questioned me was so inappropriate for the circumstance and I hadn't expected him to still be angry. He saw that he was upsetting me and it appeared that he got off on it. He had asserted his dominance and shown the "uppity woman," once again, who was boss.

—∞—

As I mentioned previously, the deadline to file an individual claim within the class action was in the summer of 1999, so, from a claimant's perspective, we didn't have to deal with the lawsuit for another year and a half after the settlement announcement was made. I will get to the details of the lawsuit in the next chapter, but, suffice it to say here, the suit included two parts. One part was the individual claims, which I haven't gotten to yet, and the other was organizational culture changing actions that Smith Barney agreed to implement. These I know were discussed during manager meetings and corporate conference calls, and a part of these changes was the immediate hiring of women as brokers; hence, the several female brokers who were hired in our branch after November 1997.

Another one of those actions was to hire a cultural consultant to "clean up their culture," so to speak; her name was Dr. Cole. I attended one of the meetings Smith Barney put on specifically for its female brokers where Dr. Cole was one of the featured speakers. It's no secret that being treated positively has a significant impact on one's performance. Dr. Cole got up in front of hundreds of women and stated, "We all know that the most important person in a broker's career is her manager!" I felt so angry, defeated, and cheated to have a representative of the company, finally, after so many years of pain, say out loud and acknowledge that what I had experienced and had complained about wasn't crazy or hysterical but a legitimate complaint and huge hindrance to my career. Of course nobody spoke to me personally. I was in a crowd of hundreds. Nobody there knew of my personal situation, and many of those women were newly hired after 1997 and had no idea what women like me had gone through. Smith Barney knew all about downtown Los Angeles 662 Branch, which got worse after I left, and at least a few executives knew about Lyndsey— yet, to this day, nobody has apologized to me.

—⁓—

I didn't want to join the lawsuit until the last minute before the deadline in the summer 1999, because, in spite of things improving, it was still a mixed bag with Lyndsey, and I was still scared to death. I wanted to put it off as long as possible. Since work life had gotten better, I didn't want to rock the boat by alerting Lyndsey that I had definitely joined the suit. I was afraid that he would find out and retaliate more or even fire me, but the class action lawyers in Chicago asked me not to wait until the last minute.

I had to be convinced again that it would be OK. One of the partners explained to me that there was more to the process than just filling out the claim and faxing it. After a claim was faxed in, Stowell & Friedman had to put it in a proper legal format, send it back to the claimant for her OK, and then submit it to Smith Barney. Stowell & Friedman were inundated with claims. Close to two thousand female employees or former employees had joined the suit, and Stowell & Friedman had to go through each claim. In spite of my fear, I submitted my claim in April 1999.

My social life had been pretty light ever since I started working at Smith Barney but I still found a little time and money to go out with friends, both male and female. I sailed about once a week out of Marina Del Rey, rode my bicycle at the beach, or went to restaurants or out dancing with friends. On my way home after a rare night out, I met Sabastien at a stoplight. He was a knockout, a beautiful man to look at. He asked me to roll down my window then asked me for my phone number. Playing it cool, I asked him, "Why should I give you my phone number?" So he asked me to take his number down instead. The friend I was with was smarter and faster than I. While I was still thinking about it, she already had a pencil and notepad in hand and was hitting me with it, urging me to "take his number, take his number!" That eventual relationship ended up being for only a couple weeks because he had a serious and overwhelming legal problem in his life as well, which precluded him from really being able to maintain a normal relationship. We ended up being friends for several years.

I was so fearful about joining the suit that I was paranoid somebody might see me at a public place faxing my claim form. I trusted Sabastien, and his machine would print out a receipt, so I went to his apartment to fax my claim. On the claim form it asked to indicate dates of employment. I wrote "6/91 to Present" and I highlighted "Present." It also asked for work and home phone numbers. I wrote down my home phone number and in the space for the work number I wrote, "Please don't ever call at work." I was afraid someone might just get the number from directory assistance if I left it blank. Then in the middle of the page where there was space, I wrote: "Please don't divulge my name to SSB (Salomon Smith Barney) until the last minute." I was completely petrified of Smith Barney.

In the meantime, since the lawsuit was announced and Lyndsey was behaving somewhat better, I did feel relatively protected and was doing much better. Work life for me had improved and my commission totals showed it. In 1998, I moved from a very dumpy apartment in Los Angeles about ten minutes outside of Beverly Hills to a cute little apartment in Beverly Hills just a half block from my office. Within a year of the settlement announcement and the small change in Lyndsey's behavior, I was doing so much better that I bought myself a brand new E320 Mercedes Benz four-door sedan. In spite of my progress, Lyndsey just couldn't help himself. This is when he made the threat that the new sales manager was allegedly going to be all over me. He still definitely intimidated me, and I took his threat to be true, so for several months I avoided Jason, our new sales manager.

It turned out that Jason was never "all over me." In fact, he was a very nice guy. Several months after he joined our office, he finally approached me and said he wanted to meet with me once a week to go over my production numbers. He started off that first meeting by saying, "Tameron, you've been in the business for a long time and didn't do well for a long time, then you took off. What happened?" I got visibly upset. I could feel the tension rise in my face; my breathing got shallow, and I started sweating and talking fast. I just didn't want to start all over with a new sales manager with the same bullshit that I had endured in the past. I didn't want this "situation" to follow me for the rest of my professional life, but it seemed to me, at the time, that that was where things were headed. Jason had never seen me get nervous like that, and I'm sure it freaked him out a bit. I wouldn't be surprised if he thought I was a psycho. I told him I didn't want to talk about it, then I said, "Nothing has changed. I'm doing everything the same way that I always have, but the difference is that Lyndsey is leaving me alone and now I'm more relaxed."

I was sorry I lost my cool and told Jason what I had said about Lyndsey. That was all the information I gave him, but I worried about what Lyndsey may have told Jason. For all I knew, Lyndsey could have told Jason it had something to do with sexual harassment as opposed to discrimination and retaliation. Therefore, Jason might have thought I was lying or paranoid, because overt weird sexual stuff didn't happen in the Beverly Hills branch. We didn't end up having weekly meetings after that. Several months later, he tried again. I went to Jason's office to ask something, so he took the opportunity to make the comment, "You're on fire, Tameron," meaning I was doing very well. He wanted an explanation of why I was doing so well, but I just ignored the implied question.

—⁜—

It had been two years since the class action settlement announcement and my call to Stowell & Freidman. The company had time to do some house cleaning. I didn't realize it then, but Lyndsey was probably smelling that his job was on the line. His boss, Aaron Weisswasser, who had put my whole move from downtown Los Angeles to Beverly Hills together, was a broker. Lyndsey had started making jokes about how he was going to lose his job around the time of the claims deadline in June 1999. He continued to make those jokes until very close to his "retirement." Several times before a branch meeting actually got down to business, he'd stand up and say that he needed, "Just five more years, you guys, just five more years," as if he was saying, make them (his bosses) let me stay because I need five more years. Then he'd say, "The house is Marla's; I need just five more years," as if he needed five more years to pay off the house in Bel Air for his live-in girlfriend. He made the same comment many times, so apparently he thought it was really funny. I always thought it was a pathetic thing to say and that he was a dishonorable man for publicly making his long-term girlfriend seem like a gold digger.

In the office, we went through a second renovation and a merger with the branch next door. Our branch doubled in size, so we were now about ninety brokers. Everybody moved into their assigned offices. I had been assigned an inside office without a view, as I had before. Shortly after everybody had settled in, a broker in a little office with a beautiful view of Beverly Hills that looked toward the hills retired. I continued to do better and better, and I wanted to be treated as everyone else was, so I thought it was time to ask Lyndsey for a move up in offices from an office without a view to an office with a view. Requesting that little office with the beautiful view was a perfectly reasonable request considering that several small brokers who were building their business had sat in that very same space at various times, including Raymond, my buddy who had sat in the cubicle next to me when I first moved to Beverly Hills. *Ding, ding, ding*— it was time for round two of the office saga.

True to form, Lyndsey put me off. I didn't want to be too confrontational or bold with Lyndsey because I knew it could have a deleterious effect, so I waited a couple of weeks. I was also still trying extra hard to be "reasonable" and not "a pain" according to him, hoping that someday I would have a normal broker/manager relationship with him. I sent him an e-mail.

Subject: Window Office

I know you said you'd get back to me a couple of weeks ago, but I thought I'd ask again if you have made a decision about a window office for me. Since Charlie is leaving in the beginning of July, I'd like to know if I could have his old office. Just as a reminder that is the office that Raymond Gregory sat in for a couple of years before the last renovation.

Thanks,

Tameron

He ignored me. A few weeks later, I went down to Lyndsey's office to ask again since Charlie had packed and left that morning. Jason was sitting in one of the two guest chairs facing Lyndsey's desk. I sat in the other chair. While Lyndsey was on the phone, I told Jason that I wanted to talk to Lyndsey about taking Charlie's empty office. Jason then told me I didn't get the office. "Well if that's the case, I have gotten my answer and that there was no point in waiting," I said, and I got up to leave.

Jason laughed, "Sit down, Tameron, I'm only joking."

Lyndsey hung up the phone and said, "What are you in here for?"

"I came down to ask about that window office. Charlie's gone, and it's vacant, and I'd like to know if I can have it."

"No," he answered, "your numbers aren't good enough," and he launched into his same old tired excuse. "It's been 100 years…" blah, blah, blah.

I could feel that my face was showing that I was very angry. "You gave Raymond that office three years ago," I answered.

"Are you happy here?" he responded. He always meant that phrase as a threat. The next sentence would be: "You know your options." I knew the script and what was to come next, but with all the corporate changes that were being made, I had become a little emboldened.

"You've already asked me that several times before," I replied. Then I preempted him. "I love this place. I have no intentions of leaving or desire to leave, and we've already been over this before. There is no point in engaging in that conversation about going over my numbers."

He shot back that "it took too long."[5]

We started going around and around, but this time I wasn't so afraid of him and I didn't feel the need to be so sickeningly polite about his insults. But I also didn't want to argue anymore for decent treatment. He would never admit to retaliation, so as long as we weren't being honest and talking about the real issue, discussing "my numbers" was a waste of breath.

"Fine," I told him, "you're the boss and your word is final." Then I couldn't help myself, "But if you'll give me the office I'd take it." I wasn't giving up. He tried to engage me again and provoke me into saying something

---

[5] He meant that my success took too long to achieve to suit him.

or having an attitude that would justify a reason to fire me. As usual, I wouldn't take the bait. I moved to leave but also tried one last assumptive close. "Can I move today?" I asked. It was very tense in his office and I wasn't going to stay there like that.

Jason, I'm sure, was very uncomfortable witnessing the exchange and in a mediating voice said, "The system would have to be changed over first." "Fine," I said, "I'll wait till next week; let me know when to move," and I left.

The moment I walked into my own office, I picked up the phone to make a call, and Penny, Lyndsey's assistant, was already on the line. "He wants to see you again," she told me.

I walked back down to his office, telling myself on the way "Relax, relax. Dear God," I prayed, "don't let him fire me." There was no reason to fire me.

When I walked into Lyndsey's office, Jason was gone. It was just Lyndsey and me. The look on his face and his demeanor had completely changed. He was much nicer, and the first thing he said to me was, "That last conversation we just had shocked me." I had soft-pedaled my arguments with him before the company started to change in order to stand up for myself and survive. This time, I repeated my argument by reminding him that he had given Rudy an office two and a half years earlier when Rudy hadn't done diddly-squat in commissions. He gave Garrett an office, along with Keith, another guy who couldn't make it in the business and left. He responded again with his usual reply that they had not been in the business as long as I. Some of them had been, and several hadn't survived, but I was tired of arguing with him; it was useless. He reiterated all the good things he had started doing for me recently. I acknowledged them and thanked him again. Then off-the-wall he said, "This isn't discrimination."

"I didn't use that word," I answered.

"Yeah, it's implied," he said. I didn't answer him. "I'll keep ahead of you as you do better," he told me.

"OK," I said and left, even though I knew he had no intention of "keeping ahead of me" or he would have given me a window office with the view. This was the most directly confrontational I had ever been with Lyndsey. The lawsuit and the changes that I could see made me feel more confident that I could confront him more boldly. It turned out that the office sat empty for months.

A couple of months later, Lyndsey finally gave me a window office. Of course, he didn't give me the office I had been asking for with the nice view, but it was a window office, and he was going to make sure that I understood that I should be overwhelmingly grateful for his undeserved largess. I was down at the cage (the administrative area of the office) and out of nowhere Lyndsey asked me, "How do you like your office?" Without missing a beat or allowing me to answer, he continued, "You could be looking at the back; you have a nice view." I didn't understand what he was saying at first. It took me a few seconds to realize that what he was saying was that I should be grateful because I could have been given a worse window office than the one he gave me. He gave me the only window office with a big pillar between the windows that blocked the full view instead of another window office that overlooked the alley. It felt like he was saying, "Be grateful because I could have you back pickin' cotton." Here he was, in a slightly threatening manner, reminding me that I had better be grateful. He had blocked me at every turn, completely ruined any chance of my cultivating a mentor for myself, and had ruined any chance I may have had of collaborating with anyone in the office. "Bastard," I thought to myself, "It's the same old stuff."

As an aside, one day while I was in Jason's office talking to him, he made the comment to me that, "Some people around here think you're flighty." "Hmm," I thought to myself, "What am I supposed to do with that information?" If he had spent the last five years working with Lyndsey systematically trying to demoralize him, humiliate him, tear him down, and block his success at every move, he might have been a little nervous too. What is interesting is that at the beginning of my career my training managers thought very differently about me. After the first part of my formal training class concluded and we trainees were sent back to our respective offices, my senior training manager, who became the manager of the Chicago office, made a point to call my sales manager in the downtown branch, David Greenblatt ("Mr. Pull Your Balls Out of Your Wife's Purse"). He told David that the three training managers had "voted" me the smartest trainee in the class. Now, how did I go from being voted the smartest in my training class to flighty?

In January of 2000, I decided to move to round three in the office saga. I was doing well and wanted the office that other smaller brokers had sat in with the beautiful view; I deserved it. I went down to Lyndsey's office late one afternoon. He was at his desk reading a magazine. The market was closed, so the office was quiet. I knocked on the door, walked in, and sat down in the guest chair in front of his desk. In a slow, calm voice, I reminded him that the office I had wanted was still open and that I would still like to have it. He quietly said, "Yes," almost as if he had resigned and was giving in and would finally give me the office he had given so many others. But he would fool me once again. He would often be overly dramatic as an intimidation tactic, and that's what he did that afternoon. He looked up from his magazine to see my reaction.

I was so amazed that he had finally said yes so calmly, that I repeated happily, "Yes, I can have it?" with a smile on my face. I just wanted to make sure that I heard him correctly. For a second, I thought "Great, he knows how well I'm doing and is willing to be fair now." I quickly realized it was just part of his old bag of tactics, ridicule alternated with trying to break me down emotionally.

"No," he answered, with an evil smile, as if he really enjoyed his power to thwart me. I launched into my argument that I had improved by 60% over the previous year etc, etc. He answered that he "would keep ahead of me" but that "it took you too long." It was the same old thing. He said he would review my numbers and get back to me but there were other people who didn't take as long and they wanted "things" from him too. I was burning angry, and I know he saw it on my face.

The next day, he used the hallway tactic again. He called out to me. I stopped and waited for him to catch up to me. In a low voice, as if he didn't want anyone to accidentally hear him, he said, "You caught me off guard; I will look at your numbers for 1999." That was the year we had just finished. He knew damn well what my numbers were. It was so strange for Lyndsey to come back and repeat himself that I reminded him that he had already told me that the day before. He had a stupid look on his face and I couldn't believe he would make such an excuse as "I had caught him off guard." From what? Reading *The Economist*? He was losing his confidence. In retrospect, I think he was relatively sure at that point that his days were numbered, and he definitely wasn't going to give me that office if it turned out that he was going to "retire." There would be no benefit to him for being decent to me. If he was fired— oops,- "retired"— and out of Smith Barney, he wouldn't have benefited by giving me the office, and seeing me frustrated one more time probably would give him his last pathetic little pleasurable jab. This way, he could get a little revenge and remind me that he was still boss until the day he walked out.

—m—

A year earlier in the spring of 1999, after I had submitted my initial claim through Stowell & Friedman, I decided to hire my own lawyer to represent me for the rest of the process of the lawsuit, which I will get to in the next chapter. The first task my lawyer gave me to do was to ask to see my personnel file. He explained to me that I had the legal right to examine my file and that they had to show it to me. Even so, I absolutely dreaded asking for such a thing. I imagined all hell breaking loose with Lyndsey. Just in case Lyndsey did fire me, I asked my new lawyer what I should do. He told me not to say anything but to quietly go home and call him immediately.

After the last office episode, which takes us back to early 2000, I finally gathered up the nerve to go down to Lyndsey's office and ask to see my file. I walked up to Penny's desk and just asked. Her jaw fell open. "I don't think you can do that," she sputtered.

"Yes I can," I replied, "it's the law."

She didn't know what to do. "I'll have to ask Lyndsey's permission," she answered.

"OK, just let me know when and I'll come back and look," I replied. I didn't hear from Penny, so about a week later I went back down to her desk and asked again to see my file.

This time she was no longer shocked. She motioned over to Lyndsey—whom we both could see sitting at his desk, since there was only a huge glass window between his office and her desk space— and said, "It's sitting on Lyndsey's desk; he's looking at it." I looked over, and, sure enough it looked like he had a file on his desk along with other papers.

"Ok," I told her, "when he's done let me know so I can come down to look at it," and I left again.

Another week passed. I was walking down Wilshire Boulevard going back to the office after having gone to the bank, and Penny was walking toward me on her way, I assume, to do her own errand. We passed each other on the sidewalk and said hello. Then Penny stopped and called out to me, "Ah, Tameron." I stopped and turned around to walk back toward her. "About that file," she continued, "*It mysteriously disappeared*," she said, in an exaggerated voice and rolled her eyes. I was stunned because we both knew that was bullshit and that he had made it "disappear." We stood there for a second and stared at each other with looks on our faces as if to say, "Can you believe that guy?" What could I do? At least, thankfully, she told me.

A few days later, Lyndsey asked if I was happy. I told him I would have asked to see my file whether I was happy or not.

"Do you have a problem with me?" he asked.

Was he kidding me? A problem? "How about you tried to ruin my career and run me out of the business," I thought to myself, but I didn't answer his question and changed the subject. He told me they ordered my file because mine got "lost in the renovation," which, again, is not what he would say under oath. Then he said again, off-the-wall, "This branch isn't in the class action; they kept the branches out of it. I don't know if you're in the class action" and he trailed off. Again, I didn't answer him. He was trying to get information out of me, and I had no intention of giving it to him.

About a month later, somebody came over the PA system and called an immediate branch meeting in the middle of the trading day. "All brokers to the conference room in five minutes." Jeff Patch, our regional guy, was in the office; he was Lyndsey's immediate boss. Aaron Weisswasser, as I said, had already been gone for more than a year. Everybody filed into the conference room. Jeff got up and said a few nice things about Lyndsey and then gave the floor to Lyndsey. Lyndsey got up, made a couple of wise cracks, and then tried to tell us he was resigning. He couldn't do it; he got all choked up and walked out of the room. Jeff got up and said something else while everybody kind of looked at each other; nobody had seen Lyndsey emotional like this. Lyndsey composed himself in the hallway and came back into the conference room. He walked up to the podium and tried again. I remember noticing the pained look on Jeff Patch's face. It wasn't pleasant for him to do this. Lyndsey choked again and walked out for a second time. It probably wasn't pleasant for anyone in that conference room to see our fearless leader get so emotional and upset, except for me. I also remember noticing how uncomfortable everybody was. The weird part for me was feeling my own emotions. Big boys aren't supposed to cry, so when they do, I know that things are really bad for them, and, as a result, it usually freaks me out. I want to do something for a man who cries— make it better, fix it, and stop his crying. But that day, I was different; I felt like an ice cube. I had absolutely no sympathy or pity for Lyndsey whatsoever. I had to remind myself to remain as placid as possible and not show any happiness or relief because it would have been unseemly.

"Now," I thought to myself, "Lyndsey felt a little pain after all those years of his general contempt and disrespect of women, his belief in his prerogative to shit on women, his power trips, his bullying and his boys' club mentality of an aging playboy who often referred to women as 'broads.'" The universe has a way of meting out its own justice as Raymond used to tell me.

Lyndsey wrote a memo addressed to all employees on March 24, 2000, which read:

> Tim Moynehan will be the branch manager of the office beginning Monday. I will be moving out of my office today and will be on the 7th floor. I will be there for a few weeks. Pete Kelly will be on vacation all next week and Dan Baylor will be attending a management training session Monday-Wednesday so we will be short- handed next week. To help with this problem Tad Chesterfield (former Manager of the Century City branch) will be here Tuesday- Friday to help with approvals. He will be located in Pete Kelly's office. Any questions, please call me.

Lyndsey was finally gone. Thank God!

IX

LEGAL EDUCATION: HIRING A LAWYER DOESN'T MEAN YOU ARE SAVED

T he lawsuit through which I filed my claim was a class action lawsuit called Martens vs. Smith Barney. A class action is a lawsuit brought by one or more plaintiffs on behalf of a large group of others who have a common interest. The original suit was filed with the Equal Employment Opportunity Commission in 1995 alleging that Smith Barney engaged in firm-wide sexual discrimination and sexual harassment. A settlement was agreed upon between the class representatives and class council on one side and Smith Barney on the other in October 1997. The complete suit wasn't wrapped up until 2007. I don't know the exact date. I personally had nothing to do with bringing the lawsuit itself and was not a class representative. I found out about the settlement, as I said, by reading about it in *The Wall Street Journal*. The journal cited the name and city of class council, Stowell & Friedman, so I called directory assistance for Chicago and got their phone number. I was a beneficiary of other people's work and courage. That is supposed to be how class actions work, and it did work for me, just in the nick of time. As I have already described, I called Stowell & Friedman shortly after I had that last ridiculous and threatening meeting with Craig, my sales manager.

Many people, including many claimants, were confused about the nature of the class action against Smith Barney. The settlement was just the beginning for all class members who weren't representatives and involved in the settlement negotiations. The settlement established and dictated the procedure and conditions upon which the members could seek justice for their individual claims, and close to two thousand women filed. There wasn't a pool of money to be divided among the class members. Instead, the settlement stipulated that there would be up to a three-step process through which a class member could seek justice if she had been sexually harassed and/or discriminated or retaliated against because of her gender. A class action member was any woman who had worked for Smith Barney or its predecessor firms between May 21, 1993, and November 1997 excluding employees of Salomon Brothers. The entire class action process would be administrated by Duke University's private adjudication center and paid for by Smith Barney.

The first step for any class member who felt she had a claim and should participate in the class action was to submit her individual claim. This was the step with the deadline in the summer of 1999. All initial claims had to be submitted through Stowell & Friedman, the law firm in Chicago, and Smith Barney was supposed to respond within sixty days from the date the claim was received. They would either reject the claim or make an offer to settle with the individual claimant. If the claimant accepted Smith Barney's offer to settle her individual claim, she was required to sign a confidentiality agreement and agree not to sue Smith Barney again.

If she didn't accept this initial offer, she proceeded to the second step, which was mediation. Duke assigned the time, place, and mediator of each mediation procedure. Mediation was an opportunity for the claimant and her lawyer to have a more detailed negotiation with Smith Barney and its lawyers with the help of a neutral mediator. The hope was that both sides could come together to hammer out an agreement and settlement that all could live with, in order to avoid litigation. If they did come to an agreement, the claimant also had to sign a confidentiality agreement and agree never to sue Smith Barney again. If a settlement couldn't be agreed upon through mediation, the third step, arbitration, was invoked.

Arbitration in this class action was a form of litigation and was the most significant aspect of the whole class action settlement. It wasn't just an ordinary arbitration process; it was a mini-trial. The genius of the settlement was that it stipulated specific rules by which the process of arbitration had to abide, making it fairer for the claimants who were already at a disadvantage to a big corporation with deep pockets and cadres of lawyers. It leveled the legal playing field as best as Stowell & Freidman could negotiate so that we claimants had a better shot at justice. Contrary to popular opinion, sexual harassment and discrimination are extremely difficult to prove. It should also be noted that corporations possess most of the evidence, and possible witnesses are beholden to them— not only for their jobs but also for harmonious working conditions, promotions, and their reputations in the industry.

Usually, arbitrators in the securities business are just regular people who are familiar with or have worked in the industry, not lawyers or judges. In this class action, the arbitrators were lawyers or former judges who conducted the proceedings as if it were a regular trial. There had to be three panelists who acted as judges. At least one had to be a woman and at least two had to have experience in labor law specifically. Each claimant had the right to seek outside council other than the law firm in Chicago during any part of the process.

The big difference between the arbitration and a regular trial were the procedural rules. Punitive damages were also a possibility by virtue of the class action settlement, but they are not in regular federal arbitration. Grounds for an appeal on the final decision the panel rendered were very limited and would only be granted if there had been fraud or corruption.

It's true, as Lyndsey had said to me, that "they kept the branches out of it." I didn't sue Lyndsey personally. The class sued Smith Barney, claiming there was a culture and a firm-wide pattern and practice of discrimination and harassment, and I was a part of the class. Smith Barney could not argue in the arbitration that it was not responsible for an employee's behavior toward another situated in a position lower than managing director. No claimant could be compelled to undergo any medical or psychological test, and, unless the claimant raised an issue of physical, psychological, or emotional injury or distress, Smith Barney could not introduce medical records as evidence. No party would be allowed to use evidence of any person's sexual history except evidence of sexual activity between any person accused and the alleged victim. But these rules, designed to aid the claimants, would also prove to be tricky for the average person such as me. It seemed to me that even some of these rules were thrown to the wayside, as well as the time frame in which each step was supposed to have occurred.

Another important part of the settlement, especially for all female employees of Smith Barney hired after November 1997, was the part dealing with diversity programs and initiatives. The settlement required that Smith Barney spend $15 million over the four years following the settlement on diversity programs and initiatives designed to promote equal opportunity for all persons and to educate about harassment, discrimination, and retaliation. They were also meant to foster recruitment and mentoring for women and minorities in the securities industry.

Several times during my tenure in Beverly Hills, several people, including my compliance manager, made the comment that, "Usually women and minorities don't do well in this business." Hmm, I wonder why that would be? Is it because women and minorities, black and Latino men included, are naturally stupid, lazy, or incapable? Or, is there another reason, another explanation of why they don't do well? I don't think there are any serious arguments anymore against the fact that there is a direct relationship between how one is treated and employment performance. These initiatives were put into place as a start to change the dynamics of discrimination and to take away the prerogative that white men have had to treat and think of others as inferior, which is what discrimination is. Class council had the right to monitor the implementation and success of these diversity programs. The firm also agreed to set goals for increasing the number of women it hired and promoted in various positions in retail sales, including brokers, branch managers, and assistant branch managers. If the firm failed to make reasonable efforts to meet these goals, the $15 million would be increased by a specific dollar amount. Looking back, these initiatives at least partly explain why Lyndsey's behavior toward me changed that first year and a half before I actually filed my claim.

Smith Barney also agreed to form an Office of Diversity, which would periodically report back directly to the CEO and Executive Committee. Its primary functions would be to periodically review annual promotions and raises for consistency with the goals of promoting equal employment opportunity; to foster a diverse workforce; and to maintain a company free of harassment, discrimination, and retaliation to ensure that real change happened at Smith Barney. One of the results of the agreement was that branch managers' pay was somehow related (I don't know the details) to how many women they hired and cultivated to success. There were many other aspects to the settlement that are too numerous to detail here; however I can say without question that the environment at Smith Barney toward women changed significantly. There are, I will concede, still those who disrespect women. They feel it is their right to engage in discrimination by treating women unfavorably and are deeply resentful of the gains women and minorities have made. Such people have also learned from the experience. They watch themselves and make their efforts more covert because politics and cultural changes won't allow them to engage in the old, overt behavior anymore. There was still discrimination, but the environment was much better than it had been before. I was happy with the changes and certainly willing to take the gains, even if there were still problems.

The three-step process acted as a sifting mechanism. Originally, almost two thousand women filed individual claims against Smith Barney. Many of those women accepted the company's first offer and settled their lawsuits. However, for a lot of us, the offers Smith Barney made in the first round were so low they were a joke. More women settled during the second step, which was the mediation process, leaving only about one hundred women to go through the third step of arbitration. Class council's goal was to facilitate and encourage as many women to settle during the second step of mediation as possible, as they assured Smith Barney they would do in the settlement document. Settlement is definitely the easier, faster, less stressful and least hurtful remedy in comparison to a trial. I did try to settle during the mediation but quickly realized Smith Barney was disingenuous with me. It is my feeling that more women didn't join the class action out of fear of retribution, but once they saw that those who did join were OK and didn't necessarily have to quit their jobs or get fired were sorry in retrospect that they hadn't joined. I also know that many women who did settle during the second step had settlement remorse, wishing they hadn't settled but had gone on to arbitration instead.

From 1999 onward, there was a lot more going on in my life than just having to deal with Lyndsey. I had to be an active participant in the entire lawsuit process, in addition to dealing with Lyndsey and his successor and running my business. We operated on New York time, which meant that I was up early every morning and at my desk at 6:30 a.m., running my business, building my business, and managing my client's assets as if none of this was happening. I never once let on to any client that there was ever a problem of any sort.

—⁂—

Class action representatives in Los Angeles thought it would be helpful to have one of the partners conduct an informational meeting for any potential claimants who cared to show up. The meeting was to be held on April 21, 1999, at the Four Seasons Hotel close to Beverly Hills. I was so afraid that someone would be there and somehow inform Lyndsey that I was there that I almost didn't go. I desperately wanted to talk to one of the partners face to face, so as the meeting was adjourning, I walked into the room. I did see one woman who had been an assistant in the Beverly Hills office, and she looked very surprised to see me there. I didn't really know her, and we had never interacted in the office, so I ignored her. The meeting was over, so I walked up to Mary Stowell and sat down next to her in a chair that had already been vacated. I introduced myself and asked my first questions. She answered me, but there was something in her attitude that bothered me. I felt that she had a "who do you think you are barging in here asking questions, after the meeting is over?" attitude, and I might have. I'm sure that most of the women there, if not all, had been support staff, not brokers, and the truth is, in most cases, brokers are different animals than other people in the industry. We are competitive, independent, self-motivated, self-starters, confident, and problem solvers who can take much more heat and rejection than most. Maybe I went in there asking questions as if it were my show, and it may have taken her aback. But, as far as I was concerned, my life, my experience, and my claim were my show. Now that I had some recourse, I had some serious questions to ask. As far as I was concerned, the war was beginning, and I wasn't interested in warm and fuzzy or girls making nice. It is OK that she subtly responded as she did, because I took it as a very helpful and early warning that I was really on my own.

Stowell & Friedman had other lawyers working with them in their office, and I also hadn't been comfortable with the lawyer who originally helped me with my claim form. It could have been that I was stressed out and had a sharp edge myself, but, ultimately, I decided that Stowell & Friedman was overwhelmed, too busy, and too far away. I wasn't going to get much individual help from them; therefore, I needed to take appropriate action and hire my own lawyer, as I was allowed to do, according to the class settlement. My problem was that I didn't really know anyone.

—⁓—

I decided to go back to Gloria Allred's office. Her office is famous for fighting for justice for women, so I thought that now that I was involved in a real and nationally-known case, Allred's office would talk to me. Well, not really. I called and did make some progress. This time I got to talk to a real lawyer, but the problem was that he was very rude. I asked him if he had heard about the Smith Barney class action settlement, and, in an annoyed voice, he said, "No." He spoke as if he was sorry he took my call and that I was wasting his time. He told me to send him the information I had and he would get back to me. I sent him copies of all pertinent information I had already received from Stowell & Friedman along with a letter. I called him to follow up, but he never took my calls again; second strike out with Allred's office.

My friend Sabastien had had a serious legal problem himself and was eventually granted political asylum. I had gone to his court trial every day for a week to support him and had met his attorney who specialized in civil and human rights. I figured Sabastien's lawyer might know labor lawyers to whom he could refer me, so I called him. He gave me three numbers, two women and a man. I interviewed the first woman in her downtown L.A. office. It was the kind of setup where you rent a small office and share reception, conference, and copy room with all the other tenants on the floor. It made me uncomfortable. We discussed what I understood about the class action and what the procedure was going to be. I also asked her some questions about her legal background. I wanted to make sure that whomever I hired was experienced in labor law. She told me she had been a corporate lawyer for many years. I asked her what she did exactly as a corporate lawyer. Basically, she used to be in the same position that my new legal adversaries were in at Smith Barney. She also still had their attitude, which was that the corporation would prevail, to not expect much, and that it's just the way it works, though she would help me and do what she could. Her strongest asset, as she said was that since she had been a corporate attorney for so long, she knew how they thought and the strategies they use. I told her I was interested in strategy and wanted to know more about what she thought about my case. She already had a defeatist attitude as far as I was concerned. She was a pleasant person but as I walked to my car after the meeting I thought to myself, "No way."

A friend of mine, familiar with law, suggested that psychologically, in terms of fighting the opposition, it would be better to hire a man. I guess there are several ways to look at it, but his perspective was that I needed one of, "them," a powerful white guy, to face off with them. They would relate better to one of their own, rather than a perceived screeching hysterical woman or a bulldog man-eater of a woman. Conversely, they would probably use a young female lawyer with me for the same reason, which is exactly what they ended up doing in the mediation or second step in the process.

I called the male lawyer next. His name was Maxwell Prague in the Century City area of Los Angeles. His office was near Beverly Hills, about three minutes from my apartment. He was white, in his very early 50s, about 6'2" tall, had his Yale University diploma on the wall, and seemed to be a very nice guy. His office was fabulous. He was on the top floor of one of the tall office buildings in Century City. There was a sitting area with magazines straight ahead as one walked into his office with a counter to the left. Behind the counter sat his receptionist/secretary, I thought, along with several other people whom I took to be paralegals and legal secretaries. The administrative area behind the counter ran almost the whole length of the office. Running parallel to the counter was the hallway, and on the other side of the hall were the lawyers' private offices. If their doors were open, one could see that all of the lawyers' private offices had windows that looked out over the golf course and, in the distance, Beverly Hills. Maxwell had the corner office with two sides of it being almost floor-to-ceiling windows. He had a couple leather couches with an oriental rug on one side and his desk and computer on the other side. His office was comfortable and the view was breathtaking. Being in his office was very calming to me.

I asked him the same questions I had asked the female former corporate lawyer downtown. Maxwell's responses were completely different. Right off the bat he started talking about strategy. That was exactly what I was thinking about and what I wanted to hear. After I had made my original pitch to Maxwell, he got up and left his office for a minute then returned with his law partner Jeremy Cope. All three of us had a discussion. I wanted those guys to understand exactly where I was coming from and where I wanted to go with this endeavor, so that we were all on the same page. I didn't want there to be any surprises in the future. I told them I was in this for justice and was going for broke, willing to forfeit my career if that is the way it turned out because if I didn't give this everything I had I wouldn't be able to live with myself. It was a matter of self-respect. If I lost, at least I could say I tried my best, but the world isn't always fair. Yet, if I hadn't tried to stand up for my own dignity and self-respect, I wouldn't have ever forgiven myself and would have lived with unbearable regret.

"Guys," I told them, "$100,000 doesn't motivate me."

"Gee," Jeremy answered, "I wish I was in the position to say a $100,000 doesn't motivate me." It wasn't that $100,000 wouldn't have been pleasant; in fact I could have really used it, but $100,000 would not have come anywhere near to making up for what I had lost. I preferred to take the risk of trying to hold Smith Barney accountable and possibly get nothing rather than settle for that amount. A settlement like that would have meant that after lawyers' fees and taxes I would have had fifty grand in my pocket. After what I had gone through, fifty grand wasn't worth it and would have been another stab to my heart. I felt very good about Maxwell and felt a sense of relief when I walked out of his office. I decided to hire him and never did meet the third referral.

—⟋⟍—

I was doing much better financially but there was no way I could pay a lawyer's fees up front. Maxwell took my case on contingency. However, he knew that even if I lost my case or won without being given a monetary award, Smith Barney was on the hook to pay reasonable lawyers' fees. According to the settlement, as long as a claimant's case wasn't judged frivolous, Smith Barney had to pay the fees regardless of the end result. He didn't know if I would win or not but he knew my case wasn't frivolous and that eventually he would be paid. That was another legal leveling of the playing field aspect of the class action that Stowell & Friedman put together. I hired Maxwell and signed the retainer agreement in September 1999. My first assignment from Maxwell was to look at my personnel file and write notes about everything that was in it.

Originally, there had been a specific timetable for each step in the process to occur, but both sides were overwhelmed with the nearly two thousand claims. Eventually the timetable for all three steps in the process seems to have been thrown by the wayside and that is why it took almost ten years to conclude the entire suit. According to the original settlement, Smith Barney was supposed to have come back with offers within sixty days of filing. I filed in April of 1999 and received my offer for the first round on November 22, 1999. Smith Barney offered me $34,000 and included a release form with a confidentiality agreement. On December 20, 1999, Maxwell and I rejected the settlement and demanded to go to the second step, mediation.

The second task Maxwell gave me was to write down all the ways in which I received compensation. I made a grid for him. On the top row going across, I indicated the years I had worked starting from 1991, and on the side row going down I indicated the type of compensation that square represented, for example, commission earnings, 401k contributions and fund performance, stock options, pension plan, etc. The third task was to start thinking about a witness list.

—◊—

Between February and June 2000, letters, e-mails, and faxes seemed to be flying back and forth among Maxwell; Stowell & Friedman; Smith Barney's outside council in New York, Paul, Weiss, Rifkind, Wharton & Garrison; and the Duke Private Adjudication Center. Stowell & Friedman had hired several experts[6] to analyze the data Smith Barney agreed to produce during the class action. I was told that claimants would be able to use these reports during mediation and arbitration.

Finally, after requesting a date for mediation several times, a date was set for November 17, 2000. The mediator in my case was also a lawyer, and the mediation was to be held in the office of Munger, Tolles & Olson in downtown Los Angeles at 8:30 a.m. and to conclude by 6:30 p.m. I was told that several of the mediations taking place before mine lasted late into the night where the women were so tired and exhausted that they couldn't think straight. I heard one woman, at some point late into mediation, literally laid down on the floor during the negotiations. How ridiculous is that! I told Maxwell, in no uncertain terms, I was leaving at the end of the day and would not keep negotiating late into the night when I was tired.

Maxwell hired the accounting firm White, Zuckerman, Warsavsky, Lane & Wolf to do the forensic accounting on my case. Our contention and the logic of my case was that I was a competent, intelligent, courageous, and accomplished individual before, I started working for Smith Barney and that if I had not been harassed, discriminated against, and then retaliated against then my total income over the years would have been commensurate with the top 20% of brokers who had worked at Smith Barney for the same amount of time as I. Since I had been a high achiever before I started working for Smith Barney, we contended that I would

---

[6] I can't tell the reader what the class-wide reports contained because I signed a confidentiality agreement regarding the contents of those reports. For a general description, see *The Boom Boom Room : Women VS Wall Street* by Susan Antilla p 285.

have continued to be a high achiever had it not been for the obstacles put in front of me.

Smith Barney keeps track of broker production by quintiles (20% segments), so there are five different quintiles to which a broker can belong at any particular time. This information was disseminated monthly to its brokers, so we all knew, on a monthly basis, how our performance stacked up to our peers. The reports were called focus reports. Maxwell and I gleaned the numbers we used in our argument as best as we could from these focus reports as well as other records and documents Smith Barney had given to me over the years. We assumed that I made the average production number of those who were actually in the first quintile and who had been in the business for the same amount of time as I. Then we subtracted what I actually made from that number. That was my economic loss that Smith Barney caused me. Then using the same logic, we extrapolated into the future what my retirement savings would have been but wasn't because of Smith Barney's treatment of me. This calculation was done not only for the top quintile (the top 20% for those in the business since 1991), but also for the second quintile (top 40%) and third quintile (top 60%). The sum total for any of the individual quintiles was in the millions.

I knew I had to prepare myself for the mediation so I listened to and took notes of an old cassette tape of Herb Cohen's *You Can Negotiate Anything*. It gave me the idea that someone with real authority had to be at the mediation. Smith Barney agreed in the settlement that they would make a good faith effort to settle with each individual in mediation, but I still wanted to make sure that whomever they sent to my mediation had real authority to make a decision. I did not know whom Smith Barney would be sending over as their lawyers and negotiators, and I was concerned about it, so in addition to sending my initial claimant submission, interim claim, and class-wide allegations to the mediator, Maxwell wrote a letter reminding Smith Barney of their good faith agreement and warning them that we meant business. He wrote, "Tameron Keyes makes a multi-million dollar claim against Smith Barney. Even in the context of this class action, the conduct she experienced and the economic injuries she suffered were exceptional. For the mediation to be successful, it must provide an opportunity for Smith Barney to appreciate that it will not avoid liability and to take a considered measure of Tameron Keyes's actual damages...."

I also took notes of friends' advice, and reviewed all it several times. Often, participants in mediations like this are kept in separate rooms, and the neutral mediator moves back and forth between the rooms. I saw this mediation as my opportunity to be able to confront somebody at Smith Barney, even if that person was just a Smith Barney representative who didn't personally have anything to do with what happened to me. I needed to get my feelings off my chest, and I felt I could speak and negotiate for myself, so I wanted the negotiations to be face-to- face instead of in separate rooms.

Maxwell and I met a few days before the mediation to prepare. I was also very worried about crying and kept bringing it up. I think Maxwell got tired of hearing me worry. "So what if you cry, Tameron, then you cry; it's normal," Maxwell finally said to me. Those few words made me feel better, as if I needed permission to cry in front of people and that it didn't make me a wimp.

I wanted to convey an image, at the mediation, of a person who was successful but also relaxed— someone who knew how to operate in the world. With that idea in mind, I wore a feminine, navy Armani cashmere jacket with a conservative lighter blue silk blouse, dark blue Armani pants, and camel-colored, pointy-toed, and high-heeled mules. Maxwell and I met an hour early in the lobby of the building, bought coffee, and then went up the elevator to the law firm's office on the fifteenth floor. At the appointed time, everybody met, shook hands, and filed into the conference room. Smith Barney people sat on one side of the table, and Maxwell and I sat on the other side with the mediator, at the head of the table.

Smith Barney had sent three young female lawyers all in their twenties and thirties to the negotiation, just as I suspected they would. The oldest, and the one with the alleged authority, sat in between the other two, very young lawyers. As the oldest, she looked to be in her early thirties.

It was my mediation, so I had the right to speak first. I wrote a statement out on paper to read, instead of memorizing it, in case I cried. I didn't want to take the chance of getting upset, losing my train of thought, and verbally stumbling. I took my pages out and started to read:

"I believe it might be helpful to let everyone know who I am and why I'm here. I am someone who has been driven from a young age toward success and independence; failure is something in which I have always refused to participate. My parents had a gourmet food shop as a side business so I started working for them in the eighth grade at thirteen years old. I experienced more economic success, thus independence, than I had ever had before and was hooked. I worked so hard at thirteen that I developed something our family doctor called walking mono, which is a fancy way of saying I wore myself out working and going to school at thirteen! After high school I went to college, I also worked and took some adventures: I lived in Hawaii for a while ...and graduated from UCLA in 1987. I went to graduate school at Columbia University and finished in January 1990. I came back to California, because at that time, none of the major investment firms were hiring. I waited tables from 1990 through 1992."

Somewhere in the middle of the reading, I started to choke up. I tried to stop myself but couldn't and began to cry. I didn't just cry; I was sobbing, and it felt terrible. I remember looking up and seeing the faces of the three Smith Barney lawyers. The two younger lawyers flanking the older one in the middle had looks of pain on their faces. It must have been terrible for them to have to sit across the table and watch a grown woman sob her heart out. The older lawyer sitting in the middle had this tense, uptight look on her face, almost as if she was angry. I remember her mouth all tensed up and thinking that her mouth looked like a little slit mouth of one of those outer space alien characters. I continued to read as I cried:

"I started working at Shearson Lehman brothers in 1991. This guy with a hole in his pants and shoe and a missing tooth hired me, really by accident. Once I had my foot in the door that's all it took. They gave me $5 an hour so I cold called from 6:30a.m., starting in New York and cold-calling across the country, until 1:00 p.m., then I'd jump into my car and zoom down to Orange County to wait tables at a twelve-table dive restaurant with cockroaches until about 10 p.m., 12 a.m., on the weekends. Then I'd jump back into my car and drive back to LA where I rented a room from two unsavory people. I'd get up at 5:30 a.m. and do it all over again. I used to study for my Series 7 license parked in the restaurant parking lot between 2 p.m. and 4 p.m. I can't tell you how many times I fell asleep. I did that for a year and a half until I got into the training program. What I experienced in the downtown branch was unbelievable. Sexual harassment, intimidation, and discrimination was how that place functioned. The guys took pride in how they behaved. They believed they were tough guys for it. I'll never forget one of the closing lines my sales manager used to brag about using when he was in production, and it goes: "Mr. Jones, reach deep into your wife's purse and pull out your balls and buy this stock." Destroy the stupid client and destroy the stupid girl was their motto. I endured it because I wanted to be a broker so much. However, it became impossible, so I politely asked my branch manager to help me move to a branch that would be more conducive to building my business. I requested to move to one of the three branches that were in Beverly Hills at the time. They moved me into Lyndsey Shanahan's branch. I believe Aaron Weisswasser, the regional director, chose Shanahan's branch specifically, because they believed that an old dog who 'knows where all the bones are buried,' as one of his colleagues characterized him to me, would be able to grind me out of the business. Well, obviously he couldn't do it. Here I am and I still have lots of strength in me. I'm here to get justice, and I'm determined to get it one way or another, and I'm confident I'll succeed."

I think the degree of my anguish and heartbreak surprised Smith Barney's lawyers. After I had sobbed that hard the mediator wanted to take a break and so did Smith Barney's lawyers. A twenty-minute break was called almost immediately. At the agreed time, we went back into the conference room to start the negotiation again. It was Maxwell's feeling that they needed a break in order to call New York. Once we were back in the negotiation room, they made me an offer, right off the bat, of $100,000. The mediator indicated that that was it, their top offer, and that there was no chance of Smith Barney increasing it.

Maxwell and the oldest lawyer were discussing something back and forth for a minute, when all of a sudden Maxwell said to me in a stern voice, "Get up, Tameron; we're leaving." I shot up like a rocket and grabbed my purse. A few words continued to go back and forth as we were moving the chairs out of our way to leave. The oldest lawyer made some comment about our behavior insinuating that we were somehow behaving badly or Maxwell had said something unprofessional or unkind. I remember Maxwell smiling at her, as if to show her she was full of it. He denied her accusation then said, "We just hope you have to pay a lot of money." We hadn't been in that law office for more than an hour, and, as we were leaving, the mediator looked lost. I, on the other hand, was very happy to be out of there and happy with Maxwell as well. "Yeah!" I thought to myself, "he's not going to take their crap."

Maxwell told me that he had concluded that Smith Barney had not treated us right because this was supposed to be an honest, good faith negotiation with someone who had the authority to really negotiate and make decisions for the company, even if that entailed serious numbers. We had come to the mediation sincerely ready to settle for a reasonable price, yet Smith Barney had sent lawyers who were only authorized, we suspected, to offer $100,000 maximum. This tactic of Smith Barney's was not the way they had agreed to conduct the mediations in the settlement agreement. An impasse was declared, and we invoked the right to the third step, arbitration.

—⚏—

Back in the office, it was now 2000. Lyndsey was gone and almost all of the weird comments had stopped. Tim Moynihan took over as branch manager in March 2000, but as far as I was concerned, he was an unknown. I had been through so much I didn't trust anybody. I believed the company saw me as an enemy within and am sure they briefed my new manager about my situation, so I was fearful. For months, I tried my best to stay away from him. He made the first move to get to know me. He actually asked me to go to lunch with him! He asked many people in the office to go out to lunch, often individually, in an effort to get to know his brokers and for them to get to know him. Actually, he took me to lunch twice during the years I worked for him. It's true that I would have liked anybody who, at least on the surface, treated me as a professional and as an adult, but I really liked my new manager Tim. He didn't have that smart-ass, bully demeanor that Lyndsey had. Tim was more intellectual, laughed at my jokes, and was just basically polite, but, even still, I'm sure any and all managers associated with the Beverly Hills branch wished I would just go away.

My feelings were accurate. Tim was professional and polite with me, but I knew I wasn't going to get much from him. He tried to block a partnership I had established with a female colleague of mine, Charlotte, from the downtown office, who was hired after I had moved to Beverly Hills. Eventually, Charlotte had moved to London to work as a broker there. She gave me some of her California clients to take care of since she couldn't do it herself from London, and we shared the commission. Tim had already given me permission. All managers involved had also given their permission, and thank goodness, I had it all on e-mail. This setup was a big to-do, which involved New York, corporate lawyers, and the compliance department because it was international. I needed Tim's approval again as a very last step, perhaps to get the joint production number and open the accounts in our branch. He welched, and he didn't have the courage to face me about it himself. He sent our fourth new sales manager, Stanley (Jason had been promoted and moved to another branch), to try and put me off. There was no way I was going to let this happen. I printed out all the e-mails and made notes in the margin showing Tim's OK, all the other managers' OKs, and all the e-mails that were written between managers and copied to everybody involved. It was obvious he was trying to squelch something that took a lot of time and effort from many people and that he had already approved. It was too obvious, and, when I laid it all out to Stanley, he took it to Tim. Tim could see that he couldn't back out and withdraw his permission without something looking very wrong. I got my partnership. If he hadn't given in and allowed the partnership as he had already approved, I would have gone to HR again because I felt protected by that time.

Another time I got a 401k plan from a very famous restaurant in Los Angeles. A lot of their employees were Spanish speakers so they wanted to make sure that some of the 401k enrollment meetings were done in Spanish. I told my new client that it was no problem. I had a colleague who spoke fluent Spanish who would do the meetings for them in Spanish. My old friend Mitchell was a fluent Spanish speaker and he did do some of the meetings in Spanish, expecting that we would be partners. It was all a done deal. The 401k was up and running, the enrollment meetings were done, and the plan was funded. I just needed a joint production number with Mitchell so we could get paid.

Getting a joint number takes five minutes and branch manager approval. Tim wouldn't do it. It was so outrageous that even my sales manager, Stanley, couldn't believe it. Again, Tim wouldn't face me and sent Stanley up to my office instead to tell me the news. Stanley was not an ally of mine because, I am sure, he was also "briefed" about my history. A colleague told me one day that Stanley flat out told him, "I try and stay away from Tameron." We didn't really know each other and barely interacted with each other. But even Stanley felt badly about this. He came into my office, closed the door, and sat in the guest chair opposite my desk. "Tameron," he said in a low, serious voice one uses when giving bad news, "I don't understand it myself; it doesn't make any sense, and I have no answer why for you, but Tim won't let you have a split production number for that 401k plan, and he doesn't want you to bother him about it either. It makes no sense to me."

It was outrageous, but I knew very well what Tim was doing. Smith Barney and I were going to court and they were trying, as best as they still could, to interfere with my success in order to show that Lyndsey wasn't the reason why I hadn't been successful but that I just wasn't good at my job. I didn't say anything to Stanley because he didn't need to be involved. I kept the business, but my buddy Mitchell got screwed. I called him and told him what happened. He was a good sport and a good friend. He knew, blow by blow, what had been happening to me all these years. He was the colleague who had told me in the very beginning not to run away from those guys with my tail between my legs and who had given me the HR telephone number back in 1993. He took a chance by doing business with me, the company pariah, bless his heart, but he lost. I got the business from this particular client, but Tim's action precluded me from getting referrals I may have gotten from this client for other restaurants that needed a Spanish speaker. Is that important? Yes it is. Again, just as when a partnership with Georges was blocked, whether I would have gotten referrals is not the point. The point is that they blocked me from the opportunity, and a broker's business grows the same way a snowball grows rolling downhill. It was obstructionist. Even though things had gotten much better and Lyndsey was gone, things still weren't as they should have been.

—⁂—

Maxwell and I had no doubt that Lyndsey had made my file disappear, but there could and should have been a copy someplace else, so we kept asking for it. Maxwell wrote a formal request asking for my personnel file to Brad Karp, Smith Barney's lead lawyer at Paul, Weiss, Wharton & Garrison. Of course, Lyndsey was gone by this time, but before he left he had come up with a couple of different excuses. One was that it "got lost in the renovation." During his deposition and under oath, Lyndsey abandoned all the stories he had told about my file and testified that he didn't know what happened to my file. He said that when he retired from Smith Barney everything stayed with the firm. Again, I had no doubt he was lying. It's probably still sitting in his garage.

While he was still working for the firm, I had kept asking to see my file, even though he had made it "mysteriously disappear," in the words of his assistant. He started a new one and eventually allowed me to look at it as he was legally obligated to do. Needless to say, everything that had been in my file such as my original employment contract and notes about my transfer were all gone. There were only a couple of pieces of paper in the "new file" relating to recent insurance transactions and some insurance licensing stuff. He had me sit at a little table across from his desk and look at the file. I wasn't allowed to copy it, but I was allowed to take notes. Maxwell told me to write everything down that was in the file, so I did even, though it was meaningless. Lyndsey was sitting there watching me look at my file, trying to pretend that he was busy and not watching me. I looked over at him and caught him looking at me; he raised his eyebrows and shrugged his shoulders as if to say, "I don't know." What made me really angry is that Smith Barney never sent the copy that was stored someplace else. Instead, in 2002, after Maxwell kept after them for it, Smith Barney had the audacity to blame 9/11. They sent a letter stating that, "to the extent that certain related files were maintained in New York, it is likely that such files were destroyed in the events of September 11." We had been asking for that file since September 1999! Smith Barney was despicable for trying to hide behind 9/11.

—m—

Early in April 2002, we received notification that a law firm in San Francisco, Orrick, Herrington & Sutcliffe, would be representing Smith Barney in the arbitration and that Terrence Paolucci would be their senior lawyer. Maxwell sent me a letter informing me that his partnership with Jeremy Cope was ending and asked me to sign another retainer agreement for him as a sole practitioner. Then, in August 2002, we finally got a list of three people proposed by the Private Adjudication Center to be on my panel.

Per the settlement agreement, I had the right to refuse panelists under certain circumstances, so I asked for more information about them. I figured it couldn't hurt and it might help. Two of the arbitrators sent us letters stating that the arbitrations they were involved in were confidential and that the information we received was all they were divulging. Maybe it was the language or the tone, but it felt to me that they were telling me to jump in a lake. In contrast, even though arbitrations and mediations are often confidential, the third panelist at least tried to be more helpful and wrote a letter to us including a reference name and number. Maxwell called the reference and had a chat with the referred person. I kept the third panelist who tried to be more helpful and rejected the other two, as was my right per the settlement agreement, since they had already participated in the class action's mediations. I figured I had nothing to lose and that the next two appointees might be more helpful.

My case was assigned two new panelists. One of them was more helpful and I wanted to keep that person, but I didn't have the option to reject the last panelist so the panel was set.

The year 2002 proved to be what I would call my year of legal hell. It was very difficult to work on my case, maintain myself at work as if nothing unusual was going on, manage my business, and take care of my clients, all at the same time. It felt like a covert war, and I was vigilant about making sure that nothing blocked my way. I had a cardboard file storage box labeled "Fire Box." In spite of the fact that I had papers and files all over my apartment that year, I kept all my most important papers regarding my case and my original notes in that one box. If there was a fire or disaster of any kind, I could just grab that one box and run. Everything I owned could have burned or been destroyed, but, if I could help it, I wasn't going to let even any unforeseen disasters thwart me in my effort to fight back against Smith Barney. There is a Middle Eastern saying that says, "Trust in God, but tie your camel first." I was tying my camel with triple knots.

X

WITNESSES AND DISCOVERY: SMITH BARNEY DIGS IN THEIR HEELS

As I have mentioned, the arbitration or third step of the class action settlement agreement turned out to be a mini-trial. There was a discovery period, depositions were taken under oath, and witnesses testified. However, what made it a mini-trial was that there were certain limits such as to how many written detailed questions each side could ask and how many depositions could be demanded. These limits don't exist in a regular trial. Preparation activities heated up significantly in early 2002, which ended up being the hardest year of my life. Thank goodness I lived only a half block away from my office in Beverly Hills. I had never hired a lawyer before I hired Maxwell and had never before been in a lawsuit. I had no idea how much work it would be on my part, and I'm not sure I should have had to do what I did. I did a lot of work and was constantly running back and forth from my office to my apartment during the workday. Often I needed to make calls from my home phone, get information from the boxes of material I had, or get something done quickly that came up unexpectedly or while it was on my mind.

For those who have never been involved in a lawsuit before, discovery is a detailed investigation process or period during which each side tries to discover any and all information relative to the case from anyone. Copies of any and all documents related to the case are requested and all questions are asked. It takes a lot of time. For example, each side had a deadline before which they could submit written questions to the opposing side. Then each side had a deadline in which they were supposed to answer those questions in full. If one side refused to answer those questions as Smith Barney refused to do, then the opposing lawyer went to the judge or, in my case, the panel of judges and asked them to compel compliance from the other side. Events were continuously happening like this that I will detail later. Lawyers disagree with each other on procedure or application of law; they misunderstand each other, play games, and sometimes a lawyer will flat out mislead the other. There could be and, in my experience, were many disputes that necessitated going in front of the panel, all in preparation for the trial. My lawyer and Smith Barney's lawyers kept going in front of the judges to file motions, make objections, and argue points of law just as in a regular trial. They did the same thing during the actual trial; the lawyers cited specific cases as precedence to back up their arguments and argued case law application. A year passed from the time I invoked my right to a trial to the date of the actual trial.

The three panelists on my case were lawyers, knowledgeable and experienced with respect to employment-related claims. One was a retired judge from Iowa, and the others would report to new judgeships in January 2003 after my trial. Of those two, one had been voted into a state judge position in Florida and the other had been appointed to the federal bench in Washington State. The panelists had the authority to grant any relief they deemed appropriate to the same extent that a court would have. The panel supposedly also had the authority to compel relevant and material testimony and the production of relevant and material documents, but I'll get to that later. Witnesses would testify under oath and be cross-examined. The scope, timing, and methods of discovery would be determined by the panel. Punitive damages were also available by the burden of proving by clear and convincing evidence if the panel chose to award them. Punitive damages are awarded as punishment to the defendant and to deter the defendant or others from similar acts in the future. They may be awarded only if a defendant's conduct is malicious or in reckless disregard to a plaintiff's rights. Conduct is malicious if it is accompanied by ill will or spite or if it is for the purpose of injuring another. Conduct is in reckless disregard to a plaintiff's rights if, under the circumstances, it reflects complete indifference to the safety and rights of others. However, punitive damages are not awarded in regular federal arbitration. Lastly, the panel's decision was final and binding. Either party could appeal but only on limited grounds of fraud or corruption.

I called one of the class representatives whom I knew from the downtown LA branch, Claire Santiago. Claire was a sales assistant, and I remembered her as being very sweet and helpful to me as a new broker in the downtown branch even though she didn't actually work for me. We ended up having a nice chat during which she suggested that we meet with Melanie, another woman who was also a class representative and had also been hired in the downtown L.A. branch after I had transferred. The three of us made an appointment to meet one Saturday morning at the International House of Pancakes on Santa Monica Boulevard in West Hollywood. Melanie was tall, about my height, blond, wore a fabulous dark navy blue suit, and at first glance seemed professional. We went inside the restaurant and had breakfast, chatted, gossiped, and exchanged information. At some point, Melanie started to tell a particular story of an event that used to happen to her in the office on an ongoing basis. She said that a broker she cold-called for named Brian used to habitually strip in his office and change into his workout clothes without bothering to go change in the restroom. She said that the day he "stripped down to his gonads," as she called it, she had had enough. She complained and was also transferred to another Beverly Hills branch that was located across the alley from my office. She also claimed she was retaliated against.

I gasped when she told that story. "I saw him do that too," I said, "many times. Brian used to strip down to his boxer shorts in the middle of the office, although I never saw him strip naked," I clarified.

I believed her stories because much of what she described I had also experienced. But there was something about Melanie that bothered me from the very beginning. She came on just a little too strong and with a hint of being a bully herself. At one point during the conversation she was talking about something and, it seemed, trying to act authoritative in the process. So she tilted her head down and looked at me as she spoke with her sunglasses slipping down on her nose like an old-fashioned Hollywood movie star. The problem was that her sunglasses were pinching her nostrils together, so, instead of sounding authoritative, she sounded like an animated cartoon character. "Oh my God, how ridiculous is this woman," I thought to myself. What was even more uncomfortable was that she took herself so seriously and kept talking like that without pushing her glasses up. She was so self-involved that she must not have realized that she sounded like a cartoon character and didn't come across as authoritative. Her dramatic ways, it would turn out, were a precursor of what was to come.

A date was set for the first conference call to take place among all the lawyers involved and the three-judge panel, during which the schedule for discovery was agreed upon. Shortly after that first conference call, Maxwell served Smith Barney with a list of what are called interrogatories and a request for production of documents, and Smith Barney served us with the same. Smith Barney asked me to answer nineteen questions or interrogatories. The questions were long and detailed. The answers to those questions covered an eleven-year period and were often overlapping. I made sure that I answered them as thoroughly as possible, but having to relive those eleven years of events, over and over, and wanting to make sure that every word was correct was a horribly stressful task. I had to deal with a lot of memories and a lot of papers associated with those memories.

I gave Maxwell the original papers I had accumulated and made copies of everything for myself. It required a lot of concentration, and, again, I was simultaneously running my business in the office, calling clients, making trades, managing portfolios, having client meetings, and doing everything else it takes to be a stockbroker. It took me weeks to answer their questions. I reread my copies many times in preparing the answers to those questions and for the whole trial in general. Boxes were everywhere in my apartment. There were piles of papers with pieces of yellow Post-it notes stuck to various piles of notes all over the place. They were all over my living room, stacked on my desk, coffee table, couch, and floor. I would group a pile of notes together because they contained the answer to one question, then some of that group of notes would be connected to the answer for another question, and the remaining notes of that same group might be related to a third question. It felt like a mental labyrinth.

A sampling of Smith Barney's interrogatories went like this:

> If claimant complained to any person regarding the alleged hostile work environment, sex discrimination, retaliation, or differential or unfair treatment Claimant was allegedly subjected to when employed at SSB (Salomon Smith Barney) state all facts supporting this assertion, including when this complaint was made, if it was an oral complaint or written complaint, to whom the complaint was made, and the outcome or result of the complaint; or, state all facts supporting Claimant's allegations that Chad Porter discriminated against or harassed Claimant. Or, state all facts supporting Claimant's allegation that Lyndsey Shanahan discriminated or retaliated against Claimant; or, state all facts which support Claimant's allegation that Lyndsey Shanahan "treated Tameron Keyes badly," including when, where, how, and under what circumstances Lyndsey Shanahan treated claimant "badly," including but not limited to the details...etc.

Answering interrogatories and submitting requested documents was not supposed to be optional; the panel was supposed to have the same authority as a court. However, in our legal system, each side can also object to specific requested documents and/or questions. They can go back to the judge or judges to object to the request and explain why they don't want to comply. The judge or judges then determine whether the objecting side must comply or not for those specific requested documents or questions.

My response and objection document to Smith Barney's requests stated that I would comply with each of the thirty document requests they demanded of me in a timely manner except three. It also stated that I would eventually comply with the remaining three at the appropriate time but, because they were about damage and expert exchange, it was premature to submit them at that point. I gave them every piece and scrap of paper I had that related in any way to my claim. Conversely, Smith Barney dug in their heels and refused to fulfill a good portion of my document requests. They claimed that much of what I requested wasn't available, using several excuses including that if I had that information I might go running to current Smith Barney employees in an attempt to influence them or bother them somehow. They also claimed that the information I sought was proprietary information or private third-party information such as how much male brokers made in comparison to female brokers. Getting information out of them was, in several circumstances, very difficult or downright impossible. They just wouldn't comply, period. I answered every one of their interrogatory questions in as much detail as I was capable. Smith Barney objected or made a non-response to almost every single question of the nineteen questions that Maxwell asked of them. Maxwell took the issue to the panel to compel Smith Barney to comply. I wasn't privy to the arguments that Smith Barney and Maxwell made before the panel, but I do know that whatever motion Maxwell made, it was granted, as he told me. This was the beginning of my confusion because, even though Maxwell won the motion to compel them to produce documents and answer questions, we still didn't get a lot of what we originally requested. Throughout this year of preparation, as you will see, I asked Maxwell questions about what was happening and why. Sometimes he answered me and sometimes he didn't; sometimes his answers made sense and sometimes they didn't.

Maxwell told me that it was agreed upon with Smith Barney and the judges that I would be allowed to depose up to four witnesses: my original manager, James Ayala; my second manager, Lyndsey Shanahan; their boss who granted my transfer, Aaron Weisswasser; and the HR manager involved Carol Farmer. Smith Barney deposed me and the forensic accountant I intended to call as a witness. The goings-on went back and forth for months and didn't seem to be working the way I thought the law dictated, such as when Smith Barney didn't comply with the motion to compel them to produce documents. I couldn't understand it. I would realize much later that Maxwell wasn't informing me of everything that was going on while it was going on, and I didn't catch on to that fact until it was too late in several instances. It took me a long time to realize these things because, first, I had never been involved in a lawsuit before and trusted Maxwell, and, second, I had a business to run and other tasks to take care of regarding my trial, like finding witnesses who would testify for me. I was too overwhelmed to catch on any faster than I did.

Trying to get witnesses for my case was another unexpected wild ride. Growing up, I had been taught to tell the truth and that lying was wrong, even telling little white lies. I didn't have the nerve to lie, because if I had and my parents had caught me, they would have made hamburger out of me, so I just didn't do it. I was also taught to stand up for what is right. In spite of my life experiences where circumstances often contradicted this "worldview," I continued to maintain a child-like naiveté. I was so naïve that, even after all I had been through with Lyndsey, I told Maxwell several times that I thought Lyndsey would come clean during his deposition and tell the truth! I sincerely believed that one day my former manager would have a crisis of conscience and just tell the truth. I repeated my belief to Maxwell often enough that, one day, he looked at me with a slightly annoyed smile on his face. He needed to set me straight, once and for all, about Lyndsey and set my thought processes on a more realistic course. "Tameron," he said, "he is not going to do that, and that is not going to happen."

It also never occurred to me that people wouldn't help me even if they had information that was helpful and would bring about justice. The reality that I eventually came to grips with is not that simple, and my ordeal definitely taught me a more mature understanding of the mechanisms of real life. This may seem like a ridiculously simple life lesson for many people, but for those of us naïve people in the world, it is and was a difficult, shocking, and depressing lesson. I don't blame people; now I realize that people must protect themselves. Work life is hard enough; one cannot expect others— especially people who may barely know you or even your friends— to risk making their own jobs more difficult, being passed up for a promotion, getting on a powerful person's bad side, getting an unsavory reputation in the industry, or, at worst, losing their jobs. It's a small world. People have families, responsibilities, and their own struggles in life.

—·—

The first person I tried to reach was Victoria (she was the one who at eighteen had punched her boss in the face). I looked her name up on the NASD[7] website, but she was no longer in the business, Next, I looked her up on the Internet 411 directory. I found her address without a telephone number, so I wrote her a letter. I received no response, but the letter also did not come back. If she had moved, the letter should have been returned to sender. I didn't get it back, but you never know; maybe whoever was living at that address just threw the letter in the trash.

I knew Victoria had also sued Smith Barney, as I mentioned previously. James Ayala, our downtown branch manager, had transferred to another branch since I had left and then, I heard, had been fired. The gossip was that Smith Barney had started to crack down on that branch's business

---

[7] National Association of Securities Dealers

umm… "irregularities." Someone had to be the fall guy, who turned out to be the compliance manager, Fritz the Rottweiler. James was ordered to fire Fritz but refused. Management in that branch had all been in it together, and James didn't think it was right to fire Fritz. James was responsible for the branch, so they transferred James and then fired Fritz. James eventually moved to another firm in Santa Barbara County.

The manager that replaced James was the manager over whose behavior Victoria sued. I heard he was worse. James was a personally polite and well-mannered man, but Harland the next manager apparently was an animal. Victoria had told me years before that Harland had withheld her paycheck for a couple weeks demanding something sexual. I heard that many women brought suit against Harland, and it was rumored that he had had sexual harassment problems in other offices. Victoria also told me that Harland had been neighbors with Aaron Weisswasser, the boss of both my downtown and Beverly Hills managers.

As it got closer to the trial date, I started feeling more and more desperate and tried harder to find Victoria and others. There was a fine art dealer who worked out of his home across the street from my apartment in Beverly Hills. He had bragged one day about his superior skill in tracking down rich people since they were his clientele. I went to him and asked if he would help me find an old friend. After I convinced him that I wasn't a stalker or a killer, he agreed to help me. First, I had to remember Victoria's boyfriend's name because she had gotten married. There was a guy whom I had worked with in the downtown branch that now worked in my building in Beverly Hills at a cheesy discount firm that had been raided by the FBI. Every once in a while I would see him in the elevator or in our building's lobby. I knew he had been friends with Victoria's boyfriend, so the next time I saw him, I casually asked if he had heard from Victoria and asked how she was doing. He said something to the effect that he hadn't seen her boyfriend for a long time, then I took the opportunity to ask what her boyfriend's name was again. He told me and that's all I needed. I looked him up on the Internet but found nothing, so I took his name to the art dealer. A couple of days later, the dealer had an address for me. It was the same address to which I had mailed the letter. I got in my car and drove.

The address was about an hour's drive from Beverly Hills. I knocked on the door. No answer, and it didn't feel like anybody was home, but I wasn't quite sure. It seemed like someone had looked through a little opaque window that opened up to the front porch, but I could have been imagining things. I left but went back a few days later. This time a silver BMW was in the driveway. It had customized plates that I remembered to be Victoria's. I knew now that she positively lived there. I knocked on the door again then turned my back to the windows. If anyone were home they would see a woman but wouldn't see who it was. As far as I was concerned, she had received my letter and was avoiding me. I thought she would yell and be unhappy to see me since she ignored my letter, but I didn't care. Let her yell and curse, I thought; at least then I could tell myself that I tried my best. Again, there was no answer.

A week later I drove out there again. I rang the bell, and this time I heard Victoria calling out to her husband to answer the door. He seemed to have been watching a game upstairs, and she was doing something in the back of the house. I rang the bell a couple more times. She answered the door, opening it up wide, and was totally stunned when she saw me. She stood there for a couple of seconds, but it felt like an eternity. It seemed to take so long for everything to register that I felt I had to say, "It's Tameron... Tameron Keyes from Smith Barney." She didn't act as if she was angry or annoyed at all. She gave me a hug, which surprised me, and asked me in. We sat in her living room and chatted for about an hour. Her husband poked his head out and looked at me from the top of the staircase, but he didn't come down. Victoria said to him, "This is Tameron; you remember Tameron." We had all worked together downtown although I didn't know Donnie at all. I was out with Victoria the night they really got to know each other and got together. Charlotte, Victoria's cold caller, was out with us as well. Donnie grunted something and went back into the room.

I told Victoria what was going on and about the class action. She was not a part of it because she had already sued on her own. When I told her about Chad, the sales manager in the downtown branch who had basically caused all this legal action, his threat to fire me, and the other things he had said about me to more than one person, she responded with a vehement, "No Way! Chad isn't like that!" She had been friends with him to some degree, so I wasn't going to argue with her. I was there to ask her to testify about the environment and to gather any information that might be helpful for me. She told me she couldn't testify because she had a confidentiality agreement with Smith Barney. I knew her excuse was baloney, and Maxwell later confirmed I was right. A confidentiality agreement is between two private parties, and those types of agreements don't trump federal law. She could have been subpoenaed, but, strategically speaking, it is not wise to subpoena a hostile witness or somebody who really doesn't want to talk. However, I do recognize that she'd had enough trouble with Smith Barney. I don't blame her for not wanting to go up against them again or stir the pot in any way. They have deep pockets with which they could easily pay lawyers to bother her, and she did not have deep pockets to defend herself. In addition, I am sure they said a lot of horrible things about her during her own lawsuit against them, so the emotional toll hassling with Smith Barney would have taken wasn't worth it for her.

However, my trip was not a waste of time. My goal was to find anyone who could corroborate my stories of the environment in the downtown branch. It didn't matter if we had worked together or not. What was important was the corroboration. In fact, if someone who worked in the downtown branch after I left corroborated my depiction, it would have been even better, because it would have shown that Smith Barney didn't fix the problem as they were required to do by law and that their negligence was woeful. Victoria told me that Charlotte, her cold caller, had transferred to Idaho and that Emma, one of her other cold callers, had gotten married in Walnut Creek and was living up there. I never let on that I intended to track these women down. I acted like Victoria and I were just old work friends chatting. The conversation started to lag and I left.

I made a beeline to my computer. Thank goodness Walnut Creek had already computerized to the extent that many marriage licenses could be researched online. I found Emma's marriage license and her husband's first and last name then I called Walnut Creek's directory assistance; he was listed. I called her and told her what was going on and asked her if she would be willing to have a chat with my lawyer. She agreed, so I gave Maxwell her telephone number. Maxwell did talk to her and reported to me that she had given some "very helpful information," but she also informed us that she wasn't able to come to L.A. to testify, that she would sign an affidavit, but things had to be quick. Part of the class action settlement specified that affidavits would be accepted as long as the opposing side had a chance to cross-examine the affidavant. Emma told both Maxwell and me that she was very ill, had a lawsuit pending against the doctor who had hurt her, and would soon go to trial herself. She didn't have the time or the physical wherewithal to linger over this. She had gotten a nose job during which the doctor had cracked her skull inside. She had cranial fluid dripping out her nose and was in constant pain. They had tried to do a corrective surgery, but it didn't work.

Her husband told me during a subsequent conversation that he had married a smart, bright, happy woman who had earned a Ph.D. and that now she was reduced to an incapacitated invalid. He had to give her pain-killing shots himself several times a day. There was no question about it that they were in the fight of their lives and very stressed out about the circumstances in which they found themselves. Apparently, the insurance company was playing very dirty with them. The fact that she would even want to do anything for me was very generous of her.

I have no idea why, but Maxwell didn't send her the affidavit. I kept bugging him and bugging him. I called her again a couple of months before my trial. This time she wouldn't take my calls. She was too sick and stressed out over her own trial, so she referred me to her husband. I had a couple conversations with him. Really, I was politely begging him to get Emma to complete the affidavit or talk to Maxwell again. The husband wanted to get rid of me, and I have to say he wasn't the sweetest, but who could blame him. Then he dropped the bomb. He asked me to pay them money. I played stupid and said, "I don't know if that's legal." He complained that "hired liars"— i.e., legal experts— were allowed to be paid in his wife's trial and that my lawyer could figure out a way to pay him. His voice got really nasty, almost sinister, and I got the point. Of course, I knew that what he was asking was highly illegal and unethical, but I told him I would ask my lawyer and we hung up. I never called him again. I felt that Maxwell had lost a potential witness who at one time had been willing to help me.

Next, I tried to find Charlotte. I knew she had also gotten married but I didn't have her married name. Victoria had told me she had transferred to a Smith Barney office in Idaho, so I went to our company computer system and looked up all the Idaho offices. There weren't many, so I just started calling. I asked the receptionist at the first office I called if they had a Charlotte Cannon in their branch. She told me she didn't know a Charlotte Cannon, so I asked to be transferred to the branch manager's assistant. I asked her the same question. No-go. Nobody knew her. I called the next branch and asked the same thing. The receptionist had never heard of such a person, so I asked to be transferred to the branch manager's assistant. Bingo! The assistant knew Charlotte. She told me that Charlotte had gotten married and had transferred to London. She gave me the spelling of Charlotte's married name.

I looked her up by her married name in the company directory and there she was, in London. "OK," I thought, "time to go to London; I want to see Eva anyway." I called her from California and told her I would be in London soon and would love to hook up with her again. She was happy to hear from me, and we agreed to meet. When I arrived, I called again and we arranged to meet after work for drinks at Mirabelle's on Curzon Street in the Mayfair section of London. We had only gone out together a few times in L.A. and hadn't seen each other for six or seven years. We weren't sure if we would recognize each other. Actually, we didn't at first; we passed each other on the sidewalk, but, since I was scrutinizing every blond that walked by, I turned around for a second look at her. It took us both a few seconds, then she said, "Tameron." I said, "Charlotte," and we gave each other big hugs. We had a lot of fun drinking, gossiping, and talking about business and the old times when she, Victoria, and I would go out on the weekends. I'm sure a couple of reserved British patrons were annoyed by these two loud-mouthed American women talking about wild Smith Barney and their business.

At some point, I told Charlotte about the class action and asked her if she would testify for me. She could have testified about the environment and to the fact that the problem had not been fixed, even though we had never worked together.

"Tameron, I have a good job now," she answered, in a low but sympathetic voice.

Bless her heart; at least she was honest with me. I completely understood how hard it was for her to get where she was. She didn't want to jeopardize that and I didn't begrudge her decision. The trip wasn't a loss however. I had fun with Charlotte again. She's a good person, and it would work out that I got more business from the trip. Smith Barney had changed their minds about the setup she had in terms of taking care of her stateside clients while she lived in London, so she needed to get a partner. After our meeting in London, she asked me if I would take over some of her California clients, and we would split the commission. I agreed, and we became business partners. This partnership with her is the situation that

I have already described when my new manager, Tim Moynihan had tried to nix the deal after he and several people in the organization had already set it up and approved it.

Over a period of several months, I tried to find many people simultaneously including Penny, Lyndsey's assistant who had told me my file had "mysteriously disappeared." It was to no avail. In her case, I knew some of the sales assistants in our office had her phone number, but I didn't want to ask them directly for it because that would have tipped them off that something was up. I had to weigh the likelihood of getting a willing witness against the risk of causing more overt animosity in my workplace, which as I have also already described, had started to subside.

———

Next I tried to find Georges, the first guy I had tried to partner with, and the cold caller who actually was allowed to partner with him. I found Georges at some type of hedge fund company and went to his office in Santa Monica unannounced. He wasn't there, so I went back another time and told the receptionist I was an old colleague who wanted to surprise him. He came out into the lobby and was surprised. I was also very nervous because I had kind of ambushed him, and I never knew how people would respond to my requests. I braced myself just in case the worst happened. He was actually very polite but said he didn't remember anything. I left, but I had Maxwell call him anyway. Maxwell thought that Georges might have been playing both sides, telling me he didn't remember and telling Smith Barney whatever it was that would keep him out of this. I found the cold caller. We spoke, and he agreed to sign an affidavit, so then I went back to Georges. There was a different receptionist there and I fooled her too. A guy came to see who it was. He must have gone back in and reported something to Georges because Georges came out to the lobby a second time, I suspect, to find a woman that he thought was going to be a pleasant surprise. He was surprised again, but this time he was obviously not happy to see me.

"Georges," I pleaded, "I thought I would come back and ask one more time if perhaps you could remember and talk to Maxwell."

"Tameron," he answered firmly, "I don't remember anything and I can't help you." It was a twenty-second encounter, and he wasn't amused that I had come back to ask him again. He wasn't going to be helpful. I was more embarrassed this time around, but, what the hell, I had to try at least one more time. The cold caller had gone his own way selling insurance products at a small firm. He was willing to help me, but he really didn't know anything that could help me. He was never told about my pitch to Georges. He was given the opportunity to work with Georges and probably thought Lyndsey was a great guy for it at the time.

I also wanted to find Moses, the cold caller who had worked for me for one day but had left after the stripper incident, and Jenny, the female cold caller who told me Chad was telling people that women shouldn't be brokers and that he was going to fire me. I didn't know anything about them except their names, that Jenny went to USC, and that Moses had been an economics or finance major at UCLA. I went to UCLA's alumni association and told the clerk whom I was trying to find and why. He told me that kind of information is private and that in order to obtain it UCLA first needed to be subpoenaed. Even though Moses had graduated from UCLA, it didn't mean he was a member of the alumni association, so I asked the clerk if he would just look the name up and see if it was in his records. The clerk confirmed that there was information about him in the system, but he wouldn't give it to me. I asked him if I wrote a letter and put a stamp on it if he would mail it for me. He agreed to do that. A couple of days later, I went back with the letter in an unaddressed envelope with my return address and a stamp on it. I gave it to the clerk who had said he would put the proper address on the envelope and mail it for me. I never got a reply from Moses.

Next, I had to find Jenny. I went to Madeline, a friend of mine who had graduated from USC and had access to its alumni association. She was Sabastien's sister, the guy with the legal problem I had briefly dated. She was a lawyer and had done a lot of work on his case herself. I had tried to help them as much as I could, so she and I had become good friends for four or five years. I asked her if she would go to USC alumni association and see if she could find Jenny. There was an online service that she suggested I look at first, but she would not do it herself, even though it would have taken her three minutes to do so. I had helped her a lot with Sabastien's case, running errands for her, picking up and delivering tapes, making copies, going to his lawyer's office to help organize papers, going to demonstrations, and protesting at the city council. I got their story into a small newspaper and onto TV. It was a small local channel, but TV nonetheless. I went to court with them every day and helped her entertain people in her home that were somehow connected to the case. In addition, I was a supportive, listening friend. In spite of all that, I had to drive the half hour to her house to use her computer, while she sat there, to look on the online service. Her attitude and reluctance to help me, even just a tiny bit, disgusted me. It literally took me three minutes. I didn't find anything, but the listings on that site were limited. The majority of alumni information was on campus, she told me, and one had to be alumna and go to the campus to get it— but she couldn't be bothered.

I didn't just ask Maxwell to subpoena UCLA and USC; I nagged and nagged him. I couldn't understand why he was dragging his feet. Finally, he told me that when you subpoena someone the opposition gets to see whom you are subpoenaing and that it might give them an advantage somehow. Regardless, I felt they were too important as witnesses, so Maxwell and I went around and around about it and basically had it out. It was a very unpleasant conversation, and the tension between us was turning to animosity on my side. This unpleasant conversation took place in his office on the day that we took Lyndsey and Carol's depositions (I'll describe those depositions later). I'm just not a quitter; when one road is blocked, I try and find another road. During the lunch break of that deposition day, in spite of how much I was beginning to dislike Madeline, I ate humble pie and called her again. I asked her for a second time if she would help me find Jenny through the USC alumni association. That meant she would have to go down to USC with me. She grudgingly agreed, and I mean grudgingly; she didn't sound at all sincere. She told me she would meet me in front of Taco Bell but wouldn't give me directions and was very hesitant about setting the date and time. I wasn't sure if she'd show up, but it was the best I could get from her. The moment I walked back into Maxwell's office after lunch, his assistant showed me the subpoena requests. Maxwell had thought twice after our tiff and made the subpoenas. I called Madeline back and told her I didn't need her help after all.

Shortly before the trial, I received the contact information for Moses through the subpoena. I called him, but he told me he didn't remember any such incident and that he had not received my earlier letter that the clerk from UCLA was supposed to have sent. I don't believe him because I don't believe that someone would forget, in ten years, the scene that took place with the stripper practically at his feet that day. In fact, for most people, it would have been a job search "war story." If he didn't want to help, he didn't want to help, and what could I do about it? A lot of people will not stick their necks out especially for a stranger on the telephone, and why would they? He didn't know me or my story from Adam.

—m—

I kept in touch with Claire Santiago, the class action representative I had called first back in 1999. I wanted to find another female broker named Kim. She had originally come into our office as an assistant to a broker who had been recruited away from another firm. Part of his deal, I heard, was to eventually promote her to an independent broker after she moved all of his clients over to Smith Barney. Claire was adamant that she didn't know Kim or even remember who she was. We kept talking, then after about ten or fifteen minutes, Claire exclaimed, "Yes, I do remember Kim; I forgot all about her." Not only did Claire remember who Kim was after a few minutes, she also remembered that Kim's husband was a lawyer and that his last name was Peterson. I went to the California Bar Association's website and found his phone number. I called his office and left a message with his secretary. He called me back and I explained to him why I was calling and what I wanted. He gave me his home phone number and invited me to call his wife. I did and left a message. Kim never returned my call so I called her husband again. He told me that she told him that she'd had a very good time in that branch and didn't want anything to do with this lawsuit. I knew it was a long shot asking Kim, but, again, I was desperate after all and had to try. Kim had failed at being a broker and had been a wild woman in the branch. I know she had a lot of skeletons she wanted to keep in the closet.

Claire also gave me a couple of women's names who had worked in the branch after I had left and who were in the class action. Any of these women, I think, could have helped my case because their testimony would have corroborated my description of the environment, would have shown Smith Barney was cultivating the hostile environment and had failed to fix the problem once they were legally obligated to do so, and that they had in fact retaliated against others just as they did me. I had no idea how to reach a couple of them. Claire told me one was a dog walker in Orange County, so I copied the pet care section of the yellow pages where she supposedly lived and called dog walkers, dog groomers, and veterinarians asking if anyone knew her. That was a big dead end.

The next person to ask was Melanie, the drama queen at the International House of Pancakes. I did think she was a nut, and, stupidly, I must have let that slip to somebody. She had become friends with a lawyer who had been trying to insert himself into the lawsuit and, I suspect, he is the one to whom I let it slip that I thought Melanie was a bit of a nut. She never let on that she was hurt or angry with me. She and I had several telephone conversations in the intervening years between 1999 and 2002. Melanie was so gung-ho about the whole class action suit and had stated over and over that she would do what she could to help the class members, so I thought that her testifying for me, if I needed her, was in the bag. The next event took me totally off guard. Again, even though she and I had not worked downtown at the same time and we had even had different managers, she could have testified and corroborated, as the other women could have, to the hostile environment and to the fact that Smith Barney had not fixed the problem as the law required. She particularly would have been helpful to me because we both could testify to a very specific behavior— i.e. Brian stripping. I called to ask her if she would testify for me. She shocked me out of my socks and said no. Her reason, she told me, was because I had disrespected her husband and bad-mouthed her.

Her husband also worked for Smith Barney in the Beverly Hills branch next to mine where she had transferred. There were two incidents where I allegedly insulted him. I saw him at a Smith Barney function for brokers. I did not ignore him as he accused me of doing, but I also didn't stop to chat. We passed each other in the lobby where everybody was mingling with coffee and bagels. I said hello to him but kept walking. It's true, I didn't want to make life in my workplace more difficult than it already was. Everybody knew he was Melanie's boyfriend or husband (I don't know if they were married at that point or not) and that she was a class representative. The other incident was that I had invited both of them to call me anytime they wanted but to please call me at home and not at work. I had good cause to be worried about my work phone given my experience downtown and that conversation with Victoria. At the time, I still hadn't figured out how Lyndsey had known I had talked to Victoria the day before he came over and told me not to talk to the people downtown. Melanie's husband disregarded my request and called me at work anyway to talk about the lawsuit. It did upset me, and I probably did cut him off and end the call. These "insults" to her husband were unforgivable; therefore, she would not testify for me!

Immediately I called her husband to apologize, to explain what I did, and to say that I didn't mean to insult him. Then I called Melanie again. We called each other a few times, I begging her to testify and she refusing, then giving me a rash of shit. During the last call I had with her is when I cried on the phone. I couldn't believe Little Miss Crusader for Justice would not testify for me. I think she enjoyed the bullying and the power tripping, otherwise why would she have wasted her time returning my calls or taking my calls? The last communication between us was a message that she left on my machine. Her message was ten minutes long; my machine kept cutting her off so she called back three times to continue her tirade. I thought the message was so incredibly psycho that I kept the tape. It sounded to me as if she knew she was being mean and not acting right toward me, so at first her voice was breathy and nervous, but as she got into her tirade her voice got angrier and hysterical. For ten minutes she repeated the same things over and over again:

"Tameron, it's Melanie. Umm, this is going to be a long message because I have a couple of things you're going to need to ask Maxwell to get. Umm, I cannot testify for you. I was not there at the time you were there, and you need to get your facts straight. Umm, Barry was not the one undressing" (When I was on the phone crying and very upset, I slipped and said the name of the partner of the actual guy that stripped), "so you're going to lose your credibility if you don't get your facts straight because he was not the one doing that. Umm, I can't testify because I wasn't there, that's the main reason but, umm, I talked to Claire Santiago; she knows how I feel. Umm, you were really, really rude to my husband for no reason at Smith Barney functions and he's the nicest sweetest guy, and the paranoia was just ridiculous, and I know for a fact when this case first started you bad mouthed the hell out of me on the street. Umm, and so, if I hold a little resentment, yeah, I'm pissed… But I cannot testify. I was not there, and Barry was not the one. I'm telling you, you're going to lose credibility if you don't get your facts straight and umm, you know I'm sorry, but yeah, I'm pissed. I mean I busted my hump on this, I was right on my case, I was right with my facts, I knew what happened to me, I know what happened to a good chunk of women in this case, and you know, I'm sorry, Tameron, but you really bad-mouthed me in the beginning of this case and for no good reason. I will tell you this, just because I'm saying I'm not testifying do not even THINK of bad mouthing me again on the street because umm, I will make sure that that is addressed. It wasn't addressed when the case first started. Umm, but I don't deserve that. I worked my butt off on this case and you and a lot of other people like you have taken advantage of umm, the work. Umm, all I want to say is look, I don't deserve being bad-mouthed. I didn't deserve it years ago and I don't deserve it now. I'm just saying I can't testify for you and I can't testify if you don't have your facts straight, but I wasn't there when you were there. I did not deserve and my husband did not deserve the treatment we got." Finally, she was finished. "Alright," she ended with, "so you have my e-mail address. I hope everything progresses successfully for you, and I hope you win your case by millions. Thanks."

What a nut! I couldn't believe my ears. She also had thrown in some legal rambling, none of which were helpful or accurate. Even as a class rep[8], it didn't seem she understood the process. Honestly, I think she was downright jealous that I was going to get my shot at arbitration and she

---

[8] She was paid an extra $75,000 for being a class representative in addition to the amount she settled her claim for.

was still burning with resentment that she had settled. I moved on.

There was one more woman, a sales assistant whose name Claire had given to me. I found her number from directory assistance. I called and she was very nice and agreed to testify for me. After we hung up, she must have called Melanie, because she called me back and in a very nasty voice told me that she would "never testify for a woman like me" and then hung up on me. I couldn't get one single word in. Strike out again. Not only would Melanie not testify for me, but, I believe, she was talking others into not testifying for me as well.

—◊—

I didn't know what Kevin (the guy who had sent me supportive poetry) could say, but I decided to contact him anyway. I was searching for any corroborative help, and, as another friend had said, you don't know what you'll discover in discovery until you discover it. I called Kevin, who had always come across as very straight-laced. He always looked nice and corporate in his suits and talked about God all the time. He was divorced but seemed to be a very devoted father. As I mentioned before, the odd thing about Kevin was that he was unbelievably terrible on the phone. He just didn't know how to talk to people. Every phone call sounded as if he was inviting someone to a party.

I called him ostensibly to say hello, to see how he was doing, and to see if he wanted to have a drink. My bigger motive was that I wanted to pick his brains. I wanted to know if he knew anything that could help me. He agreed to meet for drinks, but he wanted me to pick him up in my "Benzos," as he called my new car. He had seen me struggle, and I believe he was genuinely happy for me since I was obviously doing much better. He gave me his address and set a time that I was to pick him up. I realized as I drove that I was getting deep into a neighborhood that made me very uncomfortable. I saw women shuffling on the sidewalk in house slippers and gigantic pink curlers in their hair, and it seemed like graffiti was everywhere. "Where is this guy taking me?" I thought to myself. Finally, I turned on to his street, but it wasn't any better. I found his address and pulled into the driveway. It was somewhat of a relief to see that his house was, by far, the nicest house on the block. In fact, it was cute, the old thirties-style California architecture. The house was clean and white with a manicured lawn and beautiful rose bushes. The whole property was entirely surrounded by a chain-link fence that seemed to me to keep the rest of the neighborhood out. I parked in the driveway and walked through the gate up to the front porch.

Kevin was so happy to see me. He jumped all around acting a little odd, and he looked terrible. He had jams or maybe cut-offs on and was all greasy and sweaty. He didn't look or act like the Kevin I had known in the office. He introduced me to another guy who he said was his best friend from childhood. The house turned out to be the friend's, not Kevin's. Kevin pulled out a dining room chair and asked me to sit down, then he ran and got a camera. He came back in the room, handed the camera to his friend, and asked him to take a picture of us. Then he promptly sat on my lap, crossed his ankle over his knee and called out "Yee-Haa". His friend took the picture, but it all happened so fast and didn't feel right. I was taken aback by this different Kevin I saw and felt creeped out.

Kevin cleaned himself up and we left. We drove down to a hotel on the beach in Santa Monica, had drinks and hors d'oeuvres on the patio, and chatted for several hours. I concluded that he didn't know anything that would help me, but he did tell me an interesting story. Leon Tiller was an enormous broker who had been in the business so long he had worked with Sandy Weil, the CEO of Citigroup, at a branch way back when. Kevin told me that when he had been walking passed Leon's very large office, the biggest in the branch, bigger than Lyndsey's, he saw a suitcase full of cash. He said he couldn't believe his eyes and had turned around and walked by again to make sure his eyes weren't deceiving him. They weren't; he swears he saw a suitcase full of cash on Leon's desk. That story never made sense to me because brokerage firms, cannot by law, take in or give out cash, and in addition to that, we don't have the facilities for cash. I have always wondered why so much cash would be in a suitcase on Leon's desk. I told that story to someone who had been in operations for many years and who had worked with Leon. That person told me that the story was believable, because Leon and his crew had been such shysters over the years that anything was possible. Who knows why a suitcase of cash would be on a broker's desk, but I do believe Kevin because I don't think he had any reason to lie to me, especially in the light of what he was about to tell me.

I concluded that Kevin didn't have any information that would help me in my lawsuit and we had spent enough time together, so I decided I wanted to go home. I don't know what made him tell me this stuff, but he decided to tell me about himself and his family while we drove. He told me his father had many children by several different women.

His mother was white and didn't want him, so his black father's sisters ended up raising him. His brother had killed a woman and then had sex with the dead body. This brother was on death row for the crime in another state and Kevin didn't want to see him die. He didn't say his brother had been shafted or wrongly accused. It seemed to me that Kevin believed his brother had committed the crime. "What kind of person is in my car?" I said to myself.

Then he went on to tell me a story of his own. I had wondered why someone would tell such an unflattering story about his family to someone he didn't know well, but it may have been a warm-up to the next unflattering story. In the world of criminals, maybe this is status stuff. He was bragging when he told me that he had committed every crime in the book. I didn't react, so just in case I didn't understand, he leaned toward me as I drove and said, again, with emphasis, "Every crime." He told me that he believed that he had never gotten caught except for once because God protected him. He continued his story by telling me that he had also been a drug dealer for a time and that he thought one of his friends had gotten jealous of his success and had ratted on him. Consequently, the police raided his house and, as the cops barged in, Kevin shot one of them. "Oh my God," I said to myself, "I am driving in the car with a full-on criminal." I was so freaked out over realizing whom I was driving with that the details are a little fuzzy, but I think he told me he had a plea bargain and ended up getting very little jail time. After he had done his time, the judge expunged his record because it was a first-time offense. Of course the judge didn't know about his other crimes because God protected him and he had never been caught. Kevin felt that the judge did what he did because, again, he still had God's protection.

Smith Barney requires that job applicants take a psychology test, a math test, undergo a credit check, and an FBI background check. Kevin had managed to get hired by Lyndsey, and he knew that even though the crime had been expunged from his regular criminal report, as he explained to me, it would show up on an FBI report. He also knew it would take some time to get that report back. Lyndsey hired him, then Kevin studied for and passed the exam for his Series 7 license and went through the one-month training period. He also knew when he got back that Lyndsey would have the FBI report on his desk, so, as he told me, he thought it was better to go to Lyndsey "the moment he set foot back into the branch" and tell the story himself, rather than have Lyndsey call him into his office to fire him. So that's exactly what he did. He also knew that Lyndsey would not have access to the details of the felony. Kevin went in to Lyndsey's office and gave him some shuck and jive story of how he shot some guy by accident.

Lyndsey didn't fire Kevin even after he found out Kevin had a felony record. At the time, private offices didn't have locks on the doors, and all client personal information such as Social Security numbers, addresses, and financial information were kept in black books that most brokers kept on their desk out in the open. By allowing Kevin to remain employed, which was definitely against Smith Barney policy, Lyndsey exposed all those wealthy Beverly Hills clients to a convicted felon who bragged that he had committed every crime in the book. Kevin told me he " had Lyndsey over a barrel." Kevin may have thought that he had Lyndsey over a barrel, but he didn't really. I couldn't imagine a more lazy, dishonorable, and unethical man than Lyndsey who didn't seem to care about anyone except himself. It was probably just easier for Lyndsey to keep Kevin and delayed him from having to find another minority or woman candidate.

I tried to remain as calm as possible while driving with Kevin in the car and show no fear. But I was scared out of my wits. It was a surreal experience, and it seemed it took forever to arrive at his friend's house. I quickly dropped Kevin off and high-tailed it out of there and away from him. I drove home in shell-shock and worried for months afterward that Kevin would try to find out where I lived. Eventually, I moved into a safer apartment in my same building. It is amazing that Lyndsey would put so much effort into trying to thwart my career and get me out of the business, yet he allowed a known criminal to stay in his branch.

—m—

It was time to find Craig, my former sales manager, who had blurted out in a moment of frustration, "You're the only one Lyndsey treats this way; you must have done something wrong." Craig had gotten a management position at another firm so I called him in his office. I told him my story briefly, which explained Lyndsey's bad treatment of me and that I was suing. At some point I started to cry. I just couldn't help it, and it would turn out that for several years after my trial I cried every time I got to certain parts of my story, mostly when telling of the day I first called Stowell & Freidman. I felt at the time that Craig was thinking, "Oh brother, this woman is pulling that girl thing and crying crocodile tears to get sympathy and to get her way." He was polite but not sympathetic, and in fact he repeated the Lyndsey party line which was that he had been generous by allowing both Kevin and me to stay at the firm and implied that we didn't really deserve his generosity.

Craig also told me he didn't remember making the comment that I said he had made. I asked him to think about it because after my experience with Claire, who had not only remembered somebody after she swore she didn't know them but then had remembered that person's husband's name and occupation, I thought he might remember later. I called him back the next week. He wasn't too happy to hear from me again. It is important to know that Craig had been Aaron Weisswasser's personal broker when Aaron was the regional director, and I believe he had hired Craig to the firm as a broker originally. Craig understood the importance of corporate alliances, power, friendships, and support within an organization and an industry. As I said before, the securities industry is a small world. He politely didn't want anything to do with my situation.

Very close to the time my trial was scheduled to start, Craig lost his job so, eventually, I did call him to try again. However, instead of calling him directly, I called his wife. She was a successful broker who had joined our branch for only a few weeks through the branch merger, then had moved to another firm. The rumor was that she couldn't stand Lyndsey and refused to work for him. I told her who I was, what I was doing, and why I wanted to talk to her husband. She seemed to be very supportive. She told me that Craig would "definitely" talk to me and gave me their home phone number. I called and left a message. Eventually I spoke to Craig again and asked if he would talk to my lawyer. This time he said he was willing to talk to Maxwell but that he didn't have any helpful information. Again, he said he didn't remember making the comment.

When I think about it, you cannot expect anyone to remember blurting out a comment in passing in a hallway years before, even if he wanted to remember. It's reasonable that he wouldn't remember. That day Craig was under the gun, frustrated, and stressed out about something else. I was the last person he wanted to see or deal with, someone he knew was on Lyndsey's shit-list. This was my life and my experience, and I alone in that office knew why Lyndsey behaved the way he did toward me. It wouldn't be reasonable to expect people to remember comments like that made years before when there was no reason to cause them to remember. Also there was no advantage or reason for me to confide in any of my colleagues, so I didn't. It had been a long shot, but I had to try.

—∞—

There were several other women who had worked in the downtown office at some point and who could have corroborated my depiction of the environment. They had also sued Smith Barney, and Maxwell and I were in contact with them. I asked him over and over about them. He would either give me the run around or he would say that we were OK with downtown and didn't need any more, meaning that the evidence we had was good enough to prove my case. We had received evidence from Smith Barney through discovery and the testimony of Carol Farmer, the Los Angeles HR manager, which had corroborated my allegations and testimony, and Maxwell didn't think we needed anything else to convince the panel I was telling the truth. We didn't exactly agree on tactics.

One of these women was named Denise. Claire introduced me to her because she had worked in the downtown branch, albeit after I had transferred. Many women who had worked in the downtown branch at one time or another, but not necessarily at the same time, were in contact with each other. We had agreed to help each other as much as we could, and I had no problem helping anybody and everybody that I could truly help. Conversely, I appreciated any help that came my way. Unfortunately, there was something about Denise that made me uneasy. My conversations with her seemed to go nowhere and didn't make sense to me. I felt like I was going around and around when talking to her. She told me that she never actually read the stipulation of the settlement and didn't seem to know or care about what was going on. I thought to myself, "Why would she bother with me then?" It seemed strange. She would call me to talk yet had no interest in working on her own case or understanding the rules of engagement in this class action. It was a very complicated settlement, and I still don't think any woman would have won without her own active participation.

Instead, she repeatedly asked me for documents of my individual case. I kept explaining to her that each woman had to prove the specifics of her case individually and that my documents would not help someone else's case. After her repeated requests for my documents, I finally told her I preferred if documents were exchanged between lawyers. I assured her that Maxwell would help her lawyer in any way that he could and that her lawyer should call Maxwell. That shut her up and she never asked for my documents again. I don't think she was being honest with me, and, in the pit of my stomach, I believe Melanie had put Denise up to it for her own power tripping reasons.

A couple of the women had suggested that there may be another way to be able to have testimony on my behalf and that was by showing the panel or introducing into evidence a tape of a *60 Minutes* TV segment and of another TV program that had aired about the class action. I never saw the tape, but Melanie told me she was on it and talked about her experience in the downtown branch. I repeatedly asked Maxwell if a taped TV program could be used and if I should try and get a copy. I didn't get a definitive answer from him for months. Then he said no. Then a few days before my trial, when it was too late to get a tape, he said yes, so I never got it.

In the end, after all my efforts, I would not be able to get a single witness to testify for me. I did not call one single witness on my behalf except one expert witness, the forensic accountant. I don't blame my colleagues still in the business because they had their own careers to protect and absolutely no concrete benefit in testifying for me. I also understood any fear they may have had or reluctance to stir up past memories and cause problems or humiliation for themselves. I didn't hold it against anyone except Melanie, who was a class representative and wasn't in the business anymore.

XI

DISHONEST GAMES: SMITH BARNEY STILL IN THE BULLYING BUSINESS

Testifying is done on two different occasions— first during what is called a deposition, then, again during the actual trial. A deposition is an information-gathering technique through which the lawyers from each side ask the parties involved on the opposing side even more questions than they asked during discovery. Deposants testify under oath and penalty of perjury, but without a judge present. If the witness says something different during deposition than he or she says during trial testimony, the opposing lawyers can use this difference to impeach the witness' credibility; therefore, depositions are a very important and serious part of the process.

My deposition was videotaped and lasted for three days. It was held in the Los Angeles office of Orrick, Herrington & Sutcliffe. Terrence Paolucci, Smith Barney's senior lawyer, was sitting across the table when I entered the room where I was going to be deposed. He smiled in such a way that I imagined he was saying to himself, "Ahh, look at her, isn't she cute? I'm gonna eat her for lunch." "Humph," I answered back to my own imaginations, "We'll see about that."

I had never been deposed before, so I had nothing to compare my experience to, but I assumed my deposition would progress normally. I also assumed that Terrence was gathering information from me so that he could sort out— in his own mind and for his client, Smith Barney, in New York— what had happened to me during my employment. But something else happened. I began to notice, through Terrence's questions, a pattern of thought. He was interested in gathering information from me, but he was also interested in making my statements conform to beliefs that he already held. At times, his questioning was so illogical because of his effort to try to make my testimony conform to his beliefs that it flabbergasted me. "Is this guy for real?" I thought to myself. "He's trying to bully my testimony into what he wants to hear." It was as if he had an ideological template that he was going to force my testimony onto, whether I liked it or not. He would fixate on an idea in that template and then ask question after question, regardless of how ridiculous they were, as he tried, in a lawyerly way, to force me to say what he wanted me to say. It was easy for me to stand my ground, because what he wanted just wasn't the truth.

One of those thoughts that Terrence fixated on was the idea that Carol Farmer, the HR person involved, had "helped me." There wasn't a minute during my whole ordeal when I thought or felt that Carol Farmer had helped me. She was firmly with the opposition— which had surprised me, since my friend Mitchell had lead me to believe in 1993 that HR is there for employees. As I have already described, as negotiations progressed, I realized Carol exercised no power; she completely went along with management and just acted as their messenger. I was hurt— I even cried in her office— because she was a woman in a position where she could have done something. Instead, she was absolutely spineless.

At one point, Terrence asked me, "Did you regard Carol Farmer as being helpful to you in your request to move to a Beverly Hills branch?"

"No, I did not," I answered.

"Why not?" Terrence continued.

Carol was sitting at the deposition table at that moment, as Smith Barney's HR representative. Why she was allowed to witness my deposition when she was involved in the lawsuit is beyond me. I don't think she should have been allowed to be there before her own deposition, but she was. I had to tell the truth, even though she was sitting right there.

I turned to her and said, "I'm sorry, Carol." Then I turned back to Terrence and the camera videotaping me and finished answering his question. "I thought she was a Twinkie."

Ed Brown, one of Smith Barney's co-counsels, let out an audible gasp— kind of like a little screech— and seemed to simultaneously jump vertically out his seat a few inches. The weird part is, even after I was absolutely adamant that I never felt Carol Farmer had ever helped me, Terrence would harp on the idea in my deposition and again during my trial. He tried to get me to say that she was helpful and that I did find her helpful. It was almost as if he had that same old male prerogative that Lyndsey had— I say it is so, therefore it is so. He would do this over and over in his letters to Maxwell and in his questioning during my trial. It got him nowhere with me. The scary part, though, is that people are susceptible to repetition. His tactic does often, if not usually, work. Repeating something over and over does make people believe it. How many other women had he done this to?

After my deposition, Terrence sent his first threatening letter to Maxwell. It did nothing but piss me off. I didn't like his game at all. He insinuated that my deposition had gone so poorly that I'd better give up now before I hurt myself. It was shocking. I didn't know whose deposition Terrence was thinking about, but if he believed he was speaking accurately about mine, he must have drifted off into Alice's Wonderland and must now be speaking in Jabberwocky. He told Maxwell that "it should be evident to (him) that based on my testimony alone there was much less to this case then there may have seemed at first." I wanted to scream at him, "Whose deposition are you talking about?" Then he condescendingly continued, "While not minimizing the asserted impact of alleged actions... Ms. Keyes' reaction to alleged conduct must be viewed through the reality of her interactions with men and women." In others words, he was basically saying "Poor little Tameron is such a nut that she thinks the whole world is out to get her. She doesn't get along with anyone. She doesn't like anyone and she thinks nobody likes her and everybody victimizes her. Obviously, she alone is the problem, just as Lyndsey and Smith Barney have said all along. In fact, Lyndsey was generous for not firing her." The last part had been Lyndsey's mantra for years. Terrence went on to say that he realized Maxwell had done very little discovery. He asked if we could settle or even go back a step and try mediation again. "I would like to explore whether we can approach settlement. We are amenable to convening a new mediation either before or after your depositions (with a mutually agreed mediator) if you believe it would help facilitate discussions. As we have enjoyed a very professional relationship to date, I am happy to negotiate with you directly...."

Observing Terrence during my deposition was interesting, but this letter, referring to my deposition, came as a big shock. I was so angry at the way Terrence fabricated and twisted my testimony in his letter that I marked each of the paragraphs of my copy with Roman numerals. Then I wrote a response sheet for Maxwell, with each of my paragraphs marked with corresponding roman numerals, in order to easily match up my responses to Terrence's absurd comments. As far as I was concerned, Terrence being illogical again and trying to twist reality to suit his purpose, and it infuriated me. "I don't care about his personal relationship with you," I ranted in my letter. "Tell him to put the money on the table. Any settlement will be spelled out in detail BEFORE I agree to anything. I have seen many people screwed in my business over verbal or partially-written agreements. The same thing will apply to the trial. If they decide to settle during the trial, I won't stop or delay unless the total and complete agreement is on the table, ready to sign."

By the time I wrote and faxed this letter to Maxwell, I was already very frustrated with him. I felt he had lost interest in my case and that his heart wasn't in it anymore. I thought that perhaps, between Smith Barney's in-house lawyers and the hired legal teams in New York and San Francisco maybe Maxwell had become intimidated by Smith Barney's legal juggernaut. Maybe he was afraid this situation might end up giving his professional reputation a black eye. It seemed as if he were digging in his heels toward me as well. In all fairness, there had been a fairly strict timetable in which the class action was supposed to proceed; but so many women joined the lawsuit that the timetable couldn't be maintained, and so it was abandoned. Maxwell probably believed, when he took my case, that it would be finished in one year at the most. Three-and-a- half years later, in 2002, we were still at it. He also could have been just plain annoyed that I wasn't leaving it all up to him and trusting that his actions would be enough. Once, he called me "crazy." And other time, he said my involvement in my own case was "over the top."

Sometimes I do think I was under so much stress that my mind short-circuited. At one point, Aaron Weisswasser's deposition was due in a few days, and I believed that we still had not received any of the discovery to which we were entitled— even though I had already briefly looked at some of it and had even discussed it with Maxwell.

Maxwell had told me in the beginning that it was agreed that James Ayala, my downtown branch manager, was one of the four to be deposed. I couldn't figure out why Ayala wasn't scheduled for a deposition like the three others, and it was bothering me. When I asked Maxwell about these things, he just gave me the run-around. I couldn't understand what was happening. I was becoming increasingly desperate. I started to think that maybe my own lawyer was selling me down the river. I did not consult with other lawyers about the details of my case or any strategy that should have been taken, as Maxwell had accused me of doing. However, I did have a friend, Matthew, who was familiar with law and who turned out to be somewhat of an emotional support for me. I called him late one night, and he suggested that I put pressure on Maxwell by leaving a pleading message on his voice mail which might motivate him to do his job.

I didn't really understand how everything worked or everything that was going on. I didn't know that conference calls had happened or that agreements had been made, but I was kicking and paddling as hard as I could, as the saying goes. I was constantly writing questions down to ask Maxwell and making lists of follow-up questions generated from questions he really didn't answer. I was writing lists of results reports I wanted from him of things he had said he was going to do. I made lists of things I had to do and lists of thoughts or new ideas germane to my case.

A lot of the time, Maxwell resisted me. In turn, I felt more desperate and got tougher with him. It became a total nightmare. Again, simultaneously, I carried on at work, taking care of my clients, managing their portfolios, and acting as if nothing unusual was going on. What made it even worse was that, after more than three years, I began to believe that Maxwell had never really intended to try the case. I thought that he really just wanted to settle, something I began to think he actually did for most of his clients.

Two months before the trial, I started looking for another lawyer. I called my dad because I just needed someone to whom I could vent.

"Dad," I told him, "Maxwell is not doing what he is supposed to be doing. He doesn't call my witnesses until it's too late; he wouldn't subpoena people. He told me he had a private detective to find some people, but he won't allow me to talk to that detective or tell me anything about it. I think he's overwhelmed. I also found out that he is a sole practitioner."

"Tameron," my dad answered, "how could you hire someone who is all by himself!"

"Dad, I didn't know," I replied, frustrated. "I saw several lawyers in his office that first day. It looked like the whole office was his and that those people worked for his law firm. I just found out that they don't work for him; they rent office space from him, and the people behind the counter work for the other lawyers. Maxwell didn't even have a legal secretary or paralegal. His secretary was just a regular secretary who is now out of the office for a long time, dealing with very serious medical problems of her own."

By that time I had several lawyers' names that I had gleaned from other sexual harassment cases written up in the news and from friends' suggestions. But first, I went back to Gloria Allred's office for the third time. Once again, I got a lawyer on the phone. I told her the situation and asked if they would take over my case. Whoever the lawyer was who took my call asked me to hang on; she put me on hold for a long time saying she needed to discuss this with somebody. When she got back on the phone, she told me in rapid fire, that they couldn't help me at all. Then she literally hung up on me before I could say a word. Strike three for Gloria Allred's office.

Next, I called several lawyers who specialized in labor law. All of them were kind and spent a few minutes with me on the phone. They all gave me the same advice: if I switched lawyers at that point, so close to my trial, I would be doing myself a disservice. They also said that Maxwell might have claims to some of the lawyer's fees awarded. They all counseled me to stick it out and do the best I could. Almost all of them knew of Maxwell or knew him personally, and all said he had a very good reputation and was a good lawyer.

The last call I made was to a lawyer who, it turned out, knew Maxwell personally and very well. That lawyer was very kind: he spent forty-five minutes to an hour talking to me about my dilemma. He concurred with the others that changing lawyers now would not be a good idea and he assured me that Maxwell was a good lawyer who knew his stuff. He didn't know why Maxwell would be behaving in the ways I complained about, but told me that I needed to "hold his feet to the fire." This also is essentially what Matthew had told me— but Matthew's idea of motivating Maxwell was that phone call. Holding Maxwell's feet to the fire was the plan, so I wrote a letter and faxed it to him in an effort to start documenting our communications.

"Unfortunately, it seems like we aren't on the same page," I wrote. "Therefore, I feel the need to write things down. I wonder if what has happened over the last three weeks has registered with you. Believing that my lawyer had not received one single piece of discovery requested from the opposition— and wasn't bothering to compel them before he started depositions— I started to panic. The phone message I left you last weekend, the phone message I left a couple of weeks prior, and all the calls in between were pleading with you to get the discovery we requested from SSB. I was asking you to get a copy to me and to allow me some time to review it before you started depositions. Any time during the last three weeks, you could have said 'Tameron, I have a lot of the discovery we requested. Come over to my office and pick up a copy.' I'm confounded by the fact that you didn't tell me you had it, and, if you did tell me at some time in the past, why didn't you tell me again during any of the conversations we have had over the last three weeks?"

Many times, after I had spoken to Maxwell, I would realize a few days later that he hadn't been listening or had given me some bogus answer so I would go away. I felt that wasn't right, so I continued in my letter, "I'm not telling you how to do your job, but I do hold you responsible to fulfill your legal responsibilities. You owe it to me, as your client, to tell me in advance what your game plan is, to set a schedule of your planned tasks with respect to my case, to set deadlines to complete those tasks, and to share that information with me. It is also your responsibility to keep me apprised of extensions, delays, your intentions to make requests for extensions, rulings of the panel, and agreements you make with the opposition. It is not unreasonable or 'over-the-top involvement,' as you said, to expect to be apprised of these types of issues in a timely manner." He never acknowledged the letter or its contents.

When I asked him about things verbally that he didn't want to deal with, he'd say things like, "I'll find out," or "I'm not sure yet," or "I have a private detective on it," but I wouldn't ever get a real answer to those questions. I would think that he understood something, such as that I wanted to be at every deposition— but then, he would seem surprised when I asked for the third time for the date and time of Aaron Weisswasser's deposition. Maxwell and I really did go around and around the last three months before my trial.

Some of the other claimants in the suit convinced me that Smith Barney didn't like publicity about the class action and that the threat of journalists might prod them to settle. Because I was a current employee of Smith Barney, I didn't want to take any chances of violating Smith Barney policy by talking to the media. Just because I was suing them didn't mean that I didn't still have to live by their rules. I had asked Maxwell many times about how to invite journalists to the trial because I was not supposed to talk to them about the company. I never got an answer. I asked him when would I have an answer, and I didn't get an answer to that question either. I started to have trouble sleeping.

The same day that I faxed Maxwell that letter, I also faxed him notes that I called "Thoughts on Weisswasser's deposition." It was a list of ideas that I thought Maxwell should be aware of or think about, along with direct questions I thought he should ask Aaron. I submitted to Maxwell a separate sheet of such thoughts and questions for each person he was supposed to depose: Aaron Weisswasser, Carol Farmer, Lyndsey Shanahan, and James Ayala. Maxwell did use many of my ideas and questions. Whether he thought all his questions up for himself or if my notes helped him is for him to say, but it looks to me as if my lists did help. During this time period, there were other motions and arguments before the panel to which I was not privy. One of those arguments was whether we could ask questions during depositions and demand information through discovery about the downtown branch after I had left in December of 1993. The panel ruled against us. I had no idea at the time that this argument was taking place or how Maxwell argued it. When Maxwell informed me about the ruling, I asked him how they could make such a ruling, since it is the law that companies must fix sexual harassment/hostile environment problems. He told me that he thought they had made a mistake. I felt that, by that time, Maxwell didn't have his heart in it anymore and consequently hadn't tried very hard and had lost the motion.

He also dropped the ball on James Ayala. Maxwell had told me at the very beginning that the panel had agreed to allow us to depose four witnesses: the three managers involved— James Ayala, Lyndsey Shanahan, and Aaron Weisswasser— and the Human Resources manager, Carol Farmer. For months, I operated on the assumption that James was going to be deposed, and spoke with Maxwell as if that were going to happen. He never was, and I have no idea why, how, or when Maxwell dropped the ball. He must have known long before the trial that James wouldn't be deposed, but he didn't share that information with me until shortly before the trial was to begin.

In October, I went to Maxwell's office to listen in on Aaron Weisswasser's deposition by speaker-phone. Aaron claimed that he was living in Connecticut and it would be too big a burden to come to California to be deposed face-to-face. I didn't believe he was living out of state full time. Remember, Aaron had been regional director for the L.A. metro region and therefore had been the boss of both my managers. He is the one who ultimately approved and orchestrated my transfer. He also was responsible for Smith Barney not fixing the problem in the downtown branch after I left. By law, a company must fix a hostile environment, even if the complainant is no longer there. The idea is that the corporation must fix the problem for the benefit of all employees. Not only did Smith Barney not fix the problem, but it got worse. I heard, as I have mentioned before, that at least eighteen women filed suit from that branch and that many were quid pro quo suits in addition to environmental sexual harassment and gender discrimination suits.

Many women believed Aaron Weisswasser knew what was going on and not only did nothing about it, but also went after other women to get them out of the organization, just as he had done to me. Many, as one woman put it, "wanted Weisswasser's head on a platter." Shortly after the class action was settled in November 1997, Aaron stepped down from his post. When managers in the securities business are fired, they often are given the option to "become a broker," so they are not truly fired. It's more like a gentleman's firing. Aaron's excuse for "retiring" was that, someone in his family was having medical problems, which had prompted him to do some introspection, and he had come to the conclusion that the stress of his job wasn't worth it— so he wanted to step down and become a broker. A family member may have been sick, but I don't believe that is why he stepped down. I believe he was forced out. His excuse implied that being a broker and building a business from almost nothing— which is what he would be doing— wasn't extremely stressful or difficult. Baloney. That was face-saving spiel.

I know that Smith Barney had not yet gone through any arbitrations, and possibly they had not yet settled many mediations. If they had fired Aaron outright at the time, he might have been able to go back at them with a wrongful termination suit. On the other hand, Smith Barney has a lot of crafty lawyers working for them, and they should have found a way to fire him. Instead, he was given the broker's title of Senior Vice President, and he partnered up immediately with two other brokers; I have heard that he did very well. He was no longer in management, but the fact that he remained with the company until the Spring of 2009 and thrived showed to all who were watching in the company that he still remained powerful. His continued employment with the firm acted as a threat and a warning to those people who were inclined to do the right thing telling them not to take action when they see something wrong. It also served as a reminder for those who continue to break the law, saying that, in the end, the powerful get away with it and nothing really changes.

In 2002, when Smith Barney claimed Aaron wasn't available for a face-to-face deposition, I called his office in San Marino, a suburb of Los Angeles, and spoke with his secretary. I asked her if Aaron still worked out of that office. She answered "yes" in a tone of voice that said, "Of course! Why would you ask such a question?" Then she said that he was "just out of the office at the moment." I don't know if Aaron was flying back and forth between California and Connecticut, but I'm sure that, even if he was in Connecticut a lot during that period, he was back in California enough so that he could have done a deposition face-to-face, if he had wanted. I believe he was trying to avoid a face-to-face deposition, and I believe he wanted to do the deposition by telephone because he planned on stone-walling us and lying through his teeth. It would be easier to lie and not have your emotions show so obviously if the deposition was done by phone. He was, however, videotaped while being deposed by phone. His strategy would backfire on him.

Aaron Weisswasser could remember the history of his employment going back to 1967, including all the numerous mergers. He had been a Regional Sales Manager or Director since 1981, responsible for Orange County, San Diego County, Palm Springs, Palm Desert, Arizona, and later, Los Angeles. Yet when it came to 1993, he had a miraculous failure of memory. He testified that he couldn't remember when James Ayala started to work for him. He also testified that transfers like mine were rare and that he couldn't remember any other transfers like mine, but he also claimed under oath that he had no memory of my transfer. He had no memory of discussions with Chad Porter, James Ayala, Lyndsey Shanahan, or Smith Barney's in-house lawyers, who we know were involved because of notes we received in discovery and information in Carol Farmer's testimony.

Weisswasser also claimed he didn't remember me downtown, ever— not the complaint I made, even though I had cried, not my transfer to another branch, and not the prolonged discussions to extend my training salary, even though all of it was highly unusual. He claimed he had absolutely no memory of events downtown in 1993, period. He had no memory of any complaints or allegations of improper conduct and no memory of any conversations. He also had no memory of basic information a man in his position would have normally known. He claimed he remembered absolutely nothing. He responded that he didn't remember or hat he had "no memory of that" 124 times during his two-hour deposition.

Equally miraculously, he suddenly remembered me again, one month after I transferred to Beverly Hills. He remembered he'd had a conversation about me and money with Lyndsey, and he also remembered stopping by my cubicle to chat after I had transferred. His testimony and the pretense that he didn't remember anything were absurd. I thought it was shockingly audacious in its dishonesty, and a shame on him.

Maxwell was obligated to find out if there might be a medical reason for Aaron's incredible loss of memory, but Smith Barney's lawyer even blocked Maxwell from questioning him about that. Smith Barney's lawyer instructed Aaron not to answer, thirteen times. Maxwell and the other lawyer disagreed about what the panel's ruling actually was, and Maxwell threatened to go back to the panel to force compliance and told her that we might have to depose Aaron again. But Smith Barney's lawyer called his bluff and told Maxwell to go ahead and that she doubted Maxwell would go back to the panel.

A day or two later, Terrence Paolucci, Smith Barney's senior lawyer, called Maxwell to request a second mediation; however, he still tried to intimidate us. They wanted a second mediation, a second step, but they wanted me to pay for it. It seemed to me as if he were saying, "OK, we will be nice to you because we know you're about to break. We will allow you another mediation, but, because of our generosity, you should not only be grateful that we're doing this for you, but you should be so grateful that you will pay for it." We would have had to rent a room and hire a mediator. They did not, in our opinion, conduct the first mediation in good faith, which they were obligated to do under the settlement agreement. If they had wanted to use their money for the extra mediation, I would have participated. But since they had already shown me they were disingenuous and were cheats and liars, as far as I was concerned, if they wanted me to pay for it they could stuff it. A formal mediation didn't really matter anyway. If they had wanted to settle, they could have picked up the phone during business hours Monday through Friday and negotiated a settlement with me. Towards the end, as you shall see, they did try to do that— for peanuts.

Two more depositions were scheduled to take place in Maxwell's office. Lyndsey's was first, and his deposition wasn't much better than Aaron's. Unlike my deposition and Aaron's, Lyndsey's and Carol's depositions would not be videotaped. I waited in Maxwell's private office until Lyndsey arrived with Smith Barney's lawyer. Maxwell greeted them while I waited and then called me out of his office when he directed everybody down the hallway and into his small conference room.

I didn't say hello to Lyndsey; instead, I ignored him. I was apprehensive to see Lyndsey for the first time, after two years, but I also felt protected by the circumstances. He couldn't hurt me anymore, and he couldn't control events or the people around him now. So after that initial look in the hallway, I had no fear. Lyndsey did look over at me a few times during his deposition. I thought I saw a very slight embarrassment in his face— because, in a way, the tables were turned. Now his behavior was going to be scrutinized by seasoned people who weren't beholden to him in anyway, and who couldn't have cared less about him and his reputation or his former power. As for my emotions, it felt like a business meeting.

Lyndsey had participated in a lot of arbitrations over the course of his career; therefore, he was skilled and practiced at testifying. He was also a very smart person, no question about it, and a very slick operator. As a result, he was cagey with his answers. I will concede that Lyndsey was an impressive man when you first met him. He came across as a consummate Ivy League-educated, powerful, white man— the foundation of our country, if you will. People respond to that image and Lyndsey was used to people responding to it. In his world, it was his prerogative, and historically speaking, he is absolutely right.

As Maxwell had warned me, Lyndsey didn't admit to or come clean about anything, as I had naively and firmly believed he would. It seemed to me that Smith Barney had long and detailed discussions with all of their witnesses and put a lot of effort into preparing several of them, especially Lyndsey, Aaron, and Carol Farmer. They also seemed to have coached Gigi Jenkins, the operations manager downtown, and Bettina, one of the female brokers in Beverly Hills. Still, they were at a disadvantage; they had to compose and articulate a cohesive, comprehensive theory and get everyone to agree with it and testify in a way that corroborated that theory with their own experiences. It was almost impossible. Maxwell told me that not even most sociopaths can keep track of all their lies. He said that, with proper questioning, a liar can be exposed in court— and he was right.

Lyndsey claimed under oath during his deposition that he retired voluntarily and that nobody had suggested that he should retire. But, he just couldn't stop his spin-doctor behavior. Colleagues of mine in the branch told me, unsolicited, that Lyndsey told people after my trial that he had lost his job because of me. I believe he did lose his job because of me and because of other reasons— but if what my colleagues told me is true, then Lyndsey lied under oath. In fact, it seemed obvious he lied about many things.

The most outrageous lie he told was that he didn't know why I was transferred! Anyone in management in the business— in fact, any Smith Barney broker who started in the business before 1997— knows that his claim of not knowing why I was transferred makes no sense whatsoever. Even Carol Farmer the HR Manager testified that, "It would not make sense for him not to know." He made it sound as if someone had called him and said, "Tameron would like to come to your branch…just because… is that fine with you?" and that he had said, "Sure, that's fine with me." He acted as if he had subsequently found out my production was low, but that he was such a generous guy he just made the best of it, and, in fact, was kind enough to allow me to stay there and encouraged me to excellence like any good manager would. His claims were ludicrous, especially since my diminished training salary had been extended for six more months. Nobody gives money away if they don't have to and then forgets about it, especially when it requires a contentious, weeks-long negotiation between three powerful men against one female broker trainee.

Lyndsey had made my file mysteriously disappear; however he couldn't make all of it disappear. Apparently, when documents were being added to my file, copies were made of some of them and sent to files in different offices. Maxwell and I don't know where each set of documents came from, but we made our requests for discovery and the call went out to various offices where documents associated with me could have been held. I assume clerks in those offices just copied what they had and sent it over.

We ended up getting multiple copies of some of the same notes. Maxwell surmised that they probably came from the HR office and the general legal office for Los Angeles. One was a note we believe was hand-written by James Ayala saying on orders from Aaron Weisswasser, to "Play Hard Ball with Tameron... She is to Move On." Another was written by Lyndsey a week or so after I transferred; it said that he thought I was "Flaky." Yet he allegedly didn't know why I transferred, but invited me into his branch and let me stay from the kindness of his heart? I don't think so.

—⁕—

Carol's deposition was held after lunch on the same day as Lyndsey's. She also tried to be cagey with her answers and spin them to fit Smith Barney's theory, but she couldn't pull it off. She obviously was not willing to make files disappear, and this was lucky for me, because many of the complaints I made were documented in the notes the HR woman in New York took from that very first phone call I made secretly from that empty office. Those notes were faxed to Carol in Los Angeles. However, I'm sure she had been coached by Smith Barney's lawyers, because she kept going back to four ideas that seemed to make up their defense theory: 1) an investigation had been done after I complained; 2) they concluded that the problem was me, poor little Tameron, and that I was such a basket case that I had sexual, social, and psychological problems, and therefore my perception of the world was deeply askew; 3) IF there had been any peculiar behavior, although they were not admitting to anything, it was just "childish pranks," and boys will be boys, and the perpetrators were part-time college boys anyway— insinuating, therefore, that Smith Barney wasn't responsible for them and that I was making spurious accusations because I had a poor performance review and I was trying to keep my job; and 4) Carol was "helpful" to poor little nut case and incapable Tameron and that she also kindly "focused' on me and my problems to make me happy and comfortable, even though I was a loser and didn't make any money for the company and should have been fired throughout my career for poor performance.

Coaching or not, Carol gave us a lot of very useful information. Maxwell first asked her about HR's procedure in handling sexual harassment complaints. She testified that Smith Barney's policy was to interview the complainant as well as others who may have been involved or who may have witnessed something. Yet she also admitted that she had never sat down and talked to me herself as an HR manager. She admitted that she didn't interview anyone else, even though the notes that Smith Barney had from that phone call were detailed and included many names of those involved and of witnesses. She also admitted that the only people she spoke with were James and Chad; she said that Chad did substantiate several of my claims, such as the strippers, and that he also had added more incidents that I did not mention, such as the whistle explosion.

Still, she revealed in her deposition that she had talked to nobody else— even though I was accusing members of management of participating directly! She also admitted that, even though some my claims were substantiated, she had never reported that back to me, as she is required to do by California law. So what, then, was the investigation? There wasn't an investigation; it was a cover up. She used this kind of tactic with every point of Smith Barney's "theory." She had notes in front of her that she couldn't deny; therefore she had to admit to things, but then she would try to insinuate the opposite. That was the spin that she tried, but she couldn't pull off. It was surreal; these were more Alice in Wonderland tactics.

Another example of Carol trying to squirm out of her incompetence was the alleged performance review. There was no performance review, and there were no notes of any kind either referring to a performance review or documenting a performance review. I never even knew they claimed there had been a performance review until 2002, nine years afterwards. I learned that they made such a claim through Carol's testimony. Chad told me to find another job if I didn't do $10,000 a month every month, starting from my ninth month as a broker, and James had told me that he wouldn't help me transfer because my production was too low— but these were not performance reviews. They were one-sentence threats. Maybe Chad or James or both had covered their behavior by claiming to Carol that I'd had a performance review after I had called HR; but there is no evidence of or testimony for this claim. If I had known about such a claim, I would have called them on it immediately and they would have found out that I had written down the production of twenty- three people in our office for a two month period (which I'll discuss later). Both Carol and other managers testified that, not only were there no notes of a performance review, but that they never saw or read any notes of a review in the past either. Of course not— because there hadn't been any review. I don't believe Chad or James even made such a claim. In spite of all this, Carol illogically clung to the performance review claim.

The third part of Smith Barney's theory that she tried to spin was the office environment. She denied there was a sexually-hostile environment. She said, in essence, that boys are boys; that they were young and part-time dialers (which wasn't true); and that it was just locker room stuff, a "young camaraderie." Then she admitted under oath that she found the office did have an "environment problem" and that she "was uncomfortable with it."

Carol also testified that she felt she needed to work with management to "change the branch issues" or that she needed to "work with management in the approach they took with respect to the environmental issues."

She testified that it took more than a year to change the branch. In fact, the branch didn't change until the class action came out. Harland, the manager who took over that branch after James Ayala, was named personally in the suit by several women. So we know that it took more than five years, at least.

The fourth aspect of Smith Barney's strategy was to claim that Carol had tried to help poor little nut case Tameron. She couldn't get around the facts that she didn't do an investigation, that there wasn't a performance review, that the environment was indeed sexually hostile, and that my wanting to get out of there was a legitimate and reasonable response. She testified that after I went to her office to ask her if she, as a representative of Smith Barney, saw my moving to the ninth floor as a solution to the problem, she involved Aaron Weisswasser. I didn't know that. All I knew is that James told me Aaron was coming into our office on his normal visits and wanted to talk to me. She said that she "focused on resolving my issue" and on "making me comfortable." She made it sound, both during her deposition and during her trial testimony, as if I had been the problem and she was just trying to help me— even though she did absolutely nothing.

Carol also unwittingly exposed both Aaron's and Lyndsey's deposition testimonies for the lies that I believe they were. She said under oath, at least three times, that she had "a number of conversations" about me with Aaron and Smith Barney's lawyers. Those conversations also involved James Ayala and Lyndsey. This makes sense, because I have a document stating that they were going to continue my diminished salary for another six months in Beverly Hills that was signed by all three managers: Aaron, James and Lyndsey. She said that the conversation was about my low production and that there were "a lot of conversations with Lyndsey's office."

Notice she said "Lyndsey's office," instead of Lyndsey. She was trying to be cagey. I don't believe for a nanosecond that Aaron or Lyndsey didn't remember or know any of this, which they both tried to claim. She testified that "local transfers (like mine) were rare and that it would have to be a compelling reason to allow one and that (she) would remember such an event." Gee, then how come Aaron and Lyndsey couldn't remember? It was money out of their pockets, and yet they didn't remember.

Last, she said that decisions about issues of sexual harassment complaints and remedying any problems were handled by local management and that this was true even if local management was implicated. Just as I had suspected all along, she had been only a witness and messenger for the men.

As I've said, branch managers were kings ruling their little fiefdoms in the securities industry. Carol's discussions with management and Smith Barney's Los Angeles-based lawyers during my negotiations with them were not about an investigation and whether there was a problem with the office and what to do about it. They were discussing me as an adversary and what to do about me. I believe they made a business decision to move me and to implement the strategy they did because, if I had blown the whistle to authorities outside of Smith Barney at that time, all hell would have broken loose, and they really didn't want that at the time. If somebody from the SEC or the NASD had started sniffing around that branch, they would have been really busted over many of their "business irregularities." They had concluded it was better to pretend they were moving me in good faith and then to grind me out of the business. Records only have to be kept for seven years, so the business records of the early 1990's are long gone. Who's to say? Maybe their strategy, from their personal and short-term branch business perspective, was the best course to take because they were never busted for those unethical business practices or for cheating all those clients I believe they cheated.

Toward the end of October 2002, after the other depositions had been taken, I was still bugging Maxwell about James Ayala's deposition. He finally went back to the panel to ask for more time to get permission to subpoena and depose James Ayala which I had thought was going to happen all along. The panel denied his request; it was too late, with only six weeks until the trial. This was another example of how Maxwell dropped the ball and had lost another critical witness for me.

In the beginning of November, Smith Barney made me another offer of $124,000. Maxwell wrote a letter to me laying out the strengths and weaknesses of my case, the possible outcomes, and the fact that I should seriously consider settling with them. A week later, Maxwell called to tell me that he had talked to Terrence again and thought there was another offer on the table for $186,000 plus lawyer's fees. Maxwell really wanted to settle. I thought this was more because of his desire not to try my case himself than because my case was weak. I still felt he was very intimidated by Smith Barney. Smith Barney now had all the documents they had subpoenaed from my doctors. The settlement document said that medical records couldn't be accessed but Smith Barney did subpoena my doctors, and Maxwell didn't try to stop them. I had seen a dermatologist for those things on my fingers that she said had been from stress. During my threatening and stressful negotiations to transfer, Carol had told me our insurance pays for counseling, so I started seeing a psychologist. I continued to see that therapist until things got better with Lyndsey in 1998, after the class action settlement announcement.

My therapist was really the only person I talked to in depth about my work life. I was hell bent on succeeding, but it was an embarrassing and humiliating situation to endure and made me feel like a loser. Being a stock broker is a marketing job, and even the illusion of success was important. I didn't want to share what was happening to me with anyone except a therapist, who would keep it all to herself.

After Smith Barney received my medical records, they wanted to depose me again. When I arrived at Orrick's downtown office for that third day of deposition, Maxwell was already there. He took me into their large and impressive conference room. He had arrived early to talk to Terrence again, and he was taking me into the conference room in an effort to try again to get me to settle for what I felt was peanuts. It just wasn't worth it for me. I would have rather tried my best and lost rather than take what they were offering. I don't remember what Maxwell said exactly, but I took it as a threatening message from Terrence. What bothered me even more was that Maxwell seemed to be going along with it. I didn't respond well. I almost jumped out of my chair and said to Maxwell, "They Can Eat My Shit!"

Maxwell was taken aback and seemed a bit upset at my language. "Maybe you should go find another lawyer," he replied to me.

"I already tried," I snapped back. "It's too late."

Maxwell wasn't going to get me to settle on their measly terms. We got up and walked to another room where the deposition was to take place, but I was burning with anger that he would pull me aside and upset me before the deposition. He could have waited until afterwards. "What is he doing," I thought to myself, "trying to save them money by not going through with the deposition?" The various lawyers I had called told me how to stay on top of him and to respond to him in writing. My letters were meant, I have to admit, to be documentation. I am embarrassed to admit this now, but, if I had lost big, I intended to sue him for negligence. I probably wouldn't have gotten far, because I didn't have any money, but I would have done my best to make his life miserable. I'm not usually a vicious person, but this was the fight of my life. I was trying very hard, and I felt it wasn't right that he wasn't paying the attention that he should have to my case.

In late November I faxed him another letter:

Dear Maxwell:

After our conversation this evening, I felt the need to make very clear to you my thoughts about the status of my case and my experience with you. I understand that part of my case will be difficult because we don't have direct evidence to corroborate the retaliation portion of my claim. However, panelists are human, and there is plenty of evidence that casts doubt on Smith Barney's behavior and motivation. There is also evidence that my experience corroborates the class action statistics. The fact that Lyndsey Shanahan was surreptitious and sly in his retaliation is at the center of my case! It is your job as litigator to convince the panel of that. I'm sorry to say this, Maxwell, but my experience with you so far is that you have acted as a lazy lawyer. As I told you Wednesday, November 13, I feel you have been remiss in your responsibilities toward me and that you have not done right by me. My concern is that you will not appropriately prepare for this trial/hearing. You have two weeks, so I'm telling you now, prepare for this case to the fullest extent of your abilities. I will, as I have all along, cooperate to the fullest. My concern is reasonably founded..." (I reiterated my complaints to him about losing witnesses and strategizing about my case.) Your response to my concern, and your excuse about losing an important witness, were to say the evidence with the regard to sexual harassment complaints after I left the downtown branch is solid and that we are OK there. What conscientious lawyer would strategize like that? The panel denied discovery from the downtown branch of sexual harassment complaints after I left that branch. I was the first to complain and leave. Without that discovery, and now, without that important witness, I have nobody to ask about the environment to corroborate my testimony. Carol Farmer admits during her deposition that there was a problem but her testimony in no way conveys just how unbelievably terrible it was. Without understanding how terrible it was, the panel won't believe Smith Barney and Lyndsey Shanahan had much motive to retaliate. I'm sure they will call somebody to testify to refute my characterization of the environment, so that, even though the environment was so outrageous that eighteen women filed suit, the panel may very well conclude that my perception is "overly sensitive" because you lost my one very powerful corroborator. (I also accused him of lying.) You specifically told me on more than one occasion that we had four depositions, the two branch managers involved, their boss, and the local HR executive involved, to my one deposition (the panel allowed Smith Barney to depose me only) …. Now I find that they (Smith Barney) claimed they don't know where he is. If you had shared the original agreement with me when you should have, I could have given you James Ayala's home and work contact information in three minutes! The fact that you would allow this situation to develop because you didn't keep me apprised is outrageous. His complete home information is listed in the 411 directory and his complete work information is listed on the NASD website, as all registered professionals must be by law. If you had kept me apprised from the very beginning, as you should have, this would have never happened.

I complained that he had missed deadlines and that he wouldn't answer questions such as how to handle the journalists issue since I wasn't allowed to talk to the press as an employee of Smith Barney. There had been two TV programs about the class action, one on *20/20* and one on *60 Minutes*. I had asked if getting tapes of those programs would be helpful and about discovery that we had requested but never received, but he hadn't answered me. I complained that we didn't get all of the discovery we had asked for, that he wasn't familiar with the details of my case, and that I needed a press release before the trial.

I have told you, from the very beginning, what I would not accept and what I would do if Smith Barney refused to negotiate at a reasonable level. Three years later, I remain true to my word. I also still hold you responsible to fulfill your legal responsibility and obligation to me… You have a lot of work to do on my case, but it seems that you have several other cases you're working on simultaneously. It's not right that after I sign a contract with you, you put little effort into my case. I'm not telling you how to do your job, but, as I previously told you, I want to read your brief well before the deadline to submit it. I know you're smart and that you know the law, but I'm telling you again in no uncertain terms to prepare this case to the full extent of your abilities.

—⁓—

The two weeks before my trial, I was very upset. Maxwell had dropped the ball so many times, I really did feel like he was selling me down the river. At one point, I thought I was going to have a heart attack driving down the 405 freeway on the way to see a client in Seal Beach. My mind just clicked into a fantasy world, I guess, as a survival response. That had never happened to me before, and it felt very weird to observe my own mind do that.

—⁓—

Terrence wrote Maxwell another letter, one week before my trial. His accusations were ridiculous, and the letter was meant to threaten me. He twisted reality so much that the letter read like another episode of Terrence in Wonderland. And, again, it had the opposite of the desired effect. I was fuming. Terrence accused Maxwell of being the obstacle to a settlement, but he really had no idea. "You have suggested," he wrote, "that we have 'jerked around' your client in negotiations and that you will not respond to our last offer. I will not undertake to explain why I believe you may be the obstacle." It wasn't Maxwell who refused to respond to his offer. It was me! And Maxwell was passing on the information. Terrence made another offer to settle for $325,000, which was to include all fees and costs.

Maxwell sent me his letter, conveying his idea about the offer, and then we discussed it. He warned me that I might lose the arbitration hearing and would then get nothing. That idea really didn't bother me. In my mind, I was using the stable, home-owning lives of my colleagues, with whom I had gone through training, as a comparison. I felt Smith Barney had taken that opportunity away from me, and that is what I thought they should restore to me. I instructed him to counter offer with $635,000, which would not have even bought a small house on the West side of Los Angeles at the time. I thought my counter offer was more than reasonable, and I would not accept anything lower.

I had nagged and nagged Maxwell about the journalists and the necessity of making a press release. I wrote a release; Maxwell probably thought it was so pathetic that he finally told me he would write one himself. I asked him to show it to me. I was still confused about what I could and couldn't do with respect to journalists regarding the class settlement, and I was absolutely paranoid that, if Smith Barney found out that I was speaking directly to the media, I would be fired. I enlisted my good friend, Eva, the investment banker in London, and my sister-in-law, both of whom have foreign accents, to call journalists back East. Someone had suggested that I call Pamela Martens, the originator and namesake of the class action lawsuit, so I did. Pamela was very nice on the phone and gave me several names of journalists who originally had been interested in the class action when it was settled in 1997. By this time, Eva had filed a suit in London against Nomura for discrimination and had a few media contacts of her own. I wasn't taking any chances. Smith Barney had a policy against employees talking to the media, and Maxwell had never gotten back to me about the proper way to invite journalists to the trial as the class settlement allowed, so I found another way.

Eva and my sister-in-law contacted journalists at *Dow Jones*, *The New York Times*, and *The Wall Street Journal* as well as Susan Antilla, formerly of Bloomberg, who had written a book called *The Boom Boom Room* about this class action against Smith Barney. I got most of the journalists' names and numbers from Pamela Martens— and thank goodness I listened to her. In the end, none of the journalists she recommended wanted to bother getting on a plane and coming west, which turned out to be a good thing. When I arrived at the hotel where the arbitration/trial was held and walked into the arbitration room, after at least a year of sweating the issue, I was completely relieved that journalists were not there! After being so worried about media attention and trying so hard to get somebody to show up, I realized, once I got there, that their presence would have changed the atmosphere of the arbitration into something unproductively tense and hostile.

I went to Maxwell's office a few days before the hearing to prepare for an hour or so. He gave me an agenda of the questions he would ask me and I practiced answering in his office as if I were already on the stand. He also gave me some pointers to testifying. He told me to speak in the first person and not to use "frankly," "to tell the truth," "honestly," or "the truth is." Those phases make people think you're not telling the truth. He also told me not to look at Terrence. I don't remember exactly why, but it had something to do with respect and power. He said that when Terrence asked questions, I should look up, look around, or look at the panel. "Just don't look at Terrence," he told me "and don't look down, either." He also told me to make one sheet of crib notes. "I don't know if you'll be allowed to use them," he cautioned, "but make them anyway, just in case." I was prepared as I ever would be. The day before the trial, I did nothing but try to relax.

XII

THE TRIAL

On the morning of my trial, I thoroughly expected Smith Barney's lawyers to stop me in the hallway of the hotel where the arbitration was being held and try to settle with me again, but they didn't. The arbitration was held at the Bonaventure Hotel in downtown Los Angeles, which is a large hotel with several fountains and lots of plants in a central atrium. As I walked through that atrium area with Maxwell, the sound of running water and smell of chlorine and mildew were very strong. We walked past a restaurant and down another hallway lined with conference rooms to our assigned room, which was the last one on the right. After the long struggle I had been through it felt really weird to finally walk into the arbitration room.

I watched everybody greet each other and chat, and then settle down in their seats as if it were any normal day for them. The room was configured like a rectangle. There was a snack table in the back, left corner that was stocked with coffee, tea, and breakfast foods. To the right, three long tables had been set up in a kind of square horseshoe configuration. Looking into the horseshoe, Smith Barney, who had sent four lawyers, were on the left side; Maxwell and I were on the right; and the three panelists sat at the long table that connected the two side tables. The court reporter sat in the middle at the open end of the horseshoe with the witness chair and a small table.

As the panelists sat down and started the proceedings, I thought to myself, "Oh, my God, here we go; we're really going to do this." The panel chairperson began the proceeding. "Good morning, my name is Megan Clarke and our panel this morning to my left is Mr. Dale Blaine and to my right is Ms. Mercy Tyler… We are here this morning on the Tameron Keyes matter, and, before we get started, I just wanted to go around the room and have everyone again state who they are for the record… so I'll start on my right in the corner."

Each person spoke in turn: "My name is Pauline Cervantes and I'm in-house counsel for Smith Barney."

"Elizabeth Cardenas with Orrick, Herrington & Sutcliffe for Smith Barney."

"Edward Brown of Orrick, Herrington & Sutcliffe on behalf of Smith Barney."

"Terrence Paolucci, P-a-o-l-u-c-c-i, Orrick, Herrington on behalf of Smith Barney."

"Maxwell Prague, representing the claimant Tameron Keyes."

I didn't understand the procedure but also didn't want to drop the ball. It seemed for a split second that they were going to forget about me, so I called out, "Tameron Keyes."

Edward Brown, the lawyer across the room, let out a little suppressed laugh. This was a legal proceeding. Claimants don't speak unless they are on the stand or a judge addresses them directly. I hadn't understood that, and was so embarrassed that I had called out like that. *"Tameron, you idiot,"* I scolded myself, *what were you thinking? That we were sitting in a summer camp fire circle, introducing ourselves and about to sing Kumbaya?"*

First the panel conducted what they called "housekeeping" by discussing the trial schedule and procedural issues. Then the panel chairwoman announced… "the other thing, just to kind of set the tone, we have discussed this morning that we would like to make this efficient and effective, and to that end we ask you to minimize your objections. We are all lawyers. Ms. Tyler is just about to become a federal magistrate. I was just elected circuit judge. Mr. Blaine is a former judge"….

I was happy to find out that at least two of my panelists would not be arbitrators anymore after my arbitration. The criticism against arbitration is that each industry— like the securities industry— for example, supports its own arbitration system. Securities companies have been accused of keeping track of arbitrators in its system and whether they rule for or against corporations. The accusation is that if arbitrators rule in favor of a plaintiff too often or too strongly, they are not invited to arbitrate again. No matter how honest an arbitrator wants to be, everybody is human, and if ruling in favor of a plaintiff against a corporation is going to cause you not to be invited to work on another case, even if it is subconscious, you might lean toward the corporations. In my case, two of my panelists were becoming judges after this arbitration; that meant that even the possibility of them having a conflict of interest had been eliminated. As they would reveal later, both had been required to clear their dockets in order to start their new positions as judges, so they wouldn't be able to arbitrate even if they had wanted to. That was a lucky break for me.

From the beginning, Smith Barney desperately tried to keep four specific expert reports out of my trial. These reports had been generated by as a part of the class action. In order to get a copy of these reports, I'd had to sign a confidentiality agreement that stated that I wouldn't reveal the contents. To this day, I have never read them; I left that up to Maxwell. I was told that the use of these reports in the individual arbitrations had been agreed on between class council and Smith Barney and that the use of statistics was specifically allowed on page 40 of the *Stipulation of Settlement,*— yet Smith Barney tried to double-deal with sleazy, illogical, and disingenuous arguments. First they claimed that they weren't notified in time. Maxwell called them on that lie; it was blatantly not true. Smith Barney knew about these reports from the very beginning and, in fact, had issued rebuttal reports. Then they tried to claim that the contents were not relevant to my case, saying that the Martens class action was "primarily a claim brought by sales assistants and other staff." That was a laughable statement since Pamela Martens, the class action originatorand namesake, was a broker in the Garden City, New York branch. In addition to that fact, Smith Barney, at that time, had approximately 10,000 brokers, of whom 5 percent were women! [9]Five percent! Later in the proceeding, one of Smith Barney's lawyers specified that 10 percent of claimants were brokers. Hmmm, let's think about that number. Ten percent of an approximate 2000 claimants is 200. If 5 percent of 10,000 brokers were women then 500 women were brokers. Two hundred is 40% of 500; that meant 40% of all female brokers sued Smith Barney.

"In addition," Mr. Brown continued, "the class-wide evidence has no relevance to the claims that Ms. Keyes is bringing herein. Ms. Keyes is claiming that she was subject to a hostile work environment while she worked at the downtown L.A. branch prior to December 1993. She is also claiming that when she went to the Beverly Hills branch, Mr. Lyndsey Shanahan, the branch manager, subjected her to discrimination— not the firm, but Mr. Lyndsey Shanahan." Again, he was purposely misrepresenting the class settlement. On page 34 of the *Stipulation of Settlement*, it specifically stated that Smith Barney could not claim that it was *not* responsible for the actions of managers and brokers.

Brown went on to say "...and what goes on, on a class-wide basis, has no probative value as to whether or not Lyndsey Shanahan, as the branch manager in Beverly Hills, took any action which was in any way discriminatory against Ms. Keyes on the basis of her gender or retaliated against her based on her complaint in Los Angeles. So I believe the expert reports or any rebuttal reports that we would offer in opposition to that have no probative value for this panel as to whether or not Smith Barney is liable on the claims made by Ms. Keyes."

Maxwell looked as if he couldn't believe his ears. "If I might respond just very briefly," he said. Then he began to clarify the agreed rules to

---

[9] I have seen several varying estimates of the percentage of female brokers in the early 90's. It is very difficult for outside observers to make such a calculation. I believe, and many of my colleagues agree, that in Shearson Lehman Brothers in the early 90's, women comprised about 5 percent of brokers. That number started to change while negotiations were going on in 95 and 96 and doubled after the settlement in 97.

Chairwoman Clarke, saying "714.10a is "the section that deals with hearsay, and the very first sentence says 'hearsay evidence relevant to the particular ADR[10] proceeding may be offered by claimants or the firm at the ADR hearing and shall not be excluded by the ADR panel on the grounds that the evidence is hearsay.' So that is the basic rule. Then the rule goes on to provide a particular format of notifying the other side and providing copies or affidavits or videotapes. Now, technically speaking these are neither affidavits nor videotapes. They are simply hearsay statements, but we went the extra mile and provided them… it's simply a report; it says Mr. Goldman said this; Dr. Fanning Madden said this. Those are hearsay statements. Then the question is, are they relevant? …We provided them (Smith Barney) with the names at the very beginning of the discovery process here as to who they were, and there was never any question in Smith Barney's mind when we listed those names as to those individuals. I never got a call from anybody at Orrick saying, 'Who are these people? I've never heard of them before,' because of course they had heard of them and had the reports at that point."

"The second question is, 'Is it relevant to the claim?' and I heard Mr. Brown say something that is frankly astonishing, given what our hearing complaint says. The hearing complaint is that there was sexual discrimination against Ms. Keyes in the form of hostile environment, harassment, and unfair treatment; that she was treated differently than other brokers; that the unfair treatment occurred both in the Los Angeles office and in the Beverly Hills office… that, in addition, there is evidence that Mr. Shanahan, who was the branch manager in Beverly Hills, was conducting himself in a way that was retaliatory because Ms. Keyes had complained about the behavior in the LA office… So the notion that somehow hostile environment claims are different than discrimination claims not only misstates what our hearing complaint says but misstates what the evidence is going to be… hearsay."

---

[10] ADR stands for Arbitration Dispute Resolution

Mr. Brown also claimed to the panel that Maxwell had threatened Linda Friedman, which Maxwell adamantly denied.

"On the contrary," Maxwell said defending himself, "Linda Friedman is willing to testify over the phone about the agreement to use the reports..."

The panel left the room to deliberate. Five minutes later, they came back into the room. "We have made a unanimous decision that the reports will be admitted," the chairwoman announced, "and we will also accept Smith Barney's rebuttal reports." *Whew!* I thought, and let out an internal sigh of relief. The panel had ruled in my favor on a major point.

—⁓—

Smith Barney was also very adamant about trying to keep the panel from hearing anything that went on in the Los Angeles branch after I had transferred. The office had gotten worse after I left; that information would have been explosively damaging, so Smith Barney didn't want the panel to hear one word about that branch after 1993. Consequently, Smith Barney fought tooth and nail, from the beginning, to keep it out and for the most part they succeeded in doing so. Since the panel had already ruled that discovery would not be allowed from the downtown branch that occurred after December 1993, Smith Barney argued that no testimony (from depositions, for example) should be allowed, from either before or after I worked at the downtown office. Maxwell explained to me that discovery orders do not preclude live testimony from being offered— but Smith Barney was trying to make sure we could not even do that. They claimed that what happened after I left had nothing to do with me, so it was irrelevant to my case. Of course, it was relevant; not only did the company not fix the problem which is required by California law, but the environment got worse. The manager following James Ayala had several quid pro quo sexual harassment complaints lodged against him personally in addition to hostile environment complaints.

Smith Barney and Maxwell argued in front of the panel about it. ... "A ruling about discovery certainly is not a binding ruling as to what evidence is appropriate at the hearing," Maxwell rebutted. "In this case there is a very critical issue, which is how did Salomon Smith Barney respond to Tameron Keyes' complaints of discrimination and harassment in the Los Angeles office? Those complaints were made at the end of 1993... She was moved out of that office in December 1993, but the case law is very clear. An employer has an obligation, actually independent of the person who makes the complaint, to effectively investigate charges of harassment, to report back to the person who made the complaint, to take effective action, including discipline... Failure to do those things, or any one of those things, is not only evidence of discriminatory motive, not only evidence that the later complaints that someone might have may not need to go through a complaint procedure that's been shown to be bankrupt... It is also evidence of willfulness, which goes to the issue of punitive damages."

This was an extremely important part of my case. "When Smith Barney learned of a problem," Maxwell continued, "it had an obligation to fix the problem and to bring it to an end, and to the extent that there is evidence that it failed to do that— even if that evidence occurs when Ms. Keyes moves from Los Angeles to Beverly Hills— that evidence is admissible. It's particularly important in this case because the regional director for Smith Barney, who had responsibility for the entire Los Angeles area, was personally involved in the decision to move Ms. Keyes. He was personally involved in overseeing the investigation— or lack of investigation— and he had responsibility for offices. He had direct communications with Mr. Shanahan, the branch manager in the Beverly Hills office. Mr. Shanahan reported to Mr. Weisswasser, the regional director. And so what happens in the Los Angeles office, post-December, is directly relevant to the continuing treatment of Ms. Keyes after she leaves the frying pan of the Los Angeles office and moves into the fire of Beverly Hills."

Chairwoman Clarke asked a question. "Correct me if I've misunderstood, but did you not say that the evidence you intend to offer addresses what happened to Ms. Keyes's complaints and that this was related to whether the complaints were acted upon, investigated, and effectively resolved, and what action or discipline was taken or not taken in connection with her complaints in the L.A. office?"

"That is what we intend to offer," Maxwell answered.

"And to that end, panel," Ms. Clarke asked the other panelists, "are you interested in hearing those issues?" They were, so she ruled, "Anything that goes far afield from that, however, into other areas, would be, I think, beyond the scope of this hearing."

Maxwell subtly reminded them that they had ruled against us on the discovery motions months earlier. "We were not able to do discovery because of the panel's ruling on discovery issues as to behaviors that continued after Ms. Keyes left by the remaining managers, replacement managers, and by Human Resources people, as to other women in the office, which does go to the question of whether they fixed it, whether they effectively brought the problem to a halt."

Ms. Clarke clarified the ruling "to the extent you can connect it to this case, we will allow it."

Thank goodness; the panel had ruled in my favor again.[11]

Smith Barney tried to block us one more time before the trial had even started. They didn't want Maxwell to be able to show the panel Weisswasser's deposition video in its entirety, which Maxwell had informed them he planned to do. Of course, I was silent during all these arguments. It became obvious to me that there had been a lot of "lawyering" going on between Maxwell and Smith Barney that I had not known about. The motions and arguments that seemed to have occurred up to that point and that were still being made as the trial started were all news to me. I was so happy when I realized that Maxwell wanted to show Aaron Weisswasser's entire deposition to the panel. Maxwell had

---

[11] Melanie's testimony could have helped me enormously even though she had worked in the Downtown branch after I had transferred.

said that Weisswasser's lies were so incredible, he wanted the panel to see the whole, videotaped deposition for themselves. Reading excerpts from the deposition, as normally would have been done, would not have shown the significance or the magnitude of his lies. Smith Barney argued vehemently against it and accused Maxwell of "accusing Weisswasser of a number of things and making comments," suggesting that his questions had been inappropriate.

Maxwell stood his ground. "A couple of things on that, he said. "When you take a deposition of a party, and Mr. Weisswasser was the regional director at the relevant time… it may be used for all purposes. And the second thing is that he made some very telling admissions at his deposition. The panel is entitled to hear and see that without having them clean it up first, and I think it is critical. There are some limited objections that are made. They don't interfere with the flow of the questioning and they are almost entirely instructions not to answer or objections about vagueness. The entire tape, start to finish, is two hours long."

Again, Smith Barney argued against it. Maxwell was about to respond again, but before he could get his words out of his mouth, Ms. Clarke interrupted. I think the panel saw that something was up.

"The panel doesn't mind to look at the video, and we will take the objections as they are raised," Ms. Clarke said. "So we can proceed with that." I was poker-faced, but inside I shouted, "Yay! They ruled for me again!"

It was time for the actual trial to start, and, because I was the plaintiff, Maxwell got to go first. He began his opening statement and delivered it in a calm, measured, and self-assured manner. He summarized what had happened to me and laid out my case to the panel in a way that made me very happy. He did an excellent job, which brought back my confidence in him. After all the tension, anger, suspicion, and frustration between us, he ended up coming through for me. His statement was precise, linearly logical, and articulate. I calmed down after hearing it.

—⚏—

After opening statements, I was the first to take the stand. Maxwell asked me questions that allowed me to tell my story to the panel. First, he asked me about my personal history before Smith Barney, including details of my education and travels. Then we moved to the details of my experience downtown, the complaint I made to Human Resources, and the details about my conversations with Aaron Weisswasser, James Ayala, and Carol Farmer. We ended my testimony with my describing the problems I had in the Beverly Hills office with my second manager, my earnings, my feelings about the whole experience, and the impact it had on me.

When Maxwell was finished, Terrence got to cross-examine me. I was, and still am, dumbfounded by Terrence's line of questioning. Maxwell was right when he said that Smith Barney "didn't have anything" and that "Terrence was grasping at straws."

Terrence's line of thinking was amazingly illogical. Several times, he asked me a question he had asked during my deposition. I gave the same answer I had given during my deposition, but he would still direct me to a written copy of my deposition— as if he were going to bust me for giving a different answer. Then he'd look at the deposition again, realize my answer was the same, and withdraw the question. Another time, he straight-out accused me of changing my testimony. We looked back at what I had said during my deposition, and my testimony was the same. He continued to hammer me, even though the written transcript was right in front of us. "Are you now changing your answer?" he accused me.

"No," I answered.

Then he said, "So was your testimony in your deposition true or is your testimony here today true."

"They both are true?" I answered back.

I sat there thinking to myself, "What a nut he is! The written testimony is right there in front of him."

At another moment, he was hounding me, and we were getting nowhere. My honest answer just wasn't what he wanted it to be; it didn't fit into his planned strategy. Maxwell finally objected, and the panel chair sustained the objection. "I think you've asked that question three or four times," the panel chairwomen said. "Let's move on."

Terrence's strategy seemed to concentrate on "themes," let's call them, during both my deposition and the trial. I thought this was downright bizarre. He pretended that things were done or said that weren't. His mindset reminded me of the character Rosanne Rosannadanna on the classic TV show *Saturday Night Live*. There is a skit in which Jane Curtain plays the serious newscast journalist asking a guest commentator Rosanne Rosannadanna played by Gilda Radner— her opinion on the subject of Russian Jewry. Radner goes on and on about Russian jewelry until Jane gets frustrated, interrupts her, and blurts out, "What are you talking about, you idiot? The topic is Russian *Jewry* not Russian *Jewelry!*" Radner turns, looks at the camera with a dumb smile on her face, and says in her irritating voice, "Never mind." It seemed Terrence had learned his litigation techniques from Rosanne Rosannadanna.

That being said, the effect of this technique should not be underestimated. As I mentioned in Chapter 11, repeating something over and over— even if it is not true, can be an effective tactic to get people to agree with you or to change their minds. Even the smartest people are vulnerable to repetition so the technique needs to be described and the public should be aware of it. It just didn't work on me.

—m—

The first of Terrence's "themes," and a subject he harped on repeatedly, was the idea that I was supposed to go to other brokers, especially female brokers, and ask them how I could "improve my performance." I told him repeatedly and in detail, at both my deposition and at the trial, that asking a question like that is not the language brokers use when they

talk to each other and that I didn't do that. What I did do, however—
and still was doing at the time of the trial— was to go over our focus
reports with my colleagues. We would compare, contrast, and break
apart the various numbers that Smith Barney produced monthly in those
individual reports which were a numerical breakdown of our individual
business and production numbers. What I would also do, I told him,
was to ask other brokers what they were working on, what stocks they
were selling, and what ideas and opinions they had to share. This was
the normal conversation brokers have with each other throughout their
careers. Sometimes I would go into older brokers' offices and ask questions
about a product I knew they worked with and with which they had more
expertise. Sometimes I would even cold call with colleagues or listen in on
their cold-calling pitches. A few times, I went out with another colleague
to an industrial area and she took one side of the street and I took another,
and we walked into businesses and just introduced ourselves.

All these kinds of activities are normal and expected among brokers
who are building their business, and even those who are established. But
one broker does not walk up to another and ask, "How do I improve my
performance?" That would be a direct question one would ask a sales
manager. In spite of my explanation, Terrence harped and harped about
why I hadn't asked another female broker how to "improve my performance."
Was that supposed to help his case? I couldn't see his point.

The second of Terrence's inexplicable themes was that I had a problem
with women in general that, somehow, affected my career— how exactly, I
can't imagine. It's not true, but even if it were, how would that relate to one
manager retaliating against me individually because of specific incidents
that had nothing to do with those women? Terrence especially harped
on the fact that I didn't know a certain female broker in the Beverly Hills
office. I didn't know her, and I still don't know her. It was bizarre and
irrelevant, and he had no testimony to back up his themes.

A third kooky theme of his was that Carol Farmer had "helped" me and that I had "admitted" that she had helped me, and was therefore, he insinuated, a liar. If she had helped me once before, his reasoning went, I should have gone to her again when problems arose— and, since I didn't, my claims must be disingenuous. This was another area about which I testified at length and in detail during my deposition. I said that she had not helped me, except to explain medical benefits which I have already mentioned. Part of Carol's job description was to go to each branch in her territory— I assume— once a year to explain the new benefits package. He ignored that fact and harped repeatedly on his own theme that she had somehow helped me.

One last crazy theme of Terrence's was this idea of training. My training complaints were derived from my experience in the downtown Los Angeles branch where I was left to sit by myself doing nothing, for months at a time, during two separate time periods. Terrence knew this and even defended Smith Barney in his opening statement by saying that my lack of training –and their treating me differently— happened under a different company; therefore, Smith Barney wasn't responsible. It seemed that he didn't really understand what I had said during my deposition; instead of trying to figure it out, he tried to use that section of my deposition to impeach my credibility. He bizarrely questioning me about training I said I didn't receive in Beverly Hills— and when he went back to my deposition, of course, it wasn't there.

Terrence's question during the deposition as to whether I had asked Lyndsey to pay for any training was another one of those Rosanne Rosannadanna moments. I did not ask Lyndsey to pay for any training, and no such thing was in my complaint. Almost any training an established broker wanted was free and freely available. I didn't have to ask Lyndsey. Instead, Terrence brought out Bettina, one of my colleagues in Beverly Hills, to testify against me, which I'll discuss in the next chapter. Smith Barney spent millions of dollars a year on analysts, economists, strategists, and all kinds of investment-type people to provide educational information, which collectively could be called research. There also are several types of designations that brokers could earn. It was all free. Where was Terrence's head?

Maxwell had said that Terrence was grasping at straws, and I think he was right. Terrence seemed very desperate. He brought up several other things that weren't themes but that were just downright incorrect. At one point he tried to say that the incident involving the insurance ticket— when Lyndsey tried to march me upstairs to the annuity coordinator's office then thought twice, looked at the paperwork, signed it, and walked away— was because I really didn't have the right paperwork. But his own client's managers and witnesses never said such a thing or testified to such a thing.

Terrence stooped to making stuff up by himself, and then tried to get me to agree with his hare-brained ideas. He said that the reason I started performing better from 1998 onward was because my attitude just changed! Poof, just like that! After years of struggling, he contended, I made a phone call to total strangers— he meant Stowell & Friedman— and I felt so much better after that phone call that… surprise!… my commission production sky rocketed. He insinuated that that phone call was such a "cathartic experience" that it made my gross production improve significantly.

He tried to get me to agree that my improvement had nothing to do with the fact that the settlement had occurred, or that once I complained to Stowell & Friedman, changes were made at Smith Barney that resulted in my being treated better— and, because of that better treatment, I wasn't working under the same pressure or fear. Nope, not in the world according to Terrence, even though his own client's managers who worked with me and were in the position to know my attitude testified to the *opposite*.

Even Aaron Weisswasser, who had that incredible lapse of memory, had testified that my attitude was "enthusiastic," "upbeat," and "dedicated." Lyndsey characterized me in his testimony as "bright," "intelligent," "worked hard," and "believed in what she was doing." Pete, my compliance manager, testified that I was "always positive," "very professional," that he "always enjoyed working with (me)" and that "(I) really cared about (my) clients and (his) interaction with (me) always displayed that; it's rare that you get that consistency." Those words were from the mouths of Terrence's client's managers under oath!

—∞—

During another brilliant moment, Terrence produced my first focus report from December 1993 and pointed to my business Return On Assets or ROA— a number which shows the firm how often assets are transacted. Traditionally, the firm makes money every time a transaction occurs, so an ROA is one way the company can see how profitable a broker is to the firm. ROA's are calculated by a formula that is described by amount of assets divided by gross commissions. Terrence accused me of "churning accounts," which means excessively buying and selling investments. My first full month of production was November 1993. The first month's ROA is meaningless. One would expect new brokers bringing in assets and transacting them for the first time to have a very high ROA, precisely because the assets have never been transacted before. He accused me of churning accounts because my first month's ROA was expectedly high. Again, he accused me of this even though his own witnesses had never said such a thing. He was trying to use information about which he had absolutely no understanding.

I suspect Terrence got this idea from Bettina who had a large bond clientele. One day a few weeks before the trial, I was walking past her office and saw Edward Brown, Smith Barney's co-counsel, in her office with her with the door closed. They spent two hours talking. I am sure they were talking about me, and I assume he was coaching her to testify against me. She must have told him that an ROA above a "1" indicates churning. If you primarily managed bonds, it might indicate those assets are turning over excessively, but one cannot make a blanket statement that all ROA's over one indicate churning. It doesn't mean that. Yet, Ed and Terrence took that idea and ran with it, even though they didn't understand how ROA works.

The ROA is also affected by the broker's length of service. A new broker's entire book of business would have been newly transacted, simple because he or she is a new broker and is bringing new assets to the firm. New brokers always have a high ROA. By contrast, a broker who had been in the business for a long time and whose business was heavily skewed to fixed income such as bonds, like Bettina's would have a low ROA. For example, if a client bought a twenty-year bond to hold until maturity, the turnover or opportunity for the firm to make money on that specific asset would obviously be very low. Conversely, you would expect a broker whose business was 100 percent stocks to have a higher ROA, because most people often have no intention of holding a stock for twenty years. A broker whose business was primarily options would have a very high ROA because options expire every three months or so; that asset would be transacted again and again. Terrence obviously didn't understand any of this. Yet he made up the idea that I churned accounts because my very first focus report's ROA was expectedly high. Those who are in the business understand that this bumbling move was worse than grasping at straws.

But Terrence couldn't seem to help himself; he bumbled some more and made himself look really bad in the process. One condition of the class action settlement was that a claimant's sex life could not be brought in as a part of the case unless a part of her claim involved having sex with somebody in the company. Part of my claim was for emotional distress in that my social life and happiness had been compromised because I had to put all my energy, time and emotions into dealing with a job where they were trying to get rid of me for illegal reasons. Because of this, I could be asked questions about my social life. My deposition had been three days long. Terrence had asked me about the guys I went out with on both the first and the second day of my deposition. Dating somebody doesn't mean you're having sex with them but I was a little confused, because I didn't think he could ask such questions, but Maxwell didn't object, so I had answered Terrence's questions. On the second day, Terrence asked me again about whom I had dated.

"Well, this goes back to that whole dating thing again," I responded. "I'm not sure what you mean by 'serious dating relationships.'"

"Have you dated anyone for longer than three weeks?" he asked.

I assume he asked that question because I had told him I had dated Sabastien for about three weeks in 1996.

"No," I answered. Then I made a mistake. I said "Let me qualify." I tried to explain the nature of my relationships with men, because the idea of a "date" wasn't clear to me. I mentioned sex. I told him that I was friends with the guys I had mentioned earlier whom I had gone out with, but that I didn't sleep with them. No! No! No! I shouldn't have done that! I don't think Terrence could have asked me directly about sex, but, since I mentioned it, he could ask follow-up questions. After that, I became cagier with my answers and tried to back pedal because my sex life was none of his business. He asked me:

Q. You are an attractive female; you live here in Los Angeles. It sounds like you have had little in the way of sexual relationships in ten years; is that stressful?

A. Yeah, but in the age of AIDS and herpes, I am very careful.

Q. Well, you say you are very careful. What do you mean by "very careful?"

A. Between 1980 and 1990, I slept with a more men than between 1990 and 2002.

Q. Okay, that's because of AIDS and herpes?

A. That's a big problem, yeah. I think a lot of people have changed their sexual behavior.

Q. What do you do in order to be careful, in order to protect yourself?

A. Well, I believe the advertisement that says there is no safe sex. I believe that. So I am more careful about whom I sleep with, and I would turn down a lot more people nowadays because of AIDS and other sexually transmitted diseases.

That was all I said, but it was enough. Looking back I should have refused to answer and told him my sex life was none of his business, even though Maxwell hadn't objected. I learned that, in legal situations, you should never mention sex, for any reason— never, ever, ever. Corporations routinely try to use the "slut or nut" defense. They will try, if they can, to make a slut out a woman; if that doesn't work they will try to portray her as a nut. In my case, there was no way they would be able to make a slut out of me, but they did try to portray me as a nut on many levels, including by using sex. I wasn't dorking every man who came my way, so they insinuated that must be because I have something emotionally wrong with me!

The questions and answers about dating and AIDS came back to annoy me during the trial. Terrence tried to bring up the sex questions. "Now, is it true, Ms. Keyes," Terrence asked during his cross examination, "that one of your major concerns since 1990 through the present is the risk of AIDS and herpes from sexual intercourse?"

"What!" I answered, absolutely floored that he could take a simple and widely-held concern that sexually-active people need to be very careful these days and spin it into insinuating that I had a mental problem.

"Objection!" Maxwell proclaimed loudly.

"Don't answer," called out the panel Chairwoman.

"Irrelevant," continued Maxwell. "Also, the stipulation specifically provides that the claimant's sexual activities and history are not appropriate." The panel sustained Maxwell objection and I didn't have to answer that question. But why had Maxwell allow him to ask such questions or for me to answer them during my deposition? I'll never know.

—m—

Maxwell got to redirect when Terrence rested his defense questioning. Through Maxwell's redirect, I got the opportunity to tell the panel other stuff that hadn't come out during the direct questioning, such as when I saw Weisswasser in McDonalds talking to Chad then lying to me about it a half hour later about it. I was able to describe when I heard Fritz, the Rottweiler compliance manager, talking to James about getting rid of me before I hurt them. I got to say a lot more about Lyndsey's behavior towards me, including that weird first interview— the "AK-47" remark, the "I'm sick of you" remark and other instances like that.

I also got to explain about the different kinds of notes I had written over the years and why I wrote them. I am sure that Smith Barney's lawyers believed that I kept notes my entire career with the intention to sue. Colleagues of mine had told me after I won that Lyndsey was claiming that it wasn't a fair fight, because I had kept notes for years with that intention. But it wasn't true at all. I had kept notes in order to document what was happening between the time I called HR and the time I transferred. I also took notes after I called Stowell & Friedman. I had made a few little notes in the intervening years that were like diary entries, such as the notes I made about the inexplicable pains I was having that first year after I transferred. But I did not keep notes throughout my career with the intention of suing Smith Barney, as Lyndsey accused me. The thought of poor little Lyndsey, the victimized man he portrayed himself to be, complaining that it wasn't a fair fight because I had kept notes for years, makes me sick.

Not everything came out during my time on the stand, but I did get to tell them how I had been naïve in the beginning, hoping that Smith Barney had moved me in good faith. I told them that, week by week, I began to realize from the incidents I had with Lyndsey— from the way he talked to me, the way he behaved toward me, and the things that happened— that the move hadn't been in good faith at all. I got to tell the panel that I wasn't given a chance to start over, as Smith Barney had agreed and that it wasn't reasonable to expect me to go back to the people who had lied and intimidated me and complain again, as Smith Barney contended that I should have. I wanted my job, and I had thought the best course of action was to suck it up, be quiet, and do my best under the circumstances.

Until the very end of my testimony, Terrence was still trying to make stuff up, intimidate me, and get the last word in. He threw out what I took to be a veiled threat, insinuating that I was lying about my notes and that he'd bust me when he introduced them into evidence. I felt like calling out to him in front of the whole court-room to "Go ahead!" But I didn't; it wouldn't have been appropriate. He was a sinking ship. He made one last, threateningly snide comment at the end of the trial. By that time, I think, he was fairly sure that he had lost.

—◊—

The next witness called after me was Dr. Lane, the forensic accountant we used. First, Maxwell asked about her background and credentials. Dr. Lane had impeccable credentials as a mathematician and accountant. She had a bachelor's degree from Wellesley College in physics and math and a master's degree and a Ph.D. from Harvard University in applied mathematics. She was a Certified Public Accountant and an accredited Senior Appraiser in business valuation; she was certified as a valuation analyst and was accredited by the AICPA, the American Institute of Certified Public Accountants. She also was certified as a fraud examiner, a commercial real estate appraiser, a national forensic economist and accountant, and a management consultant. She was definitely qualified to do the mathematical calculations Maxwell had hired her to do.

Maxwell questioned Dr. Lane in such a way as to walk the panel through the explanation of her calculations. She was hired solely to make calculations from numbers and data provided to her from Smith Barney-generated Focus Reports and financial consultant compensation booklets and other documents of that nature. She wasn't hired to give an opinion about my abilities or whether I might have been more successful if I had not been discriminated against.

True to form Terrence had more Rosanne Rosannadanna moments. During his cross examination of Dr. Lane in the trial, he tried to hammer her about the assumptions she had been given to work with and, I guess, tried to get her to draw conclusions about my ability. She hadn't been given any information about any other issues. She's a mathematician and was hired to calculate numbers only, so she answered many of his questions with "that is outside my scope of analysis." He had done the same thing to her during her deposition. Both Maxwell and Dr. Lane had thought it was odd that Terrence would go after her so aggressively and with that line of questioning. We all figured he would not do that during the trial because he would lose credibility, given the tasks she was hired to do and the type of expert witness she was. But he questioned her exactly the same way during the trial, and he sounded like an idiot doing it.

—w—

The next witness was Aaron Weisswasser. Since Smith Barney had lost the motion to keep the video out, their lawyers wanted Aaron in the room when the video of his deposition was played. I believe this was so he could do at least a little damage control. He was invited into the arbitration room. This trial, I felt, was my opportunity to face and confront management at Smith Barney, who I felt had broken the law and done me deep harm for a very long time. I wanted Aaron Weisswasser to look at me when he walked into the room. I really wanted to face him— but he would not look at me. He acted as if I didn't exist. I think he was playing the same power game to which Maxwell had alluded to when he counseled me not to look at Terrence when I answered his questions.

It didn't matter, because as somebody dimmed the lights and switched on the video machine, I distinctly remember crossing my arms and sitting back in my chair to watch the video. "*Beautiful*, I thought to myself. I was so happy that the panel would see Aaron's entire deposition as it happened. Aaron's lies were so blatant and outrageous in my opinion — and, apparently, in Maxwell's opinion as well— that Maxwell thought it best that the panel see the whole deposition. Even after Maxwell's screw-ups and defeats, this was a big score for him in my eyes. I didn't know he had planned on doing this but once it happened, I greatly appreciated him for doing it.

When the video was finished and the lights came back on, I felt it was obvious to everyone in that room what a liar Aaron Weisswasser was. It seemed he knew it, too, and he tried to make up for it. Elizabeth Cardenas, one of Smith Barney's lawyers, questioned Aaron first. She asked him the normal stuff: his name, how long he had been with the firm, and what his various titles and duties were. Then she asked when he "retired from management." He told her it was the spring of 1998.

"Why?" she asked.

"It was personal, not business-related," he answered. Baloney. Lyndsey had called an impromptu branch meeting in the middle of the trading day— over the PA system— without saying what the meeting was about. It was about ten or eleven in the morning and the meeting only lasted about ten minutes. If this was a planned and happy retirement, why would Lyndsey call such a meeting. Wouldn't he have announced the retirement of a senior executive who had worked at the firm since 1967 in a regular branch meeting, and wouldn't we, who had also worked for him for years, have been given advanced notice of Aaron's plans? That is what would have happened normally. I thought Aaron was lying, and he lied because he had been asked to step down— or was "invited to be a broker"— as a consequence of everything that had happened in the downtown branch, especially after I transferred branches; and because of his actions in response to those events while he was in management; and because of the lawsuit. Of course, he wouldn't tell the truth; it was humiliating. And his lying was part of the strategy to keep anything from downtown coming to light and tipping off the panelists about what really happened there.

Next, Elizabeth asked him about his experience serving on arbitration panels for the NYSE and NASD. Now, a man I felt was as dishonest as Aaron serving on an arbitration panel was a very scary thought. I feel sorry for any client who had a man like Aaron Weisswasser as an arbitration panelist in a dispute. Elizabeth then continued to question Aaron in detail about his position of Regional Director. It's interesting that he remembered a number of conversations with me, including a very specific conversation we had a week or two *after* I moved to Beverly Hills but that he didn't remember a thing about me and downtown Los Angeles. Despite having hundreds of brokers under his command for years, during the trial he remembered my low commission production and the even quintile I was in! But he couldn't remember one thing about all the conversations and negotiations in downtown Los Angeles?

Throughout the preparation for my trial, I had been very worried about how to prove Lyndsey's retaliation against me. It was the weakest part of my case, precisely because it would be the most difficult to prove. Most of the events I claimed about the downtown branch and the fact that Smith Barney had done nothing about them and had decided to get rid of me instead were documented in Smith Barney's internal HR notes— so the downtown part of my case wasn't difficult to prove. But, Lyndsey's years of retaliation actually did the most damage, and there was nothing in any Smith Barney internal documents that documented what had occurred.

I bugged Maxwell a lot about this. He assured me he was going to "go after Lyndsey." I didn't understand and was confused about how he could go after Lyndsey, but I felt there was nothing I could do about it. I had to just accept that Maxwell would do what he said he was going to do. He told me that one technique of finding out information about someone is not to ask that person directly but to ask someone else. The logic is that if someone is asked a question about themselves and the truthful answer is not very flattering, they might lie about it. This is exactly what Maxwell did. Instead of asking Lyndsey things about which he thought Lyndsey would lie, Maxwell asked Aaron and later Pete, my compliance manager.

Aaron claimed, during cross examination, that Lyndsey had an impeccable reputation in the investment community. That gave Maxwell the right to question Aaron about the origin of his belief. This was one of the ways Maxwell revealed at least a hint of the truth of what kind of a man Lyndsey was. It wasn't much, but it came out that he was a recovered alcoholic and had been a chain smoker, both habits he had quit on his own. Aaron said that Lyndsey did have an acerbic tongue, and that he could be very scary and intimidating and that he sometimes treated people badly.

Smith Barney was trying to show that Lyndsey was just a tough guy and that he was tough with many people; therefore, his behavior toward me wasn't anything different. If that had been true, my accusations would not have fit the definition of the law for discrimination and retaliation— but of course, it wasn't true. He was a tough guy with some people. His own big broker had described him as a "prick." But what he did to me was way beyond just being tough.

Maxwell's version of "going after Lyndsey" was turning out to be too soft, as far as I was concerned, so I started writing notes to Maxwell during Aaron's testimony. Lyndsey openly bragged that he used to "run around with models," so while Maxwell was questioning Aaron, I wrote him a note to that effect. Maxwell, in turn, asked Aaron, "In forming your judgment about Lyndsey Shanahan's fine reputation on the westside, did any of your information include the fact that he used to run around with models, date models?" Smith Barney's lawyers, all at once, jumped all over it and objected. "We were not asking about sex," Maxwell said. "This isn't a matter of sexual conduct. It's a matter of the statement that the man had a wonderful reputation in the community as a respected business leader and his public image. I'm entitled to test his knowledge of that reputation." The panel sustained the objection, and we moved on. It was a silly move on my part, but I couldn't stand Aaron's portrayal of Lyndsey as an upstanding, honorable man. Besides, I was conveying information that Lyndsey freely gave out when he was bragging about himself.

Aaron's testimony made him look more like the liar I thought he was, but the running with models comment got Aaron's attention. Now, he looked straight at me with burning anger. His eyes looked like black balls of fire. *"Yeah buddy,"* I thought to myself, *"now you're going to look at me."* I glared right back; it was my moment to face him. I felt like tearing that short, little man limb from limb. There was a very angry energy between us. It is slightly scary to know that I enjoyed the experience of him glaring at me and being so angry. Even though there were no words between us, the confrontation felt good to me after so many years. I loved the fact that he couldn't control the arbitration in the way he was accustomed to controlling events that adversely affected me. The truth was out, and there wasn't a damn thing he could do about it. He was toast by the end of his testimony. Dismissed!

—⚏—

The next witness to take the stand was Carol Farmer, the divisional Human Resource manager. Maxwell examined her as an "adverse witness." During the next break, I asked Maxwell what an adverse witness was. It turns out she was my witness after all, because Maxwell called her to the stand. Of course, Smith Barney wouldn't call her because the notes we got from her office during discovery and her testimony were too damaging to them. An adverse witness is a witness that is called to the stand by one side, but that side has given notice to the judge that the witness is expected to be hostile; therefore, the lawyer examining that person is not limited to asking open-ended questions, as he or she normally would be. Carol Farmer's unwillingness to perform her duty and instead, to go along with and protect the guys and cover up what was happening, had, shocked me out of my socks back in 1993 and still disgusts me to my core to this day.

Her testimony was a couple of hours long. Maxwell proceeded by having her read, line by line, the notes HR had in its possession. They were the notes the HR manager in NY had taken the day I made that first phone call in the empty office. The matter and the notes had been handed over to Carol, since she was HR manager for the L.A. area— but she never followed up and had done no investigation except to talk to my managers, whom, I had accused of being involved. Almost everything was documented right there in Smith Barney's internal notes. The dates were there, and the details, including some things that I had forgotten about but which had been mentioned by my sales manager, Chad.

Edward Brown cross-examined Carol. Some of it was spin, and some didn't make any sense. They harped on the idea that, because not everything was in the HR notes from that initial nerve-racking and emotional phone call— such as the "fucking you so hard that you'll have to hold your guts in by a two-by-four" comment— that I must be lying. Did that mean Chad also lying when he informed them of incidents that I had forgotten, but left out stories I remembered? His stories were also documented in Smith Barney's notes. They weren't applying their own logic consistently; to me this made them look worse. I couldn't understand why they would do that to themselves. Their line of questioning and kooky logic seemed to just emphasize the fact that Smith Barney had not done an investigation.

Then Smith Barney tried to claim that all my complaints had taken place outside the scope of time covered by the lawsuit. Carol had claimed over and over during her deposition that she couldn't remember much and would have to rely on Smith Barney's notes, which had dates on them. But during the trial, after just spending more than an hour with Maxwell going line by line through those notes— and still claiming that she didn't remember much of anything except what she could read from the notes— she testified under Smith Barney's cross examination that she knew that the events took place before May 1993 and therefore were outside the scope of the lawsuit. Was she listening to her own testimony? It was all spin.

As I mentioned earlier, Smith Barney's lawyers also harped on the idea that the company I had worked for— the company where the complaints were first made— was not the same company after the merger occurred in May 1993. And since the class settlement only covered May of 1993 going forward after the merger, anything that happened before that happened at a different company; that meant it was not relevant and was outside the scope of the class action.

Maxwell cross-examined Carol on redirect. Because he didn't work for the company, I knew he wouldn't know which questions to ask to get the truth out of her. Again, I furiously started writing notes to him, just as I had done during Aaron's testimony. Maxwell didn't catch on fast enough and didn't ask Carol the right questions. Instead, he asked her who the Chairman of Smith Barney was. Carol answered, "Sally Krawcheck," who had been hired in, 1998, after the settlement.

I believe Sally Krawcheck was hired as a result of the class-action settlement initiative to hire more women. Having a female chairwoman to counter-balance all the bad publicity didn't hurt either. This is not meant to detract from her, any other women hired after November 1997, their abilities and qualifications, or their deserving their positions. I was trying to get at the fact that Sandy Weil, who had started one of the predecessor firms to Shearson Lehman, was still the CEO of Smith Barney's parent company and that the chain of command— from Lyndsey up to the top— consisted mostly of the same guys until 1998, when men such as Aaron Weisswasser started stepping down.

The company was the same company, as we experienced the merger from the Shearson side. We had the same management teams, both downtown and in Beverly Hills, on the regional level and in New York. We maintained the same computer system, trading desks, programs, products, and program liaisons. We kept the same telephone numbers, operational systems, client statements, everything. Nothing changed for the Shearson Lehman people; it was the Smith Barney people who had to learn our system and who were swallowed up by Shearson Lehman, not the other way around. What Maxwell should have asked were questions that would have brought out the fact that nothing at all had changed for the Shearson Lehman branches after the merger.

For the record, part of the old Lehman firm went out on their own again, becoming a separate company, and our company became Smith Barney Shearson. Salomon Bros. had had a big bond trading scandal several years earlier, and it seemed they were never able to recover. So after the 1993 merger, Salomon Brothers also ended up being a part of our company, and we were called Salomon Smith Barney for a while. Eventually, we dropped the Salomon name and became Smith Barney again. We were told in the branch that each time there was a merger, the firm would do a study to determine which name was perceived most favorably by the public, and that is the name we kept. The company I worked for was always the same company, and the fact that Smith Barney's lawyers tried to say it was different was just more dishonest spin.

—ᴍ—

Finally, after all those years of his crappy behavior, Lyndsey was next up to the witness stand. He couldn't control events; he couldn't intimidate or bully anybody; nobody cared that he lived in a big house in Bel Air that allegedly looked like something out of *Architectural Digest*. At the trial, his snide remarks wouldn't be tolerated; he was no longer the king. He was just a regular Schmoe in the chair, and it was his turn to be uncomfortable and to be confronted with at least some of his actions. He would never be held accountable for his behavior or those years of demeaning and humiliating words— and, unfortunately, questioning him about that kind of stuff was not the way to get to the truth. Instead, he had to be outsmarted.

Maxwell questioned him in a calm, normally-paced, and civilized tone. There were none of the aggressive bully tactics that Terrence had tried to use on me. Maxwell questioned Lyndsey about his work history first; then, after he understood my point about the company not changing on the Shearson side, he proceeded accordingly. He asked Lyndsey about the company and his perception of it as the manager of one Smith Barney's top twenty-five branches.

Then, Maxwell slipped in the stuff we really wanted Lyndsey to reveal about the 1993 merger. Lyndsey testified that, after that merger, nobody asked him to change the culture in any way or do anything differently and that the company kept running pretty much the same, exactly as I had claimed. His testimony completely refuted what Smith Barney's lawyers were trying to convince the judges— that the company wasn't the same company and was therefore not responsible for what happened to me.

Absurdly, Lyndsey testified that he didn't recall that the problem I had that necessitated my move into his office involved charges of sexual harassment. There is not a branch manager out there, in any brokerage firm in the whole industry, who— if he'd had multiple discussions with his boss, the giving-up manager, an HR manager, and in-house legal counsel about a women who claimed harassment and then wanted to transfer to his branch— would not remember those conversations, especially, since they strategized about what to do. They discussed firing me or keeping me, continuing my draw after it had expired or not giving me a draw. That draw had to come out of one of the branches' pockets. He contended that immediately upon my meeting him, I was such a poor performer that I didn't deserve decent treatment— but he couldn't remember why I moved? It was obvious to me that he was being a team player and lying like a rug, just like Aaron.

After Edward had cross-examined Lyndsey, Maxwell got to redirect. He asked Lyndsey if he had assigned private offices to several people in the branch, naming them one by one. Again, as everybody in the room could see, I was writing notes to Maxwell. I was giving him the names of brokers' who were new or relatively new in the business. Maxwell also questioned him about giving large numbers of accounts away to a couple of those new brokers that I knew about specifically.

The room was quiet; Lyndsey and everybody else watched as I furiously scribbled notes then handed them to Maxwell. Maxwell would read my note and then ask Lyndsey the question; Lyndsey would answer, and then I would furiously write another note to Maxwell who would read it and ask Lyndsey the next question. It was obvious that I was prepared and angry and that I knew the details cold. Now I got to ask Lyndsey questions, and this time he couldn't snidely wave his hand to the outside world and tell me that if I didn't like it, I had other options. He couldn't make stuff up, such as allegedly that I stomped away in a tantrum. He was on the witness stand, and he had to answer me.

I nailed him. It was obvious that Lyndsey had given offices to everybody, most of whom had failed in the business anyway, while I continued to sit in a cubicle. Predictably, his answers were cagey, just as they had been during his deposition. He kept saying "I don't know" or "I'd have to look that up." It didn't matter, though, because his testimony was not credible. It had the effect of emphasizing that I was the one who was telling the truth.

Lyndsey's time on the stand was my time to confront him. He had this look on his face as if he couldn't believe what he was seeing. In the past, I had walked very carefully around him. He was the boss, and we both knew he could, under those circumstances, chew me up and spit me out. He had walked on me for so long that he probably had convinced himself that I didn't have it in me to go after him, even if I had the chance. But I had no fear in pursuing him at that moment and the fact that I actively challenged him seemed to surprise him.

In the end, I am sure the questions were much more benign than Lyndsey had feared. We had both thought it was going to be worse. I am sure he was worried that some embarrassing and unsavory skeleton would jump out of the closet and not knowing what or when it was going to jump out made him very nervous. When Lyndsey's testimony was over, he was visibly relieved and happy to leave the room.

For some strange reason, he waited in the atrium area for Smith Barney's lawyers when we all left the room at the end of the day. When Maxwell and I were walking by as we were leaving the hotel, I heard Lyndsey crack a joke to Smith Barney's lawyers about what a relief it was that his testimony was over. What had he been worried about? He was retired and wasn't even an employee of Smith Barney anymore. That was the end of the second day of my trial.

XIII

SMITH BARNEY'S BUSTED

On the third and fourth days of the trial, Smith Barney called nine people as witnesses: the operations manager from downtown, the compliance manager in Beverly Hills, the downtown sales manager's assistant, and six female brokers—including—Annie, the female broker I first worked for downtown, and Hope, also a broker from downtown. I had been friendly with both of them. The additional four female brokers were from the Beverly Hills branch.

I could understand why they would call the first broker I worked for, but the fact that they called all the rest seemed odd. Smith Barney's strategy was to call these women to the stand and question them about their own careers. I didn't understand why they would do that; what happened to me had nothing to do with their careers. It was more illogical strategy as far as I was concerned, and I believe it worked against them. It seemed to me that all the women had been coached or at least had had long discussions with Smith Barney's lawyers.

Bettina Crawford, the submissive foot-shuffler I had seen in Lyndsey's office years before, was the first colleague of mine called. I believe she had been coached, I had seen Smith Barney's lawyer Edward Brown in her office with her with the door closed for at least two hours. They sat at an extra work table in her private office and talking at length. Can you imagine what it felt like for me to walk to the copy machine and unexpectedly see a colleague, with whom I had worked for nine years, talking for two hours to Smith Barney's hired gun? My heart jumped. Bettina and I had always been friendly. I had gone to because of her experience with certain products and had even asked her if she wanted to partner with me regarding retirement plans. But she had stopped talking to me about six weeks before the trial; then, about three or four weeks before the trial, I saw Smith Barney's lawyer in her office. What is ironic is that Smith Barney insinuated twice that I would plot against, intimidate, talk negatively about, or otherwise try to influence colleagues. They refused to comply with discovery requests, making this claim. In November, they accused me, in writing, of planning to talk to friends in order to influence them—but I never did, not once.

Terrence had written in one of his threatening letters that he had been surprised to find out that I had not even told my buddy Raymond, about the lawsuit and that he wondered if I knew that they planned on talking to him. Smith Barney was paranoid about my plotting, scheming and influencing witnesses because influencing witnesses and engaging in retaliatory behavior is exactly what they— especially Lyndsey— had been doing all along. They wrote:

Dear Maxwell:

Per the parties' agreement, enclosed is respondent's Salomon Smith Barney's witness list for the arbitration hearing set for December 9, 2002. Respondent understands that you may wish to make *ex parte* contact with non-managerial witnesses. However, please note respondent's concern that Ms. Keyes not make any contact with the witnesses identified regarding their participation in the arbitration that may result in negative actions or comments by her and that she not otherwise engage in retaliatory conduct against any individual listed as a witness or who may otherwise participate in the arbitration of this matter.

The only person I did speak with was Raymond, about a week before the trial. Terrence said he was going to talk to him, so I felt it was only right that I tell him first. He and I went up the street to the little shop where I got my coffee every morning. I cried a bit, because it was so hard to talk about it. I warned him to know that he might be called. I told him to just be honest.

—⁓—

Bettina took the stand. Edward Brown asked her the normal questions such as her name and history at Smith Barney. Then he asked her, "In your experience at Smith Barney, especially during the 90s, are you familiar with the kinds of training seminars that the firm offers to brokers for either education or to help advance their careers?" Her answer should have been just "Yes." Then the lawyer would have asked her something like, "Could you explain your understanding of what that training is?"

But, instead of waiting to be asked, Bettina launched into a long and accurate description of the informational and product platform that Smith Barney makes available to its brokers. It was a beautiful presentation. It appeared she had been planning what she was going to say. I just thought it was odd that this is what they brought her to talk about. I never claimed that I was in any way prevented from utilizing the platform that Bettina had just described.

In fact, anyone who can remember me sitting in my cubicle should also remember that I had seven or eight notebooks lineup on my credenza. They were stuffed with information that I had learned or was learning. I am an educated person, and, I used my study skills, to full advantage of the resources Smith Barney made available. I tried to teach myself the business. I labeled my notebooks according to the subject matter contained in them. One was labeled "Economics," another "International," another "Fixed Income," another "Marketing," etc.

Smith Barney bringing Bettina to testify was another shockingly ridiculous moment.

When I understood what Smith Barney was trying to accomplish by having Bettina get on the stand and describe the corporate research and educational platform, I pulled out my business card and handed it to Maxwell. My card showed my Financial Consultant title and my designations, which indicated the extra education I had obtained.

When it was Maxwell's turn to cross-examine Bettina he approached the witness chair and handed her my business card. "Ms. Crawford, could you read this card please?"

Bettina looked confused. "But," she gasped, "she has more than…" and she stopped herself mid-sentence. I believe she was about to say "she has more (training designation) than me."

It was obvious from my designations that I had taken advantage of the educational programs Smith Barney had to offer. By that time in 2002, I was seventh in the branch; in terms of the "managed money" business I did, which is a specialized type of private money management. A couple of those people above me were in partnerships with very big brokers, which I'm sure put them above me in rank. I was all alone, and I still ranked seventh. If we had all been ranked individually, I probably would have been ranked fifth in the branch.

Bettina was dismissed. "Thank you for coming," Chairperson Clarke said.

Bettina is the only colleague in whom I was truly disappointed and by whom I was somewhat hurt because of the way she radically changed her behavior towards me shortly before the trial and continued treating me differently until the day I quit. She is an older woman whom I had liked and respected, but she showed me how willing she was to engage in petty and pathetically catty behavior by gossiping with our mutual sales assistant and others in the branch. I lost respect for her. We never spoke again; after the trial, it was if she were trying to make a show of not talking to me. It was childish and I almost felt sorry for her. I think she was ashamed of her behavior but didn't have the courage to own-up to it. I later heard that she felt Smith Barney's lawyers had misled her.

The next witness was a female broker I didn't really know. She came to our office as part of the two-branch merger, towards the end of 1998, and she worked on a different floor. She described the other firms she had worked for and how she had built her business. Her testimony had no bearing on my situation except that she testified that she had already been a successful broker when she found herself under Lyndsey's management. I believe that her testimony was helpful to me. It showed that Lyndsey didn't hire her or cultivate her career to success, as was the case with every woman they brought to testify from the Beverly Hills branch. The information she provided was irrelevant to my case; and Smith Barney should not have brought her. "Thank you very much," I thought. Next.

The third witness of the day was my compliance manager, Pete. They went through the usual name and history questions. Pete had only positive things to say about me personally. Edward Brown questioned Pete about how a branch functions in terms of distribution of accounts to remaining brokers when a broker leaves the firm; they talked about the franchise protection program, a retirement program Smith Barney has for retiring brokers and about office assignments. They asked his opinion of Lyndsey (he called Lyndsey a tough guy) and inquired about the gross commission production of the branch.

When Maxwell cross-examined him, he gave testimony that I believe also helped my case. Pete testified that he wasn't involved in the ultimate distribution of accounts; he said that the "last call was Lyndsey's" and that he wasn't involved with or aware of specific criteria required to get a private office. He acknowledged that, in the end, these decisions were up to Lyndsey's discretion. In my mind, his testimony clarified the idea that Lyndsey did have the opportunity to discriminate against me in the way I claimed.

Pete also was the one who said all those kind things about me that I have already mentioned, namely that I was "always positive" and "very professional"; that he "always enjoyed working with me"; and that I "really cared about her clients and my interaction with her always displayed that; it's rare that you get that consistency." Pete was the only manager who gave completely honest testimony.

"Thank you," I thought again. After the trial, Pete continued being his nice, professional self with me, and I really appreciated that.

Smith Barney then called their next witnesses, two more female brokers from Beverly Hills. Both testified that they were already successful brokers when they came to work for Lyndsey, but the rest of their testimonies were irrelevant to my case.

"Wow, more helpful testimony, thank you very much," I thought. Next witness."

Smith Barney's last witness of the third day was Karen Bean, the assistant to both my sales managers in the downtown office, David Greenblatt and Chad Porter. She described her job, what the office was like, her experiences working there, and her opinions about the office. Her testimony was short; and I don't think any of it helped Smith Barney's defense. Again, in my opinion, what she said did help me a little bit, because she corroborated that it was a rowdy place where profane language was normal. She also confirmed that the bull pen was populated with brokers in their twenties, thirties, and forties, corroborating my testimony and contradicting Carol Farmer's.

—⁂—

The next morning we started the fourth day of the trial. Gigi Jenkins was the first witness Smith Barney called. Gigi was a much more important witness than the other women because she was in a management position; however, I hadn't realized how important she was while I worked in the downtown Los Angeles branch. In fact, I wondered why they would bring her in to testify. She was the operations manager downtown, but for the two-and-a-half years I worked there, I had only interacted with her a handful of times. It had been nine years since we'd seen each other; I wasn't sure I would even recognize her.

I was surprised when she walked in the room. "Is that Gigi?" I asked myself. "No, it's somebody else. Maybe this person works for Smith

Barney's legal team and is coming in late for some reason. Or, maybe she works for the hotel and is delivering a message or something." All those thoughts took place in a split second, followed by: "Oh my god, it is her. She looks great, much better than when I worked with her. What did she do to herself? She must have had work done."

Gigi sat in the witness chair and her testimony began. When asked her position she announced her reply as if she were the commander and chief. "Operations Manager, a Senior Vice President, and second in command of the branch, I was in charge of everything, except direct sales initiatives," she boasted.

"Everything except direct sales initiatives?" I thought. "Direct sales initiatives are the whole business; we are a brokerage firm. We sell financial investments, stocks, and bonds, remember?"

Gigi may have been "second in command," but I know that in Beverly Hills, the compliance manager and the operations manager were equal. They both reported to Lyndsey directly, and they both were "second in command." When Lyndsey was out of the office, somebody had to be in charge. Both downtown and in Beverly Hills, I usually went to the compliance manager for signatures or questions. Downtown, the compliance manager was Fritz, the Rottweiller. He was a very funny man who always made me laugh. He was more pleasant to deal with than Gigi. I think all of the brokers depended on him much more than on her. Gigi handled the sales assistants mostly, or so it appeared to me.

It also seemed that, throughout her testimony, she was inflating herself to appear to do more than she really did. When women were allowed into the formerly all-male domain of Wall Street, they were given support positions such as operations or operations manager. Gigi was a help-mate, just like most the other women. Thank goodness she didn't fool the panel, as it was soon revealed.

I felt strongly that Gigi had been coached. I have a very good memory, but I barely remembered her. She would make incredible claims about remembering me during her testimony.

Early in his questioning, Edward asked Gigi to describe the layout of the eighth floor of the downtown branch. Smith Barney continued to push the idea that the area where the cubicles were located was populated with very young, part-time guys, some of whom were not even college students; therefore, they insinuated, neither the men nor Smith Barney were responsible for their behavior. The sales managers' assistant Karen Bean had already relieved the room of the delusion that the bull pen was only comprised of twenty-year-olds.[12] Again, she had testified that brokers in their twenties, thirties, and forties sat in the bull pen.

Then Gigi told the real doozy. Although she wasn't specific as to the hours she spent in the bull pen, she tried to make it sound as if she spent most of her day there! An operations manager? I don't think so. I'm guessing that this point was important in her mind because she thought she was going to refute all the stuff I claimed had happened. She claimed she knew what was going on in the bull pen because she spent all day there. Right. What a laugh! But the joke was going to be on her.

The stuff I claimed was in Smith Barney's own notes. It was uncontroverted evidence. She wouldn't have known any of that, because she was just the ops manager. It was serious business back in 1993, so I'm sure the guys didn't really involve her. I'm sure they saw to it that she stuck with her operations duties.

Edward Brown proceeded to ask her a bunch of other questions about whether she had seen or heard the things that I had reported to HR. I found it unbelievable that Edward would ask her if she saw any strippers in the office, because Chad, the sales manager, had already substantiated that fact. But Edward did ask Gigi.

She claimed that not only did she not see any of those things, but she made a point of telling the panel that she also didn't believe those things could have happened, because "she would have known." She testified that

---

[12] Besides, even twenty-year-olds are responsible for their own behavior.

she remembered some of the brokers and not others, but she remembered one "distinct" conversation she had with me. She said she remembered specifically that I told her that I was having a "hard time succeeding."

First, all brokers have a hard time "succeeding" in their first year of the business. Second, I don't remember that conversation or comment. It is possible that we spoke; many people don't remember comments they made years ago in passing, and I could have forgotten. However, I don't believe her, because I almost never went to Gigi for anything. I interacted with her less than with any other manager except the other assistant manager on the ninth floor.

Gigi smoked like a chimney, back when smoking was still allowed in the private offices in California. The amount she smoked grossed me out, and I tried to stay away from her as much as I could. I used to hold my breath when I passed her office if the door was open. I just don't believe I would have gone to her for anything, and especially not to talk about my feelings or about building my business. An operations manager has nothing to do with sales. She probably couldn't sell ice water in the Sahara.

But, Gigi wasn't finished; there was more spin to come. With regards to Chad, she kept mentioning the "rookie group," almost insinuating that new recruits were his only responsibility— as if the sales manager is not the sales manager for the whole office. She claimed that she interacted with Chad a lot because he was responsible for the "rookie group" and that there was a lot of work involving this "rookie group," "because they were learning, and required correction or maybe some, you know, additional training."

She went on to explain, "When you open an account for somebody, there are certain questions you are supposed to ask. You know, it's a learning process. People miss the boat a lot. The forms aren't filled out properly, and you have to go back, educate, say you need the total net worth, did you talk to them about their investment objectives, that kind of thing. So it's almost like having two parents, a Mom and a Dad, you know? We talked about how we are raising the kids."

"Wait a minute— did she just say '"Mom and Dad?"' I asked myself. I couldn't decide if I wanted to throw up or laugh out loud. She was trying to make it seem as if those of us in the bull pen were so green we didn't know how to open accounts. Remember, in the dialer program, one had to open thirty accounts for another broker before being allowed to go out on his or her own. Even a seasoned broker might have to ask a question every once in a while if an unusual type of trust was set up or some other type of unusual scenario occurred. Even so, as I said, I went to Fritz the Rottweiler when I needed a signature or had a question. Her answer about "Mom and Dad and raising kids" was downright silly. She should have been embarrassed to say it.

Ed Brown continued his questioning, "Did there come a point when you learned that Ms. Keyes had lodged a complaint in the branch of sexual harassment?… At the time as operations manager, do you recall what your reaction was to learning that Ms. Keyes had filed a complaint of harassment?"

"I was stunned at the time," Gigi answered. "I thought it was manipulative, because there was someone that I knew was having difficulty performing, was coached and given warning… Here was someone I knew, I had talked to, who said she was having trouble performing, who was given a written performance memo, I believe, about steps that needed to be taken to improve her performance, and it just—the timing was, in my opinion, rather quick. And I remember thinking, 'so that's how you work it.'"

Uh-oh, there was that performance review thing again and "in writing" this time, no less. Gigi didn't know that no such document had ever been produced. Nobody had testified that there had been a performance review and no notes were ever found that mentioned a performance review. There was no evidence of a performance review because I never had a performance review downtown. This was one of Smith Barney's themes. Gigi was making it up, and I believed someone must have directed her toward her "stories."

The panel was interested in her and started asking her questions directly. First, they wanted to know how she was paid. Did she financially participate in the sales initiatives like a broker or a branch manager, or was she on salary? She was on salary and got a bonus at the end of the year at the branch manager's discretion, just as I have described earlier. They also wanted her to explain again how she interacted with brokers.

Gigi answered, "I might interact with a broker, you know, if a client's spouse has passed away." Then she assumed the character of a broker asking questions: "What do I do now, what kind of paperwork do I need? What can I do with the assets or not do with the assets? Can I take orders from the spouse? Is that permissible? So and so just had a trust drafted. Will you sit down with me and the client and talk about it and help me open the account? The client is complaining. They say they didn't authorize this trade; I talked to them, Gigi , and they told me they wanted to buy this stock. Can you help?"

In my fourteen years in the business, I never once had an operations manager sit down with one of my clients. I also never saw or heard that anybody I know ever sat down with an operations manager and a client. I am not saying that it couldn't happen; I am saying that it is highly unusual, and I never saw it. I believe she was inflating her role and position in the branch. But that wasn't the end of it. The panel asked her how she interacted with brokers in terms of training.

"That was very much everyday, because when you are new, you are not sure which forms to use; you are not sure how to fill them out. You write—back at that time we were still writing physical order tickets to buy and sell securities or other investments, as opposed to typing them on them computer screen— and even filling out a ticket can be complicated to someone who doesn't have much experience doing that. So there were a lot of opportunities to correct and coach. In terms of formal training, I believe David Greenblatt— but I think Chad, too— had fairly informal get-togethers with the new brokers. He might have a topic to talk about and I might have a topic to talk about. An example would be suitability, you know, 'What is suitability? How does suitability help you make investment recommendations for the customer?' I can't really think of anything else off the top of my head."

She was trying to say that she helped conduct sales meetings. At some point in Beverly Hills, our operations manager was regularly given a few minutes during our branch meetings if a change was made in operational procedure that everyone needed to know about. A branch meeting is different than a sales meeting. The sales managers often held sales meetings for brokers building their business, but I don't ever remember her being there. If she ever was there, it was rare and only for a few minutes. Again, she was trying to sound more involved than she really was.

Apparently Maxwell also thought Gigi sounded coached. He began his cross-examination by quizzing her about any and all people she had spoken to about me before her testimony. Then he said, "Ms. Jenkins, you mentioned that you believe that Ms. Keyes had been given a written performance memo. Did you ever see that memo?"

"No, I did not," she answered. Then, he got her to admit that she didn't remember ever having a conversation with anybody who told her there had been a performance review, and that nobody had discussed a written performance memo with her.

Maxwell's questioning prompted the panel to, again, ask her more questions directly. "Where was your office?" Chairperson Clarke asked her. "It wasn't in the bull pen, I take it?"

"No," Gigi answered, "my office was to the right of the elevator bank and the bull pen was to the left of the elevator."

"You had an actual office though, right?" Chairwomen Clarke tried to clarify. The Chairwomen wasn't sure if Gigi even had an office since Gigi was pretending she was always in the bull pen! Then another panelist jumped in asking questions about whether she could see the bull pen from her office and if she kept her door open routinely.

The panel was unwittingly setting Gigi up for Maxwell to nail her with her own testimony. I was, again, furiously writing notes to Maxwell, just as I had during Aaron Weisswasser's and Lyndsey's testimonies.

Gigi hadn't looked at me when she had first walked into the arbitration room. She had ignored me as if I didn't exist, in the same way Aaron had. But now that she could see I was furiously writing notes to Maxwell, and I was out to bust her, she finally looked at me. I stared right back at her. I believed she was another liar, and I was going to show everybody in that room that she was.

Because the panel had asked more questions, Maxwell got to cross-examine her again. The dialogue between them went like this.

Maxwell: Just in terms of what you could hear— if the door was closed, you couldn't hear anything going on in the bull pen. Is that right?

A. Correct.

Q. Now, I think you said when Mr. Brown was asking you questions that you are sure that if there had been a stripper in the office you would have heard about it. Is that correct?

A. That's correct.

Q. You are sure about that?

A. As sure—yeah.

Q. So, if Mr. Porter were to say there was a stripper in the office that would surprise you— is that right?

A. Sure it would.

Q. Would you think that he would lie about that?

A. Would I think Mr. Porter would lie?

Q. Yes.

A. No.

Q. So, if Mr. Porter were to say there was a stripper in the office, and you were to say that you were sure there was no stripper in the office, maybe you just didn't hear or see that. Is that right?

It seemed that Smith Barney's lawyer couldn't stand to see her exposed, so he cleverly tipped Gigi off that there had been strippers in the office. "Objection" shouted Ed Brown. "It sort of mischaracterizes what her testimony was. She said she didn't know about it. Mr. Porter told Ms. Farmer that he knew about it." How can something "sort of mischaracterize testimony"? It didn't mischaracterize her testimony, but his objection did tip Gigi off and give her time to think.

"I'm not sure what your objection is," Chairperson Clarke said to Ed.

"I'll withdraw it," he answered. Gigi then asked Maxwell to repeat the question.

Maxwell: If Mr. Porter said there was a stripper in the office, and you are sure that there wasn't, perhaps there was a stripper and you just didn't see or hear it?

A. Perhaps if I didn't see or hear it, I wasn't there. (even though she insisted she would have heard about it.) I mean, that's about the only thing I could tell you because that would be a very hard thing to miss in the office.

Q. But you wouldn't say Mr. Porter was wrong about that if that's what he said, would you?

A. Well, as I said, if I wasn't there, I wouldn't have seen it. But, no, I don't think Mr. Porter would lie.

Q. Not about that?

A. I don't think Mr. Porter would lie.

Maybe Chad wouldn't lie, but she sure would I thought to myself. Maxwell asked her to explain where her office was in relation to the bull pen. She was trying to make it seem that there wasn't much between her office and the bull pen and that it was so close she knew everything that was going on. I started to draw a picture for Maxwell to show him that she was full of it. Between her office and the bull pen, there was the operations area, a solid wall, the bathrooms, and, on the other side of that wall, the bull pen.

Maxwell asked Gigi to draw a picture of the office. She did, and it was now very clear that she had been trying to buffalo the panel. Busted! Her drawing of the office layout was entered into the record as Exhibit 47.

Edward knew Gigi looked bad. He made an effort to salvage her credibility on redirect:

Q. Ms. Jenkins, earlier in my questioning, you made reference to the fact you got out of your office and walked around. How often during the day would you find yourself in the bull pen area?

A. "All day."

Once again, she made it sound as if she was never in her office. In reality operations managers spend most of their time in their offices. She was full of it. Operations, when she needed to go there, was four feet from her office, and both operations and her office were located on the other side of that solid wall and the bathrooms that separated them from the bull-pen side of the office.

Since Edward had re-directed Maxwell got to cross-examine her again. He went in for the kill.

Q. And what did you use your office for?

A. "Well gosh. Someone calls you, and you need to talk to them on the phone. So I used my office for phone calls. I used my office to meet with people, performance reviews[13], client meetings. I had a few of those here and there. The first hour of the day—you know, the first thing you do when you get in, there are things you have to approve immediately, that are actually on the computer, so you take care of that. I can't tell you what else, really."

Q. Aside from approving things on your computer what else did you do with the computer?

A. Well, you would—you could look up a customer account, stock research. Everybody used the computer. That was the business. And someone would say, "I don't know how to read my screen." So you go over there and say, "Show me what you are looking at" and they would call

---

[13] She was responsible for sales assistants' performance reviews, not those of the broker's.

it up and you would work through it with them. You know, it could be anything. Or "How do I find this, Gigi'" or "Where is that, Gigi ?"

Q. So, when you say everyone used the computer, you used your computer on a regular basis; is that right?

A. Sure.

Q. And you worked on the phone a lot, too, didn't you?

A. I was always on the phone.

Q. And that was in your office?

A. That was anywhere. I mean if calls came in they would transfer them to where I was.

Gigi also seemed to be aware that she looked bad. It became obvious, through Maxwell's questions, that she spent most of her time in her office, as most operations managers do— not in the bull pen, as she had claimed. She tried to back pedal. "For me to characterize something from nine years ago is a little hard."

She wasn't being asked to characterize anything from nine years ago. She was an ops manager for many years, and at the time of the trial she was the regional manager who oversaw many other ops managers. She knew perfectly well what the job description for an ops manager was, how much time they spent in their offices, and how much time was spent on the phone while in their offices. She made one last attempt to insinuate that she spent most of her time in the bull pen because all those "rookie brokers" needed her so much. Maxwell called her on that as well before he concluded.

"Nothing further," Maxwell said.

At the end of Gigi's testimony, it seemed, from my vantage point, that everybody in the room knew that she was also toast. She hadn't been dismissed or thanked and asked to leave yet, but everybody spontaneously started talking among themselves. Smith Barney's four lawyers started talking with each other, and the members of the panel started talking with each other. Maxwell and I just sat there. I remember looking over at Gigi.

She shrugged her shoulders at nobody in particular, with this look of "Oh well" on her face. She had thought she was going to "stump for the Big Boys." I think she realized that she had failed.

—∞—

The last two witnesses Smith Barney called were Hope Harcourt, one of the five female brokers who worked in the downtown branch when I started and Annie Talbot, the first broker I ever worked for. I believe that both women told the truth as they remembered it, although it seemed to me that they had preconceived notions of what the dispute was all about. It also seemed as if they wanted to help Smith Barney especially Hope.

I had been friends with these two women, as office friends go; why they would want to testify against me, I don't understand. I hadn't shared the negotiation details with Annie or Hope back in 1993 and for good reason. I still believe I made the right decision for myself not to share it. They got to hear Smith Barney's side of the dispute, obviously; they spoke with the lawyers and agreed to testify. But, as I said before, I never bothered with or tried to talk to any of Smith Barney's witnesses. The fact that neither of these two women called to ask me what was going on, just as a friend being asked to get involved after so many years, was a bit of a let-down for me.

The first one called to the witness chair was Hope, who had already worked for the firm for close to twenty years when I had arrived. She had been hired upon graduation from Stanford University by another Stanford alumnus as his sales assistant. The man who hired her was the grandson of one of the original founders of E.F. Hutton, which was one of the predecessor firms of Shearson Lehman by the time I had arrived. When he decided to start cutting back his workload, he made Hope his partner. At first, the commission of the partnership was split 20/80 in his favor, but it slowly changed as the years went by, little by little, to a percentage split in her favor. I don't know if she is the sole broker of that business now, because I haven't talked to her for years. The last time I did speak with her, which I think was in 1995 or 1996, she had well over a half-billion dollars under management. She used to brag that her benefactor was the godfather of one of the Getty kids. She was involved with old California money.

When I was made a broker, I used to go to her to ask questions and to talk about the business. She told me about municipal floaters and other instruments that could be used in place of a money market to hold a client's cash. In the course of that conversation, she showed me her cash or cash equivalent positions separate from her clients' stocks and bonds. Each page of the computer screen showed the cash positions of about nine or ten client accounts at once. These accounts would have $10,000,000; $6,000,000; $2,000,000; $5,000,000 and more in them. She paged through screen after screen after screen. It was unbelievable how much cash her clients had. I was amazed. "Oh," she said, "this is just their cash on hand. They probably all have accounts at Merrill or other brokerage firms as well. This is their lunch money." Hope had very good reasons to be happy with the firm. As Annie had told me, "Hope stepped in shit." In other words, she was fabulously lucky to be in her position. She had it made and was the partner of the grandson of one of the original founders of a predecessor firm. She was untouchable and hardly a regular broker. Hope sat on a different floor than I, separated and protected from the craziness of the branch. She never had to dial for dollars.

Like Gigi, Hope claimed during her testimony that she was "in the loop" and would have known if the events she was being asked about had occurred. However, she did testify that she visited the eighth floor mostly to chat with Annie. That is how I met her. I don't believe Hope was in the loop at all.

In spite of testifying to help Smith Barney, she made several points that actually helped me. During the time I worked with her, she had lots of little stories about the attitudes and behaviors she had to contend with as a woman working in the industry, but they didn't seem to bother her. She talked about it all in a matter-of-fact voice with absolutely no annoyance. I think Hope is about fifteen years older than I. A lot of women her age put up with stuff that would outrage younger women nowadays; they had to. The law and society have definitely changed since the 1970s.

Then again, Hope also had entrée into a crowd of extremely wealthy people. She used to brag that one year her boss/partner gave her a brand new Volvo— I think it was a Christmas gift. Who would bite the proverbial industry hand that fed them? Her boss, I'm sure, was very good to her, and I think he treated her like one of his own children and protected her. He was one of those protective "godfathers" that a few women who gotten in had, as I have mentioned before.

At one point during the cross examination of her testimony, Hope tried to launch into her own little monologue. She was going to try and lecture the panel on how she thought women should just suck it up, be tough, and not be babies by complaining about offensive behavior. Her attitude was part of the old school of thought; "If you want to play with the boys, then there is no complaining about them— or, God forbid, telling on them." Maxwell interrupted her and objected, saying her answer was non-responsive.

"Oh," she gasped surprised because she had been cut off.

Witnesses don't get to use the courtroom to state their personal opinions about the state of sexual harassment in our society. In court, witnesses answer specific questions they are asked. Her personal opinion wasn't the point and didn't matter. Her testimony didn't have much bearing on my case except to show that she'd had a powerful godfather. She was thanked for coming and was dismissed.

—⁂—

Annie was the last witness. While we had worked together in the downtown branch, I believe, she was also out of the loop, so to speak. Remember, Annie was the one who worked from 6:30 a.m. until 1:00

p.m., spending half of that time on the phone with relatives. She was never a hard-core "pitcher" in the Lehman system. Annie, like Hope, came in to the office each morning, did her thing, and was uninvolved with the craziness of the branch. It was obvious that Annie had been coached, but, despite that she didn't remember much. Her testimony was short, and many parts of it inadvertently helped me, as the others' testimonies had.

The panel seemed interested in Annie and asked her questions, just as they had asked Gigi and Hope. Like the other witnesses she didn't seem to know what the lawsuit was about. Smith Barney had been grasping at straws from the very beginning, and I think they misled all the women they asked to testify against me. If Annie had talked to me before the trial, as she had talked to Smith Barney lawyers, maybe she wouldn't have bothered testifying. But, on the other hand, Smith Barney, her employer, had asked her do something for them, so I'm not sure about that. I wish her well. I'm not upset with her at all. Once everybody was satisfied, Annie was thanked for coming and dismissed. Then the proceedings broke for lunch.

—⚊—

This was the second half of the last day of the trial, and it was the long stretch. Once everybody was back in the room, closing arguments started. Maxwell went first:

"Madam Chair and members of the panel, I want to begin by thanking you for your attention and courtesy throughout this process. The way I'd like to approach this is to go through the issues that we have presented to the panel, by way of the hearing complaint, and then to talk about the evidence that we think substantiates that complaint… Very much of what I said we would be able to prove, I believe, we have proved.

"There was a question at the beginning of this case as to what was at issue, whether it was harassment or retaliation or whether it was just about Lyndsey Shanahan. If you look at the hearing complaint, which frames the issues, it specifically alleges both harassment and discrimination in the L.A. office—indeed, harassment is a form of discrimination—and retaliation in the handling of the complaint and in the transfer to the Beverly Hills office, and it alleges both discrimination and retaliation in the Beverly Hills office.

"The legal theories that are before you are both federal and state law theories. There is Title Seven, which prohibits discrimination, harassment, and retaliation. There is the Federal Equal Pay Act and there is ERISA, which prohibits discrimination from benefits programs, but, in essence, they are all very much the same. We need to show discrimination, harassment, and retaliation. And then the second piece to all this is what is the nature of the damages that were caused by the conduct of Smith Barney, and these include economic damages, damages for emotional distress, and her claim for exemplary damages. As I talk about the evidence in this case, I want to emphasize that most of the evidence is either undisputed or uncontroverted.

"It is fact that there was a pervasive atmosphere of hostile and sexually charged behaviors and conduct in the Los Angeles office. Carol Farmer, who was in charge of Human Resources, testified that, not only was it noisy, but that the language was out of control and what she describes as "young people" in that office had a different culture. She also said that she believed it was so severe that she didn't believe she could change it in a short period of time, and she said that it would take— and it did take her— more than a year to affect the kinds of changes that she thought appropriate. It couldn't be more persuasive then the opinion of a Senior Human Resources official…

"There is a very old principle; it doesn't take any kind of modern law— the principle of evidence— if the party has control of the witness and would ordinarily bring that person and if they fail to do so, the failure to bring that evidence should be construed against them and there is an inference that ought to be drawn from that…

"Another thing that was absolutely undisputed— and, in fact admitted— was that there was no investigation. The only thing that Carol Farmer did was to talk to Chad Porter and James Ayala. She reported orally the charges to Aaron Weisswasser. There were no recommendations made about how to fix things. There were no recommendations about suggested findings. There was no corrective action taken. There was no discipline imposed on anyone, and no one was even criticized or counseled. That's their own witness.

"Now, the hearing brief that was submitted actually goes through what's required. Once an employer knows, or should know, about harassment, it has to take immediate and appropriate corrective action, and that action has to be reasonably calculated to end the harassment. The employer is supposed to do a complete investigation. It is not simply enough to take corrective action; disciplinary action is required. None of those things happened, yet all of that is admitted.

"And, having not talked to witnesses in 1993, Smith Barney comes in today and has failed to bring in witnesses whom they would ordinarily be expected to bring to controvert it. The only conclusion that is available to this panel, with all due respect, is that the harassment occurred exactly as Tameron Keyes described it to the extent that it was not controverted. Smith Barney failed to do anything about it, and in fact then chose to play hardball with Tameron Keyes.

"These handwritten notes from Smith Barney, and that is all they are, don't even approach an investigation… That is deliberate indifference, not only to Ms. Keyes' situation, but to the situation of everyone who worked in that office. The case law is very clear that the purpose of an investigation— and the purpose of requiring corrective action and discipline—is not simply for the person who complains. The purpose is partly for the person who complained, but it is also to make sure the conduct comes to an end for every employee's benefit. It has a social function. It's a basic policy that the work place not be like this…

"Carol Farmer says she told Aaron Weisswasser everything that was going on. She gave him a full report so he would know everything. Regional Director, one of the highest executives in the company— but he doesn't remember.

"So we have evidence that the problem is severe, it was pervasive, that they failed to correct it, and we have uncontroverted evidence that it was directed at Tameron Keyes. Then Carol told us, "Well, the culture between Smith Barney and Shearson Lehman was different and would take a while to change." So I asked questions and we found out, and want to emphasize, the branch manager downtown, James Ayala, was a Shearson guy. The branch manager in Beverly Hills was a Shearson guy. The Regional director Aaron Weisswasser, was Shearson guy. The only person that's a little bit different is the Human Resources person they sent out. Carol Farmer was from Smith Barney, but she was told by the people in charge— the Shearson guys— that Tameron was the problem. And they remained in charge and were not disciplined.

"There is also uncontroverted evidence of retaliation... What an employer is required to do when confronted with a harassing environment is come up with a solution that doesn't penalize the person who complains about it. But they say, "She has to take that or resign." We have in Exhibit 22 Mr. Ayala's handwriting, and it says: 'Tameron will be told: She cannot move to another office. She is to move to the ninth floor or tender her resignation.'

"That's all on October 15, 1993, after a conversation with Rebecca Eaton, who is the head HR person in New York. So when they say it was Shearson's culture, apparently Rebecca Eaton is okaying this kind of response. Carol Farmer says that when Rebecca Eaton passed it off to her an investigation hadn't been done. Rebecca was asking Carol to do the investigation, just taking down her scratchy notes. The scratchy notes, as she characterized them, documented James Ayala's statement, "We are going to tell her take it or leave it. She can resign if she doesn't like it," and

Rebecca Eaton approves of that.

"That tells you something about the policies and practices of the entire company. So we have got, "Take it or leave it; tender your resignation; play hardball with Tameron; she is to move on." That's not trying to fix a problem. That's trying to get rid of the problem. As far as they're concerned the problem is the person who complained; it is not what is going on in the office.

"So what happens when she winds up in Beverly Hills? Pete Kelly testified that she sat in a cubicle in Beverly Hills for five full years, the only broker who sat in a cubicle for five years, and that she sat there when offices were open. He said it was based on production, so I asked him, "What was the magic number?" (In other words, what number does a broker have to reach before they are given an office?) He said, "There was no magic number; it was up to Lyndsey's discretion."

"She wasn't permitted to partner. Lyndsey Shanahan says he doesn't remember telling her she couldn't partner or that she had to call him first, but Tameron Keyes said, "I spoke to Georges; I made a proposal to him, and, shortly thereafter, he partnered with Harold, who wasn't even a broker; he was a trainee, somebody that was doing cold calling." None of that is denied. They didn't bring in Georges to testify… The fact is, there is uncontroverted testimony that Tameron Keyes proposed a deal to him and a few weeks later, somebody who was far less qualified than she wound up with that deal.

"We have had lots of testimony from all the witnesses that Salomon Smith Barney brought to you that says having a partner is one of the key ways for someone to develop business, to grow as a broker, and to be successful. We saw these exceptional women at Smith Barney who have succeeded. Almost every one of them relied on relationships with other people in order to get their business jump-started. Lyndsey Shanahan admitted that partnering was valuable to junior brokers. He admitted that, for everyone else, the permission to partner was freely given. That he didn't stand in the way of people doing that— but when Tameron Keyes tried to do it someone else wound up with the partnership...

"Then there was testimony from Ms. Keyes that accounts were assigned to her when people left, and Pete Kelly came in and said, "Yes, there were." When Miller, Gasparian, and Sherr left, Pete told us Tameron Keyes got part of that book of business. I asked him when that was? Was that before or after Mr. Shanahan retired? He said it was after Mr. Shanahan retired.

"Beyond that, for Salomon Smith Barney to claim that she was assigned accounts brings to bear the best evidence rule. There is evidence that they have records of who got which accounts, of the grosses of the brokers who got them, and of the time they got them. If their argument is, and it was, that getting an account depends on, among other things, how well a broker is doing, then they should have brought that documentary evidence to us. This is evidence that is under their control— but they failed to do that. As a matter of fact, we asked for this evidence in discovery, but Smith Barney refused to produce it.

"The way Ms. Keyes was treated in Beverly Hills is not only unfair and retaliatory, but it's consistent with the class-wide evidence. I'd like to talk a little bit about the class-wide evidence. But, before I do that, I'm going to provide to the panel a copy of the case called International Brotherhood of Teamsters versus the United States. It's a Supreme Court case dealing with pattern and practice evidence and its use in individual determinations among other things.

"The site for it is 431 U.S. 324, but what the Teamsters case says is that if a pattern and practice is established— we are going to ask this panel to rule as to whether a pattern and practice is established— it provides an additional way of proving individual discrimination. In addition to all the direct evidence we have of individual discrimination, if there is a pattern and practice that is established factually, then the burden shifts to the employer to explain why Tameron Keyes was subject to those disparities.

"It's not enough for Smith Barney to say, "Well, we treated Tameron Keyes differently because she didn't produce as much." They have to explain why she didn't produce as much, and they have utterly failed to do that. They offered no evidence on that subject. The class wide evidence is quite striking[14]. ...This is a plantation system with guys on top and women on the bottom!

"The economic damages are, I will say again, also undisputed. The evidence is before you, and it's your determination as to what opportunities she was deprived of, because those are the damages she suffered. She was deprived of the opportunity. Smith Barney doesn't get to speculate, "Well, she would not have done all that well, even if she'd had the opportunity."

"The opportunity is the opportunity to succeed. We know what these opportunities are as they are provided to men. They are the opportunities to partner, the early provision of leads, and accounts from departing brokers so that you have a base on which to build, which provides a cumulative advantage. We heard the testimony that this is how it works; success begets success. When you deprive someone of that success at an early point in his or her career, it's going to have long-term results.

"The other piece we have is that, if you look at Tameron Keyes' performance over the last few years, she has been moving up steadily once the overt retaliation ended, when Mr. Shanahan was gone... In addition, Dr. Lane's report is unchallenged. They didn't challenge her expertise, and they didn't even challenge the time it would take for Tameron to catch up... Smith Barney has a very complicated compensation scheme, and I think that the calculation was a complicated one. It was helpful to me and I suspect it's going to be helpful to you and I commend it to you; Exhibit

---

[14]   I can't tell the reader what the class-wide evidence contained even if it was second hand information relayed to me by Maxwell because I signed a confidentiality agreement regarding the contents of those reports. For a general description, see *The Boom Boom Room : Women VS Wall Street* by Susan Antilla p 285 But, if Smith Barney was truly sincere about changing its culture and not discriminating against women, they would release that information. In fact, I think they would conduct that kind of research on themselves periodically and show the whole world, if they had nothing to hide.

43 is the second quintile. That's the one we believe you should use, and that is her damages.[15]

"I want to address exemplary damages… Exemplary damages are damages that are designed to make sure that this kind of behavior doesn't happen again. It's both punishment of the individual wrong-doers at Smith Barney, and it is a warning. It is intended to be enough of a financial hit so that the company won't keep doing this kind of thing. Now, do they need that? They certainly do. To this day, the testimony was that they never apologized to Tameron Keyes. They never concluded their investigation. They never reached a resolution of these things. Now, I submit to you that their regional director Mr. Weisswasser came before you and was not truthful at his deposition, and I think the reason that they did not bring Mr. Ayala and Mr. Porter and the other witnesses within their control is that…

At this point, Smith Barney's lawyer Edward Brown butted in and called out," I'm going to object to that! He knows Mr. Ayala and Mr. Porter have not worked for this company for years. I'm going to object to that. We have had motion practice on this very issue, and I'm going to object to the suggestion that they are under our control because they are not, and he knows it. He knows where they live."

As I have already relayed, when I found out that James Ayala wasn't going to be called I got angry because Maxwell had had conversations with Smith Barney without informing me and then had accepted their ridiculous excuses. Once I found out, I got James' home and work addresses in three minutes. I could have easily found Chad. Maxwell must have gone back to Smith Barney and the panel after my confrontation with him. But it was too late; Smith Barney had objected, and the panel wouldn't allow us to go back and depose James.

---

[15] Maxwell and I had agreed that we would ask for the first quintile, the logic being that I had been a high achiever before I started working for Smith Barney; therefore, it was reasonable to assume, that had I not been discriminated and retaliated against, I would have been a high achiever at Smith Barney, but he surprised me during the trial and asked for second quintile, the top 40%.

Maxwell answered back to Edward's objection. "They are available to Smith Barney. They are people who worked for them. They are people they would ordinarily call if they were going to give favorable testimony, and it's perfectly reasonable to conclude that they know that Mr. Weisswasser is lying. That Mr. Weisswasser's testimony on its face is incredible!"

Maxwell concluded his closing arguments. "Punitive damages are appropriate. It is certainly appropriate, in a case like this, to award treble damages as punitive damages, and that's what we urge you to do. There was harassment; it was severe and pervasive. And there was discrimination. Ms. Keyes was subjected to production standards in the first office that weren't imposed on anyone else. Ms. Keyes testified about all the people who weren't making $10,000 a month. All of those people's names and all of those records exist, but nobody from Smith Barney came forward and said, "Oh yes, they were" or, "Oh yes, those people were subjected to the same kind of performance review.' Clear evidence of discrimination at the time harassment was going on is uncontroverted, and there is clear evidence of retaliation... Thank you.

Ed Brown was next. I won't repeat his closing statements because, again, they were boring, full of excuses, ineloquent, and nonsensical. One statement he made was, "Mr. Prague, as I expected, spent a great deal of time talking about Carol Farmer. The issue here, of course, is not whether or not Carol Farmer did a good investigation."

"What is he talking about?" I screamed inside. "Of course it is an issue, a key issue."

His closing arguments were full of statements like that and just don't warrant repeating.

Plaintiffs get the first word and the last, so Maxwell got another rebuttal:

"Members of the panel, Madam Chair ...Tameron Keyes testified that she checked to see how many men were in a similar position and discovered that there were many brokers making less than $10,000 a month gross and that nobody else was subjected to such a standard. This is one of the things she, in fact, conveyed to management when she complained to Carol Farmer and Rebecca Eaton. It's in their notes, and nothing was done to respond to that. This is also a clear act of direct discrimination, not environmental harassment— and, as Ms. Farmer actually testified, that she never checked to find out. Smith Barney failed to provide any evidence whatsoever that men were treated similarly or to controvert the very lengthy list of names that Ms. Keyes presented. This particular action is uncontroverted direct harassment that took place during the period of time that's within the statute of limitations.

"The other piece I was going to mention, and good thing Mr. Brown said I forgot to mention it. The hissing incident[16] is an interesting thing, not just because it occurred, but because it makes it very clear that management was on notice that this kind of behavior was occurring. The notion that it was corrected consists of Carol Farmer writing a note. There is not one indication of what was done to take care of it, and that's very important in terms of the continuing violation issue. Continuing violation is clearly established, because Ms. Keyes testified it was behavior that occurred on an ongoing basis. It happened almost daily in some form or another. There was a series of events that management knew of or should have known of or that actually occurred in the offices of management, and no one contradicted these events. That is a continuing violation of harassing environment.

"First he says (meaning Edward Brown), "Well, there is a statue of limitations that only goes back to May," and he mentions continuing violations, but he doesn't give the panel any indication of how that works. If there is a pattern of behavior that goes on continually and is known to management, the law is that you don't have to complain every single time,

---

[16] This is the incident I have already related when somebody's wife or girlfriend had walked in and the office had exploded in whistling. I didn't mention it during that first phone call to HR but Chad had brought it up when Carol talked to him, and it was documented in Smith Barney's notes.

as long as the last act occurs within the limitation period. Clearly, there were allegations of several acts that occurred after May of '93. It's clear that the situation existed for a long time. Carol Farmer said, 'When I got there, I could see that this was a problem, in terms of the atmosphere in the office, and that it had been there a long time.' So, it's clear from their own admission that this is a problem, that it is a continuing violation

"Then counsel says, 'Well, it's not pervasive or severe,' and he says, 'You know, there are cases that say that just swearing isn't enough to create an environmental harassment claim.' We agree, but the cases also say that while such conduct alone is not harassing, it can— if part of a pattern, if it is part of other conduct— contribute to a harassing environment. And they are very clear on that. So it's not proper to argue, as counsel has said, that we will take each particular act, and it's not enough under the law that this particular act isn't enough and so there is no harassment.

"The standard is actually two-fold. It has to be objectively harassing and subjectively interfere with the person's ability to work. Subjectively is determined by what a reasonable person in the position of the claimant would feel. Ms. Keyes testified she couldn't work. That when people put prostitutes on the speaker-phone engaging in sex talk, she couldn't make her cold calls. She had to stop. That's not even subjective. That's objective evidence that the harassment was such that it interfered with her ability to work.

"Then counsel says, 'Why would Lyndsey Shanahan want to interfere with her success? That doesn't make sense. He makes money if she makes money.' The answer is very simple; discrimination and retaliation are not economically rational behaviors. They are irrational behaviors. It hurts the company and it hurts our country when discrimination occurs because discrimination and retaliation, by their very natures, are conducts that are not economically sensible, in either a micro or macro sense. It's bad for Lyndsey Shanahan if he does it, it's bad for Smith Barney if he does it, and it's bad for all of us if that occurs— but that doesn't explain it away.

"What you have to look at is the difference in the way Tameron Keyes was treated. And they did not bring in one woman who started with Lyndsey Shanahan and succeeded, because not one woman started with Lyndsey Shanahan and succeeded. Lyndsey Shanahan said, 'A lot of women have done well under my agency,' and he listed them. I asked him on cross-examination to tell me where they started or whom they were associated with. Not one woman has succeeded under Lyndsey Shanahan, if she started with Lyndsey Shanahan. The people who succeeded with Lyndsey Shanahan were the women he hired because they came with somebody else or with their own book of business or because they were merged into his office.

"Then counsel said that the 'expert reports have nothing to do with Tameron Keyes.' I think that is one of the strangest things I have ever heard. If there is a pattern and practice of discriminating, the Teamsters case clearly says it establishes a presumption that the same conduct would apply to individual claimants, and it creates a burden on the employer to justify its conduct. It's not sufficient in this case, since the disparity is in production, to say it's all based on production (this was my exact argument to James Ayala during the second meeting I had with him in 1993!). The class-wide evidence is actually very helpful evidence, because ███████

██

██

██████████████████████ [17]

"Then Smith Barney's argument states, 'When we get to damages there is no evidence of Tameron Keyes' ability to reach the second quintile.' As I pointed out, there is plenty of evidence that, when women are allowed to succeed, they can succeed. Most importantly, there is a history. Since Lyndsey Shanahan left, Tameron Keyes is moving up the ladder quite dramatically, and she is doing it at a time when it's a very difficult market.

---

[17] A portion of this sentence was blacked out in order to comply with a confidentiality agreement that I was required to sign concerning the class-wide reports.

So it's reasonable to think that, in the absence of discrimination, she would have had a successful career at a much earlier stage.

"If Smith Barney contributed to her failure to succeed, or to her delay in succeeding, that's part of her damages; that is not something that is 'too bad,' as Mr. Brown says. If it had just happened normally it would be 'too bad'— but it didn't happen normally. It happened because of a pattern of discrimination, different treatment, and harassing conduct directed toward her. And when she complained— and I think that is the most central thing— the way she was treated was absolutely oppressive. 'Play hardball with her. Take it leave it. Move up stairs or resign. Go to Beverly Hills, that's a good place, and sit in a little cubicle nobody sits in.' Enough said. Thank you."

—⁓—

Maxwell was brilliant. It turned out he knew labor law well and cold, off the top of his head. He could cite and apply case law and bust Smith Barney's lawyers when they tried to apply a case incorrectly. He was a strategist, just as I had felt in the beginning; and that was the reason I had originally hired him. After all the struggles between us he turned out to be the right choice of lawyer after all.

The trial was over. What a relief! I looked over at Terrence. He was holding himself with his arms crossed around his waist and was bending over slightly toward the table as if he were about to throw up. It looked like he knew in his heart, he had lost. There was discussion about the judgment and the order. The panel didn't want to write a long, detailed judgment, because everyone wanted to go home. It was Christmas, and people needed to shop. Also, two of the panelists were assuming positions as active judges after Christmas, as I mentioned before, and needed to have their dockets clear.

Smith Barney had no problem accepting just an order. As the panel and lawyers discussed it, I kept telling Maxwell under my breath, "No, I want some explanation. It's not right. This took years of my life. I want to know why they make the decision they make. I want to know why. I want to know why." I repeated this over and over to Maxwell. Maxwell said something to the panel to that effect, and the panel answered that they would write a short explanation. It was a compromise I could live with. I would be happy as long as they gave me some reason why they made the judgment they were about to make.

Everybody got up and started packing their boxes. Smith Barney's lawyers started going over to the judges to shake their hands and say thank you. I didn't know what to do, so I just stood there. The whole week, I had tried to keep my contact with the panel to a minimum. Normally, claimants and respondents don't interact with judges— but, in this case, we had been in the same room for a whole week, getting coffee and snacks at the same table. I had tried to keep my distance and not talk to them much without being rude. Maxwell said to me, in a low voice, "Go say goodbye to the panelists." I went over to them, shook their hands, and thanked each of them. Elizabeth Cardenas and Edward Brown were there, and I shook hands with them also. Then Maxwell came over and also said goodbye to everyone. Terrence was the last person to come over to the panelists' table. It seemed he didn't want to shake my hand, and I didn't want to shake his either, but I did. Because I had just thanked the panelists, I stupidly let a "thank you" out of my mouth to Terrence.

"What did I thank him for?" I thought to myself. "I shouldn't have said that." I felt more like slapping him.

Maxwell had his boxes of stuff all packed up and secured on his luggage trolley, and we walked out together. He was parked in the building, so he was going downstairs. I had parked in the $5 lot where were I used to park when I worked downtown, so I was about to go upstairs and out on to the street. I stopped before the escalators.

"So how do you think it went?" I asked Maxwell.

"I think it went well," he said.

"But, how do you feel about it? Do you feel good? Do you think we're going to win?" I needled him a little bit. Actually, it was more like pleading for encouragement.

He smiled. "I feel good about it," he said. "But you never know until it's over."

"I'm staying home tomorrow until I know what their verdict is", I told him. "Call me at home if you here any news." The next day was that Friday the 13th.

"I'll be waiting."

XIV

VICTORY

The first person I called after that morning call from Maxwell was my dad. As I have said I wasn't ecstatic. I was happy that I had won, of course; losing would have been unimaginably horrendous. But the best way to describe how I felt would be numb and subdued— angrily subdued, relieved, and grateful. Very calmly, I said, "Dad, I won, 3.2 million dollars."

"Is that right?" he answered with wonderment.

"Yes, and Maxwell wants to take me out to lunch to celebrate. But he has upset me so much, I don't want to go with him."

"Ah, Honey," my dad said, "you have to have lunch with your lawyer."

I did go to lunch with Maxwell. He took me to a nice restaurant in Century City, but I'm not sure he really enjoyed it, either. This lawsuit had been difficult for both of us.

The rest of the weekend was a total blur. I was all alone, and I think I walked around in an anti-climactic fog. I had fought this thing alone, more or less, and there was nobody to celebrate with. The whole ordeal had really hurt me, and I didn't feel like calling people up and saying, "Hey, I won 3 mill. Let's party."

I had insisted that Maxwell issue a press statement a few days before my trial, in an effort to pressure Smith Barney to settle with me. Even though no journalists showed up at the trial, they still called to find out the result of the judgment. The following Monday morning, the news broke on TV. Apparently, it was a story for several days.

The weird comments in the office had mostly stopped, but some people did give me a wide berth, and I knew there was gossip going around. Of course, there would be. I just wanted a normal work life and career, and I was still trying to downplay any negativity that might pop up in the office.

I avoided watching the news and never saw or heard any news reports. I knew I was in the news for a while because a few friends and clients called and told me. One client even videotaped a newscast and mailed it to me, because he knew I hadn't been watching. A handful of journalists called, but I didn't want to talk to them. I figured that, as a Smith Barney employee, I was still bound by the "no talking to the media" policy, and I wasn't going to give Smith Barney cause to fire me for a stupid reason like breaking that policy. I might have gotten away with it, but I badly wanted a normal career life. I didn't want to generate bad feelings from my colleagues or to cause problems.

People mostly reacted to the news positively. Many colleagues told me "Congratulations," or "Good for you." Surprisingly, even my manager at the time—Tim Moynehan, who had tried to block my partnership with Charlotte and who had nixed the one with Mitchell— told me a few days after the stick-up incident, that "I'm glad you won." He had been an executive with the firm in the early '90s and knew exactly what downtown had been like; I remembered him coming to visit in 1991 with a group of executives. He also told me Lyndsey should have been fired years earlier.

Many colleagues who were happy for me didn't say anything right away. One woman sneaked into my office a few days after the news broke and shut my door. She told me she was happy for me but "couldn't be seen talking to me." She told me she completely understood what I had gone through and recounted to me some of her experiences at another firm which had such a profoundly negative and lasting effect on her that she was still afraid— even though she was in a different industry and a totally different environment. I understood her lingering fear, and we had a nice chat.

Preston, a male broker, saw me from way down the hallway. He stretched out his arms as if to say, "Come give me a hug." He wouldn't move; he looked like that statue over looking Rio de Janeiro with his arms outstretched, waiting until I walked all the way down the hall, almost the length of our building, right in front of everyone, so he could give me a big, long hug. "Congratulations darlin', he said. I really needed that support, and it felt so good to have it. I'll never forget him— the one black male broker in the office at that time— for being so kind to me.

Several times, I heard people in the office arguing about me, but most people seemed to defend me. I heard one assistant tell another, who was trying to badmouth me, that everyone should give me the benefit of the doubt because nobody really knew my whole story. She was right, and I appreciated her defense of me.

Even Lyndsey tried to jump on the winning train. Within a few days, Lyndsey was back in our office "visiting" and trying to do more spin control! The man just couldn't stop himself. He was still trying to make himself out to be the good guy, along the same lines as saying that he had been "my savior" back in 1998. He walked around the office and told people that I *deserved to get something*! Why would he say that? He knew all along what had happened in the downtown branch, and he had been the main enforcer of the retaliation for me telling on the boys. Now he was trying to minimize his participation by appearing magnanimous and fair and by distancing himself from the losers.

I saw him in the lobby of our office. He smiled at me as if I were his long-lost friend. He wanted to talk. I couldn't believe it. He had this look on his face as if he were saying, "Hey, you pulled one over on 'em, good for you!" I wasn't going to go along with his game. I turned my back on him. "Wow, he's is a sleazy, unethical, dishonorable man, and none of his charades, maneuvering, or spin control could change that," I said to myself, as I walked away. My colleagues in the office had told me that he also walked around the office and told people that I was the reason he had gotten fired. This was a direct contradiction of what he had said just a few days before, under oath. I do believe he was "retired" partially because of me. He deserved to be.

There was some expressed negativity. Lyndsey's loyal buddy, a broker named Blake, was the only person in the office who overtly said anything negative toward me. I was sitting at my desk, and he stuck his head in my door. His whole face was shaking and he was as white as a sheet. "I just want you to know that I am very sorry and upset that you won," he told me. I smiled at him.

"You don't know the story Blake. You don't know what happened."

"Yes, I do know," he replied with emphasis. I'm sure Lyndsey had "confided" in Blake about my situation, which made Blake feel important.

I leaned toward him and smiled some more. "No, you don't," I answered very sternly. He walked away. After that, if he found himself in the elevator with me he would get out.

The nameplate outside my door was either stolen or defaced, four or five times. Several items were stolen from my private office on two occasions, including my headset and my Rolodex, which prompted management to put a lock on my door. One day when I came into my office and sat down, my chair promptly fell to the lowest possible setting with a little bump. I was surprised for a second and then laughed at the ridiculousness of it. Someone had come into my office and messed with my chair on purpose. I had the feeling Blake was doing the office vandalism. He had the corner office, two doors down from mine, and colleagues hinted that he was the culprit. He and any other possible perpetrators were cowards. "What a baby and a silly man he is," I thought.

For a while, I also received fake, anonymous complaint letters and prank phone calls. Management ignored the letters because they weren't signed but they eventually put a trap on my phone with the phone company for the prank calls. Smith Barney found out who was making the calls and put a stop to it. One woman called several times to tell me I was a liar and was going to burn in hell. Another caller phoned repeatedly with an electronic device that told me over and over that I was scum.

It is my hunch that a few women who may have been claimants in the class action also called. I believe they wanted in an immature way, to get information from me, as some had tried to do during the preparation period before the trial. I felt as if they were associated with Melanie. One woman called and stumbled around until she came out with the statement that she was doing a "technology survey" and wanted to know if I had "technology in the office." Another said she was a journalist writing an article on taxes and wanted to ask me questions. I told her she needed to call an accountant or a tax attorney.

I think there was some jealousy. Claire, the class action representative with whom I had worked downtown, was one of the first people I had called when I won. Nobody had picked up, so I left her a message thanking her for everything. I didn't hear back from her, so I figured she just wanted to put everything behind her. I didn't take it personally. Two weeks later, when she finally returned my call, I thanked her again.

A while later, another woman who had settled— the one who had tried to surreptitiously get copies of documents of my individual case under the guise of "helping others"— called me. She said, in that catty girl way, "You'd better send Claire a card or something. She's very upset that she helped you and you didn't even say thank you."

"Are you kidding me?" I answered. "She was one of the first people I called, but she didn't return my call for two weeks. I did thank her, twice." I told that woman that I thought this was manipulative girl stuff, playing games, and that I wasn't going to respond to it. If that was what Claire said and if that was how she felt, she was probably being manipulated by somebody else. That was unfortunate.

Others just kind of came out of the woodwork and tried to take advantage. A few days after my award had been announced, my phone rang at about midnight. Anyone who knows me knows that I got up very early for many years, because the stock market opens at 6:30 a.m. California time; consequently, calling at midnight is too late. When my phone rang at midnight I thought it was an emergency, so I answered it. It was not an emergency; it was Sabastien, whom I had not talked to for more than a year. He said he had just seen a story on TV about a female broker winning a sexual harassment lawsuit and that the newscast didn't mention my name, but he knew it had to be me. I confirmed that it was me and I went back to bed. I had already decided that he and his sister, Madeline could no longer be in my life. I knew that if I never called Madeline, with whom I had been friends, she would never know— but now that Sabastien had heard, he would probably tell her.

I had distanced myself from her for the last year or so because I suspected that she was an unethical and vindictive woman. She also has a license to practice law. God knows what that woman would try. I didn't want any more trouble from her, so my preferred method of getting her out of my life was to fade away. She and Sabastien had been on the outs for a long time— but I knew that family, and I realized that, now that Sabastien knew about the outcome of my lawsuit, eventually Madeline would know. I stewed about the idea of telling her for a couple of weeks. If I didn't tell her, maybe she would get angry and try to pull something. That kind of behavior was not beneath her. A friend had counseled me that it was best not to rile a woman like her up, so I decided to call her before Sabastien did. She sounded happy for me, but I just wanted to hang up the phone.

True to form, a few days later, she called me and asked if I would do her a "favor." She was thinking about applying for some international legal position and wanted to know if she could put my case on her resume and claim she had been co-counsel! I had to think fast. "No!" I said. "It's not over yet; they are going to appeal." That was all baloney, of course; I just needed to get her to go away. I hung up and sat there, stunned, for a few minutes. I couldn't believe what I had just heard. "She's a scary woman," I thought to myself. Terrence had threatened to appeal, but I knew he had no grounds. I called my friend Matt to tell him what had just happened; he was appalled.

"What do I do?" I asked him. "I don't want this woman to claim anything or associate herself with me in any way whatsoever. She knew nothing about the details of my case and was not involved at all. For the last several years, we were barely friends."

"Call Maxwell immediately and tell him," Matt advised. I did call Maxwell and told him. Maxwell just laughed, but Madeline's audacity and dishonesty had floored me.

—⁂—

I also received a lot of positive responses, in addition to those from my co-workers. I received many, many calls and e-mails of congratulations from clients, friends, and former colleagues, and many from total strangers. I want to say again that I don't hold any resentment toward those who didn't testify for me, except Melanie. My experience has made me realize that I'm not sure if I would stick my neck out for anyone anymore who wasn't extremely close to me. When Georges sent me a very nice congratulatory e-mail, I really appreciated it. Victoria, the broker I used to work with downtown, called and had a complete change of attitude. "I could have totally nailed them with all the stuff I know," she told me.

"Don't worry about it," I answered, "I won anyway."

She also told me that Chad Porter, our sales manager in the downtown Los Angeles office— who had started this whole nightmare— had called her to congratulate her! He had been misinformed and had thought Victoria was the female broker who had won the money.

"No," she had told him, "it was Tameron who won."

For some strange reason, I didn't ask how he had responded to that news.

It turned out that after all those years, Chad had started working as a broker for a company in the same building in which I worked in Beverly Hills, but I had never seen him. After my trial, I finally did run into him. Just the two of us were in the elevator. I had not yet noticed him when the doors closed.

As the elevator ascended, I looked up. At first glance, I didn't recognize him, but someplace in the back of my brain it must have registered, because I did a double take. He had already recognized me, and averted his eyes. It must have been only ten seconds until the elevator arrived at his floor and the door opened, but he looked at his Rolex watch four or five times. He was very nervous. I was caught off-guard and didn't have anything to say to him at that moment, but I just stared at him. I wanted him to look up, and, if he had, I probably would have let him have it— but I wasn't going to say my piece only for him to be able to walk out of the elevator after a few seconds and ignore me. I always felt he was a bully, a coward, and a wimp and I think he was ashamed that day and didn't have the courage to face me.

—⁂—

In the spring of 2003, I joined yet another organization as a means of expanding my circle of contacts and potential clients. With a handsome, new date, I attended its annual meeting, which was held aboard the Queen Mary in Long Beach, California. It was a formal luncheon where our seats were assigned at ten-person round tables. I was sitting there with my date, chatting and getting to know everybody at the table. When the oldest man at our table found out that I worked for Smith Barney in Beverly Hills, he asked me if I knew Lyndsey Shanahan and if he was still the manager there. My heart dropped. "Oh shit," I thought to myself, "am I never going to get away from that man? Here I am, having a lovely time— and it's just my luck that I'm seated next to one of Lyndsey's friends." I had to be cool.

"Yes," I answered, "I know him. He was my manager for years, but he retired and I have a new manager now." I dreaded having to spend the rest of the afternoon talking to one of Lyndsey's old-timer friends.

Then the man said, "I was a broker way back in the '70s. I worked for Lyndsey."

"Oh really?" I answered politely. I was trying not to encourage him to elaborate.

"I can't stand that guy," the older man said. "He was the biggest asshole; I have no respect for him." This man hated Lyndsey and went on and on about it!

"Yes, I know," I answered, nodding my head and smiling and smiling. "You don't have to tell me. You're preaching to the choir." I wanted to laugh out loud. I ended up having a lovely day after all.

—∞—

I know that I got lucky from several angles. I got lucky because the class action settlement happened when it happened, just weeks before I was going to quit in 1997. I got lucky because the specifics of the settlement agreement leveled the playing field in ways that wouldn't have been the case without it. I got lucky because two of my panelists had been made judges and would not be arbitrating again. I got lucky because not everyone in the corporation was willing to lie, to pretend they couldn't remember anything, or to make documents disappear. I was lucky in other ways, too, and I am eternally grateful.

After my year of legal hell, I would call the next year my year of decompression. The emotional damage was there, and it would take time for me to heal. After all I had been through, I was still truly paranoid that Smith Barney would try to fire me. I was afraid that they would somehow set me up and blame me for something that looked like good cause for dismissal. My fear was so strong that again I called Maxwell, asking what to do if they did this or that, just as I had called him after I had filed my initial claim.

My feelings may not have been reasonable, but there they were, and I couldn't stop them. Neither the victory nor the money made the negative emotional effects of my ordeal go away quickly, just as Maxwell had warned. My emotions that first year after the lawsuit were very complicated, and it was difficult to work and be productive. Consequently, it was not a good commission year for me.

Then one day, Raymond said— unsolicited and out of the context of our conversation— "Tameron, the people that you want to prove to that you're not a loser already know you are not." A few days later, Mitchell told me the same thing. After that, it finally sank in. I said to myself, "That's right, and they can't fire me for poor performance; the panel gave me five years to catch up, based on the forensic accountant's calculations. If they fire me, I'll sue them again."

The biggest part of me wanted to stay and hold my head up high but, even with that realization, it was difficult to stay in the company. I think what kept me there during that first year was sheer will-power. I felt that leaving soon after December 2002 would have been a concession of defeat, and I definitely still had something to prove to management. I had fantasies of triumphing by having a brilliant career.

My friends' comments surprised me, but when I thought about it, I realized they were right. If Smith Barney hadn't known before, those powerful big shots definitely knew now that I was not a weak, lazy, fearful, slow, undynamic, or unambitious person. I am exactly what Smith Barney is always looking for in a broker, as I had said all along. This is the part that I can only describe as something that makes me deeply sad. I'm not being trite, I mean it. It feels like a deep sadness.

What a waste this whole ordeal was for both sides, but especially for me. Smith Barney is a huge corporation. They are executives who check in with their corporate lawyers now and then about a long list of issues; mine used to be one of them, and that is all it is to them. The company used to have about $25 billion in cash when I worked for them, so the money I was awarded was nothing. The corporate lawyers have drinks with each other at the end of the day, laugh and joke with each other, and then go home to their families and forget all about it. For me, it was my life.

—⁓—

Once I accepted that I had grounds to sue Smith Barney again if they fired me for poor performance— at least within the five years after December 2002— made me feel a lot better. The year 2004 was the best commission year of my career. In 1998, the year following my phone call to Stowell and Friedman, my gross commission improved 24 percent. The next year, 1999, it increased 67 percent, and the year after that it increased 16 percent even though it was 2000, the first year of a brutal, three-year bear market. In 2001, I had a 1 percent decrease, and, in 2002—my year of legal hell, I had a 26 percent decrease. Something had to give. I couldn't give my all to my business and simultaneously give my all to the trial, so I chose to fight for my self-respect. In 2003, my year of decompression, I had another decrease of 4.5 percent. In 2004, I got my groove back and finished the year with a 70 percent increase, which ended up being an additional 20 percent better than even my previous record year of 2000. I finally earned the title of Second Vice President.

There is no doubt in my mind that, if I had stayed and worked my business, I would have caught up to where I should have been in 2005, two years sooner than the panel had allowed. Of course, I have no way to prove that, because I left the business. But what I can say is that I did $125,000 of gross commission, the first quarter[18] of 2005, and I already had the business lined up for the rest of the year. The average Smith Barney broker at the end of 2004 earned, according to my Smith Barney-issued focus report, $422,562 gross commission. At a 41 percent payout that would be a gross income of $170,000 a year, a very good living.

On April 8, 2005, I collected my last paycheck and quit. The 2004 year had been my best commission year ever, and 2005 looked as if it was going to be even better— but I had also just finished the first draft of this book. I had proven to myself that I was a success and, as I got closer to finishing the first draft, I lost my motivation to stay in the business. My heart wasn't in it anymore.

---

[18] The first three months of the year.

I became obsessed with telling on Smith Barney. I felt that I couldn't stay at Smith Barney and safely solicit agents to represent me or editors to help me. I thought that if word got out that I had written a book while I was still with the firm, they would fire me and then, even worse, freeze my assets[19]. Big Wall Street firms throw their weight around and make people's lives miserable all the time and get away with it, so I had good reason to be afraid.

I felt guilty just thinking about leaving my clients, especially after I had promised many that I would never leave or that, if I did leave, I would take them with me to wherever I might transfer. When I told my clients those things, I meant them. I didn't initially intend to leave the business. I wrestled with that guilty feeling for a long time, but in the end, there was nothing I could do. It was time to get this book out and to change careers. I left in the way that I felt I had to. If I disappointed or hurt any of my clients by leaving, I am sorry for that.

—⚏—

Even writing this book was not a cathartic experience. I was full of anger for years, which was not conducive to writing a good book. My dad asked me what was taking so long. What *was* taking so long? As my friend Matt said, it was "living my story." That is what was taking so long. Living and reliving my story as I wrote was very difficult. Throughout every rewrite, I spent many hours pacing my apartment trying to deal with my rage. However, now the really painful feelings are fading. The passage of time has been healing. Time has been another layer of relief, and after many years, I am not nearly as angry as I used to be.

—⚏—

[19] It is Smith Barney policy that without special permission and a good reason to do so, brokers are not allowed to have accounts at other firms, so I couldn't move my money out of the firm without quitting.

Life at Smith Barney since the class action settlement in 1997 has definitely gotten much better for women. The number of female brokers rose from 5 percent to 11 percent. Smith Barney did improve, but they didn't clean up completely, and then they stagnated. After my trial, Smith Barney issued a press release regarding my case. It stated that the management involved no longer work for the firm. That was another bare-faced lie that Smith Barney deliberately told to the public and to its shareholders. As of August 2009, Gigi Jenkins was still a Regional Operations Director with the firm, and Carol Farmer was still the HR manager for Los Angeles. Aaron Weisswasser was a Senior Vice President until the spring of 2009 when he jumped firms and moved to Merrill Lynch. The fact that he was allowed to stay and flourish signaled to everybody he worked with—above him, equal to him, and below him— that he was still a very powerful and influential man in the company.

In the end, there are no consequences for the powerful when it comes to harassment, discrimination, and retaliation against women. The perpetrators will be protected. If Smith Barney was honest and sincere, all three of these people would have been fired and put completely out of the company, as they deserve to be. I also deserve a personal apology, which I have never received.

—m—

That is not the end of the story. After spending what I estimate to be more than $100 million dollars of shareholder money on the first lawsuit, just a few months after I received my money, Smith Barney was sued again in another class action for sexual discrimination. The second case was called Amochav vs. Smith Barney and was brought by female brokers for female brokers only. It claimed that Smith Barney continued a pattern and practice of discriminating against women in terms of accounts distribution of departing brokers, partnerships, and other activities that help brokers succeed— exactly as they had continued to do to me. That suit was settled as of April 2008, and part of that settlement was an agreement on a procedure that managers must utilize when distributing accounts, in an effort to make everything transparent, fair, and non-discriminatory.

—∞—

In 2004, one of my male colleagues walked up to me in the hallway and said, "You're not one of the good girls, Tameron."

"Why do you say that?" I asked him.

"Because you didn't get as much of the assets of Phillip's book as the rest of the women in the office." (Phillip was a broker who had left the company.) My colleague had access to this kind of information and had helped me several times in the past.

"I know," I told him. I had already compared notes with some of the other women in the branch who had been hired after 1997. They were new brokers and had been given large amounts of assets, much more than I. I think this was because Smith Barney still wanted me to go away. I was having a great year, the best in my career, but I was tired and didn't want this new manager, my fourth, to be even more paranoid of me than he already was. As a result I didn't say anything. I won my case instead of settling, and I never signed a confidentiality agreement or anything promising that I wouldn't sue again. So when the call went out in 2008— for women who had been discriminated against and who had worked as brokers at anytime between 2003 to 2008— to join the law suit, I joined again. Smith Barney deserved it.

Using rough numbers, Smith Barney, at the time of the second lawsuit, now had approximately 9,000 brokers of which 11 percent are female. Again, another 2,000 women joined the second lawsuit. Those who had been part of the first suit and had settled had signed an agreement that they would never sue Smith Barney again[20]. So who are these 2,000 women?

---

[20] I was told by lead counsel that fewer than ten women went through the entire trial process like me. The rest settled, which meant they couldn't sue again or talk about their lawsuits.

I explained earlier that there were about 300 female brokers in the firm who didn't participate in the first lawsuit, and who therefore were eligible to sue in the second suit. But I am sure that this time they were not afraid for their jobs, since they had seen me sue and remain with the firm. If every single one of those brokers participated in the second suit — I am not saying that they did— that means 1,700 claimants, at the least, were women who started working for Smith Barney after the 1997 settlement. The proof is in the pudding. Yes, Smith Barney had changed a little. They had hired many more women. But they haven't changed enough.

—⁂—

There is a lot of talk out there about women's equality. One of the statistics that gets bandied about is that women and men are now paid equally. I'll accept that this statistic is partially accurate. What is not talked about is that this is a statistic for lower, unskilled and semi-skilled jobs. What is not discussed is that women, who manage to get into higher positions, where they have power and money, still earn sixty cents for each dollar a man makes.[21] Just as Maxwell said, it's a plantation system.

I am not happy with the injustice that still exists, but I hope women will benefit from my story. Am I glad I did it? Yes, I am. Am I happy today? I am happy with who I am and who I have become and what I have accomplished in my life so far. I look forward to the future. We are getting there, and we will be equal— all of us. But there is no backing down.

---

[21] See *Selling Women Short: Gender and Money on Wall Street* by Louise Marie Roth p.61